Tribal Marketing, Tribal Branding

Tribal Marketing, Tribal Branding

An Expert Guide to the Brand Co-creation Process

Brendan Richardson

Lecturer in Marketing and Consumer Behaviour,
University College Cork, Ireland

palgrave
macmillan

First published 2013 by
PALGRAVE MACMILLAN

Palgrave Macmillan in the UK is an imprint of Macmillan Publishers Limited, registered in England, company number 785998, of Houndmills, Basingstoke, Hampshire RG21 6XS.

Palgrave Macmillan in the US is a division of St Martin's Press LLC, 175 Fifth Avenue, New York, NY 10010.

Palgrave Macmillan is the global academic imprint of the above companies and has companies and representatives throughout the world.

Palgrave® and Macmillan® are registered trademarks in the United States, the United Kingdom, Europe and other countries.

ISBN 978–0–230–36882–8

This book is printed on paper suitable for recycling and made from fully managed and sustained forest sources. Logging, pulping and manufacturing processes are expected to conform to the environmental regulations of the country of origin.

A catalogue record for this book is available from the British Library.

A catalog record for this book is available from the Library of Congress.

This book is dedicated to my wonderful wife Catherine and our amazing kids, Síofra, Dearbhla, Eoghan, and Colum. Thanks for your love, patience, and support.

Contents

Tables, Figures and Boxes

Tables

Figures

Boxes

Acknowledgements

This book was inspired by the work of a number of incredibly talented people who have done so much to develop the concepts of tribal marketing and interpretivist consumer research. I would therefore like to acknowledge my debt and extend my thanks to all the authors and researchers whose work I've drawn from in writing this guide, including in no particular order such inspirational figures as Susan Fournier, Douglas Holt, Robert Kozinets, Bernard Cova, Melanie Wallendorf, Russ Belk, John Schouten, Diane Martin, Avi Shankar, and others too numerous to mention but to whom my gratitude is no less.

I would particularly like to thank my friend and mentor Darach Turley for all his guidance and support over the years.

Special mentions too to my brother John, friends and colleagues like Cathal Deavy, Joanne McDonagh, Peter Murphy, Lisa O'Malley, and Maurice Patterson, all my current and former colleagues in UCC, and Stephen, Máire, and Elaine, for your inputs or simply for your general enthusiasm for all things tribal.

I also want to record my gratitude for all the work carried out by Sumitha Nithyanandan and her team at Integra in proofing the various drafts of the book and bringing the final version to such a high standard of presentation. It was a privilege to have your input.

Finally I wish to thank Tamsine, Anna, and everyone else at Palgrave Macmillan for your patience, advice, and encouragement. It was an absolute pleasure to work with you.

1 Tribes, Tribal Marketing, and Tribal Branding

Introduction

Imagine a scenario where everyone you want to promote your brand to is so enthusiastic about the brand that they are already promoting it to one another. Instead of a situation where jaded or cynical consumers feel a sense of apathy towards your products, they feel a sense of commitment and excitement about your product that they want to share with other people. Imagine a situation where instead of only having a small team of developers trying to generate new product ideas, you had access to a huge pool of people who continually devoted their time, energy, and love to developing new ways of sharing your product with one another? What if instead of having to devote huge resources, in terms of time and money, to bring this about, you could rely on your customers to do it for free? Is this a marketer's utopian dream? Not at all. Welcome to the world of consumer tribes.

Tribes are not just loyal to their chosen brands – they are passionate about them. This passion means that they voluntarily become advocates for the brand, going out of their way to promote the brand to non-users. They organize events that celebrate and promote their chosen brands, thereby providing brand-related experiences that convert more consumers to devotion to those brands. They engage with one another online and offline, affirming each other in the practice of brand rituals that tie each consumer into a deeper relationship with the brand. Volkswagen Beetle owners swap stories online about the names they have come up with for their cars. Harry Potter fans reinforce each other's loyalty to the Harry Potter brand[1] by sharing anecdotes about their favourite passages in the books and encouraging each other to dress up as their favourite characters for book launches and movie premieres – helping to create a vibrant and authentic atmosphere around these events at no additional cost to the marketer.

Tribes also act as innovators, generating new product usages and concepts and ways of enhancing the product and brand experience for one another. The Nutella community post photos online to show each other the latest way to enjoy Nutella.[2] Mini drivers give each other advice on better ways to keep their cars in perfect condition.[3] These enhanced experiences and innovative usage practices serve in turn to renew and perpetuate the tribe's enthusiasm for the brand – or brands, if they adopt more than one. Members of tribes can also serve as an informal product support system to one another, help-ing one another to resolve product bugs or glitches, in the context of friendly interpersonal relationships that bring the goals and aspirations of relationship marketing to life. Apple owners reinforce one another's passionate percep-tion of the brand not just through sharing their enthusiasm for the product features they find most appealing, but – crucially – through positively affect-ing one another's perceptions of product quality.[4] They do this not only by repeating anecdotes to one another about how much less vulnerable Apple computers are to viruses than PCs, but also by debugging glitches for one another – for free. The outcome? Instead of a feeling developing that there is a problem with the product, a perception of brand perfection is perpetuated. Then when rumours emerge of the imminent launch of the latest Apple prod-uct, the members of the tribe whip each other into a frenzy of anticipation, ensuring that the launch will be a success.

Not that tribes always form around brands. Tribes often form around activities like snowboarding or in-line skating, shared identities and concerns like parenting, TV shows like *Star Trek*, or hobbies like photography. How-ever, when tribes emerge in a non-brand-specific way, members of tribes very often become a critical source of brand information for one another and when they feel that a brand is supportive of their shared identity and their sense of emotional connection to one another, they often become passionate advocates of that brand.

In short, tribes deliver on so many things that are of interest to the marketer that, when you consider they do all this without it costing the marketer anything, you have to ask – why on earth don't more marketers learn to practise tribal branding?

So, what is tribal branding, and what makes it different from other, more conventional forms of consumer marketing? And what does the term 'tribal marketing' actually mean? To understand both terms – in fact, to understand both processes – we first need to take a look at some key ideas that help to clarify these processes and show how they differ from more conventional approaches to brand communication and development.

The first idea we need to take a closer look at is the whole notion of consumer tribes. What is a consumer tribe? How do consumer tribes form? *Why* do they form? Who are they formed by? Only by first asking and then understanding the answers to these questions can we then understand why tribes are so important for the future of consumer branding, and why tribal branding is so effective as a way of conferring authenticity on brands and differentiating them in a meaningful and lasting way from their competitors.

The origin and emergence of consumer tribes

What is a consumer tribe? Tribes are first and foremost a means whereby the contemporary consumer experiences a sense of community. Why is this so important? As Bernard Cova first explains in his initial[5] discussion of consumer tribes in the *European Journal of Marketing*, community has taken on a new form for contemporary consumers. Even though so many traditional sources and forms of community, such as extended family or village community, have become weaker or less significant, human beings are still essentially social animals. We need to feel part of a community, or communities, because we have a fundamental need for social relationships. This is hardly news, and of course marketers have long drawn from the theories of Abraham Maslow, among others, to position brands as a means of accessing social relationships.

What increasingly differs from past experience is the means whereby we access community and feelings of belongingness. Traditionally (and I accept I am over-simplifying for the sake of brevity) consumers could derive a sense of community from ties of kin, religion, and geographic location. Identity could be constructed out of shared cultural practices, practices mutually communicated through family, through the rites of religious faith, and so on. However, in recent decades, for a variety of reasons, these traditional sources of affiliation have begun to lose their hold. The demise of organized religion and the relative demise of the nuclear family are just two of the ways in which old certainties about community and identity no longer apply. Many commentators have spoken of processes of social fragmentation that have contributed to the demise of homogenous community, as we knew it. To some extent, the effects of modernization were blamed, although it has also been observed that consumers increasingly wished to embrace their own individuality, free from the ties of tradition, organized religion, and so forth. The era of individualization – or as some called it, hyper-individualization – was born out of the desire to differentiate the self from the conventional and escape the restrictive mores and dogmas of the past. However, the fulfilment of this desire to carve out a hyper-individualized identity could not overcome the fundamental and enduring need to feel a sense of connection to others; hence the emergence of what has been termed 'social re-aggregation'.

Social re-aggregation

According to Cova, the so-called postmodern consumer, in their desire to express and complete the self through individualized consumer identity projects, still needed to feel a sense of social connectedness. The need for community could not be so easily discarded after all. Hence in the midst of this process of hyper-individualization was a process of social re-aggregation. However, this need for social connection has manifested itself in a different way to more easily defined traditional forms of community. These new communities, or tribes, are not rigidly structured or hierarchical in nature. Instead they are founded out of a shared passion for activities or objects that people freely choose to become excited about. Rather than submitting to any obligation to comply with the rules – and restrictions – of traditional communities, members of these new communities have begun to affiliate around objects and practices of shared devotion because they *choose* to do so. It is, as Cova says, 'an emotional free choice'.

Also, while Cova originally spoke about the '*desperate* search for social links', it would be absolutely in error to conclude that these tribes are made up of dysfunctional individuals whose social isolation draws and keeps them together in some kind of desperately mutual nerd-dom. Instead, when individual consumers discover that they have something important in common with each other, the social contact experienced through shared devotion to an activity or brand becomes an important means whereby their need for community is fulfilled.

As will become apparent, this sense of shared devotion is utterly critical for the practice of tribal marketing. Tribal marketing is concerned – or at least it ought to be – with supporting the twin principles of shared devotion and the need for, not community *per se*, but community with a specific sense of shared – and often flamboyant – identity drawn from collectively imagined and shared emotions, practices, and values. That's why when we speak of contemporary consumer tribes, we use the term 'linking value' to indicate that tribes gather together around what they collectively imagine or construct as sets of shared values, practices, and emotions, sometimes represented by tangible objects and brands, and sometimes not. As the tribal marketer's primary role is to support tribal linking value, this concept is of real importance to the practice of tribal marketing.

Tribal linking value

This notion of tribal linking value is absolutely fundamental to the practice of tribal marketing. Tribes affiliate together first and foremost due to a sense of shared values and emotions. Whether these shared values, when scrutinized, are more *imagined* than 'real' is not unimportant, hence we will revert later on to a much more detailed consideration of the entire notion of imagined community. For now, though, the following discussion of tribal linking value will suffice.

What it comes down to is simply this. Tribes are not held together by some sort of need to remain in a community purely for the sense of social connection that this provides. Instead, the social connection stems from the shared emotion, the shared belief, that a particular object or practice *really matters*. If you don't find the object or practice important, if it doesn't render you emotional, then that's fine, but you and I are not part of the same tribe and we won't go on to share that social connection. If you are not excited by this activity, this person, or this brand, I don't really want to form a social connection with you. On the other hand – if you *are* passionate about it, if this brand, or this activity, or this form of devotion, and what it represents *really matters* to you, and you are willing to engage with me in (potentially brand-related) public performance of this identity, then yes! – I *do* want a social connection with you. We *are* part of the same tribe.

This notion of shared performance brings us to another key concept that is central to an understanding of what tribes are all about – that concept is group narcissism.

Group narcissism

Because tribal identities and linking values are founded on shared passion, whether that is passion for a brand, an activity, or both, this shared passion must be demonstrated and upheld. You *must* show your tribal credentials and demonstrate that you too feel that the shared identity, activity, or object of devotion is personally important to you. This gives rise to the demonstrative aspect of many, if indeed not all, of these tribes. The importance of the identity is mutually affirmed through taking part, often in a highly visual way, in tribal activities. This can of course give rise to some stereotypes, such as *Star Trek* fans wearing full sci-fi regalia, sports fans decked out in team colours and facepaint, or Red Bull Flugtag participants wearing crazy costumes and careering off ramps in home-made 'aircraft' that are designed to make everyone laugh rather than make it possible for the 'pilot' to actually fly. This kind of ostentatious display, while not characteristic of all tribes, does serve to highlight the importance of participation. For all tribes, the imperative is to participate, so that there is something for you and everyone else to actually look at and enjoy. The only real taboo – if you wish to be a member of the tribe – is non-participation.

While this notion of group narcissism (so-called because of the collectively self-indulgent, self-fascinated, and gratificatory nature of these exhibitionistic displays) is thus central to the whole phenomenon of the consumer tribe, it would be mistaken to assume that *all* tribes engage in outlandish forms of playful and exhibitionistic behaviour. The dictates of group narcissism can be just as easily satisfied in ways that are much more subtle than the spectacularly public behaviours of some of the groups I have just mentioned. For the Lomography tribe, for instance, taking and sharing photos in a particular way is enough to be regarded as a legitimate member of the tribe (see Cova 1997 or www.lomography.com for more). For the Nutella tribe, it suffices to post online photos of different uses of this versatile and delicious chocolate spread! (see Cova and Pace's 2006[6] study for a more detailed discussion of this particular tribe's activities and proclivities).

In short, there are a great many variations on this theme of group narcissism and how it manifests from one tribe to the next. However, while some tribes are highly demonstrative and exhibitionistic, others may be far less so. The one key common denominator is the requirement to take part, thereby affirming the tribe's linking values and helping to perpetuate the tribal identity.

It also follows that there is a rich diversity of forms of tribal identity. Possibly the easiest way to demonstrate this is to look at a number of examples of different tribes, before moving to the question of whether all consumer communities share the same structures and manifest the same principles as the tribes we have thus far examined.

Table 1.1 therefore presents a simplified tribal typology with the names of a variety of different tribes and a summary of how they manifest (or might manifest) some of the characteristics and features we have discussed so far. In examples where there is a lack of specific research at the time of writing, I have included some examples of the likely linking value based on desk research. I've also indicated some examples of tribes that are potentially made

Table 1.1   A sample of tribes with simplified tribal typology

Tribe	Tribal linking value	Group narcissism practices	Centred on one brand? (Yes/No)
Snowboarders	Sense of adventure and difference from conventional, old-fashioned winter sports like skiing[7]	Numerous practices to emphasize sense of adventure and differentiated identity, including more youthful styles of apparel, etc.	No, but clear preference for brands sympathetic to tribal linking value
Foodies	Numerous diverse linking values, depending on specific cluster of overall 'foodie' tribe	Visiting organic farms *en masse*, shopping at Farmers' Markets, taking part in online forums, following celebrity chefs on social media, etc.	Usually not – more likely to embrace a range of different brands and in some cases shun formal brands in favour of non-branded produce
Beamish drinkers	Sense of tradition fused with playfulness and authenticity, along with a sense of difference from the boring, staid, consumers of competing brands such as Guinness	Multiple practices including participation in Beamish Tours, composition of brand-related anecdotes, and adherence to the 'Beamish Constitution'[8]	Yes – where there is a clear and exclusive relationship with one brand, this is often referred to as a *brand community*
Harley Davidson owners	Linking values include a sense of patriotism, independence, and personal freedom, along with a sense of rebelliousness and occasionally over-the-top exhibitionism[9]	Wearing of biker gear, customizing one's Harley, getting Harley Davidson tattoos, taking part in Harley Davidson biker rallies …	Yes – although many members of the community will also have a sense of affinity with fellow riders and even a sense of admiration for other brands, no other brand is as sacred as Harley Davidson

Lady Gaga's 'Little Monsters'	Complex, highly emotionally charged sense of difference – Lady Gaga is seen as affirming the collective sense of respect and love for, rather than prejudice towards, forms of diversity such as alternative forms of sexual orientation etc.	Highly visible alternative modes of dress and body modification, including tattoos, piercings, etc. Attendance at Lady Gaga concerts and other events such as launches, personal appearances, and so on. High levels of participation in related social media	Yes – although the community also serves as a collective filter through which related products and services are evaluated and consumed
Mumsnet	Mutual support and empathy for all things parental, including relationships, pregnancy, diet, lifestyle, and so on – a haven for parents Additional linking value of political consciousness/ consumer activism	Likely to be highly diverse offline – more easily identified online via participation in Mumsnet virtual community	No – but a really important filter through which multiple brands are viewed, across a rich variety of different product and service categories
Apple Mac owners	Less computer, more a statement of creativity, style, and difference from the grey and uninspiring world of the PC[10]	Celebration through discourse of the many ways in which all things Apple are superior, Apple logo tattoos, Preference for distinctive iPod headphones	Yes!
Star Trek fans	Complex sense of utopian aspirations regarding justice, equality, and progress – as expressed through the medium of Star Trek narratives[11]	Wearing of Star Trek costumes, attendance at fan conventions, participation in online forums…	Yes – although it is worth noting that being a Star Trek fan doesn't preclude you from being a member of other tribes, sci-fi related or otherwise

up of a variety of sub-tribes or 'clusters' whereby certain linking values might be better explored at the level of the cluster rather than across the entirety of the more loosely defined tribe.

There are a number of things we can infer from this simple summary. First it gives us a flavour of the sheer variety of different tribes out there.

There are so many other consumer tribes in existence and it would be futile to try to list them all – but we will look at some of the above tribes (and others) in more depth elsewhere in this book. Second, we can see that it is possible for people to have a sense of tribal identity that identifies a little more closely with a subset or cluster of people than with everyone in a wider tribe. Mumsnet is just one example of this, with examples on the Mumsnet website of everything from a blogging community to content for foodies to the Mumsnet Book Club. Another point is that tribes usually tend not to have restrictions on membership. Anyone can be a member of more than one tribe – there is nothing to stop a member of the *Star Trek* community from choosing to become a 'foodie', a 'Little Monster', or a member of the snowboarding tribe, or all four. Occasionally membership of certain tribes might preclude individuals from becoming members of other tribes. For instance, where a tribe has a singular devotion to a particular brand this might mean a shared antipathy towards competing brands (such as the Beamish community's dislike of Guinness[12]).

Another important point is that devotion to a brand or an activity does not automatically make someone a member of a tribe. A lot of people might feel quite happy to watch reality TV shows such as the *X Factor* or *Big Brother*, but might have no interest whatsoever in going online to comment on the contestants, or auditioning to take part themselves. Where there is an interest in, or devotion to, the work of a particular author such as Tolkien or JK Rowling, but no inclination towards socializing or interacting with other fans of The Hobbit or Harry Potter, either online or offline, then this orientation is non-tribal in nature. Unless individuals actively imagine themselves to be part of a community of like-minded people and actually want to interact with others who share their sense of excitement, they are not a part of the tribe. On the other hand, if nothing gives you more pleasure than meeting up with your fellow wizards and witches to exchange thoughts and emotions on all matters magical, while of course wearing either your store-bought or custom-made Hogwarts robes, then you are clearly a dedicated member of the tribe!

Three other points are worth making for now. Clearly some tribes are more active online than offline, and the online dimension of tribal identity often makes it far easier for like-minded people to make contact with one another, but offline activity is also critical to the identity and experience of a great many tribes. Second, tribes need to operate in conditions of relative freedom – freedom to create their own meanings around brands and activities, freedom to criticize the marketer's narratives and instead write, re-write, or engineer their own, and the freedom to interact with one another as they see fit. The tribal marketer's role, as indicated earlier, is to support this freedom, not to constrict it.

The third point is that in regarding all the above consumer communities as tribes, I've deliberately overlooked some of the conceptual distinctions made in the literature between *tribes* as loosely defined communities that can sometimes disappear as quickly as they emerge and *brand communities* that in some respects take on more robust and formal social characteristics. So before proceeding to identify the key elements in tribal marketing, I'll explain my reasons for this simplification.

Consumer tribes and brand communities: Similarities and differences

Fournier and Lee (2009)[13] have identified three different forms of brand community affiliation, namely pools, webs, and hubs. They envisage pools as collectives whereby members have a strong association with an activity, but a looser connection to one another. Webs consist of networks of strong one-to-one connections. While I would suggest that the difference between pools and webs is not always completely clear, in that people often develop strong ties to those devoted to the same activities as them, I agree that the idea of the hub as a stand-alone form of community is useful. Fournier and Lee propose that a hub consists of a collective whereby the members have a strong devotion to a charismatic leader, but a much looser connection to each other. They cite Oprah as an example, but other examples of such charismatic figures would, until his untimely death, have included Steve Jobs.

What I have much more of an issue with is the tendency of some commentators to effectively construct all tribes as hubs. This idea is based on the assumption that all tribes can – or indeed want to – be led by a charismatic leader, who more or less dictates the agenda for the tribe. This seems to be the model that Seth Godin[14] subscribes to in his book on tribes, for instance. However, in his 2011 paper on managing tribes, Robin Canniford[15] argues against this and asserts that tribes aspire to being transitory and free from top-down direction, albeit that certain brand communities such as Harley Davidson appear to have succeeded in the imposition of something of a well-defined, top-down approach.

In respectfully dissenting a little from both constructs, I would first suggest that the charismatic leader who ignores their tribe's linking value will sooner or later find themselves without a tribe. To some degree they *must* support their tribe's linking value. They cannot retain their leadership of the tribe without it. By implication, I also disagree with the idea that a hard and fast distinction ought to be made between brand communities on the one hand, where a top-down approach may be appropriate, and loosely defined tribes on the other, who will always insist on an absolute absence of structure. Instead I believe that brand communities can operate in a variety of different ways, with or without charismatic leadership – and so can tribes.

I think that the only possible approach to take is to assume that each consumer community has its own idiosyncratic set of linking values and its own social structures, and that these need to be explored individually with respect to that particular tribe. For this reason, I would be quite hesitant to make all the same absolute distinctions between brand communities and tribes as Canniford and other commentators. Instead I think it is more useful to consider both forms of community as variations on a related theme, whereby some tribes have developed into communities who are exclusively devoted to one brand (hence the term 'brand community' and the likely presence of stricter rules and somewhat more formal social structures), while other tribes are less brand-focused and more activity-focused, so that any one of a number of brands may be deemed acceptable by the tribe. Similarly, while some tribes pursue an egalitarian agenda, others can develop more pronounced social hierarchies without necessarily manifesting all the other distinctions that Canniford and other commentators make between tribes and brand communities. Every brand tribe is different and I would suggest the boundary between the concepts of brand community on the one hand and consumer tribe on the other should not be regarded as absolute. Hence I think it is unwise to make too many assumptions about any particular consumer community until you have researched it for yourself – using the approaches to ethno-marketing we will explore later on in this book. It remains for now to begin to address the question of what exactly it is that a tribal marketer does in a little more detail. So the next step is to introduce the key elements in the tribal branding process, before explaining how the rest of the book expands on the tribal marketing process.

Tribal branding: Key elements

Working from Cova and Cova's[16] original outline of the key principles of tribal marketing, the main elements of tribal branding are as follows:

First identify which tribe or tribes to support

This involves an eclectic mix of different methods of qualitative research to identify 'traces' of tribal behaviour. These approaches differ from survey-based approaches and include exploratory interviews, desk research, participant observation, online ethnography (or to use Kozinets'[17] term 'netnography' as explained in Chapter 5), and so on. What tribes seem to be out there, whose identities you may be able to support in some way? Remember that tribes can appropriate things we might never expect, to create and express their own linking value. Cova and Cova (ibid) cite the example of rappers and hip hop artists' adoption of the Helly Hansen brand of outdoor clothing as one such case.

Identify the basis for tribal linking value

Here the research focus is on 'anything that strengthens community links and fosters (the) sense of tribal belonging'. Sometimes this is best explored by observing and even taking part in tribal rituals, to help establish how it actually feels to take part in tribal activity. What is the nature and meaning of the activity or activities of interest? Even if the choice of tribal 'mask' seems odd, what does it represent? What are the shared values of the 2CV tribe of Citröen drivers? How do they see themselves as different from others?

Begin to engage with the community and invite their participation in the design of products and services that support linking value

The emphasis now shifts from research to development of and support for 'products and services that hold people together as a group of enthusiasts or devotees'. The greater the contribution of a product to strengthening the tribal bond, the greater its 'linking value'. Remember that you cannot take tribal participation in this phase for granted. It will only come about if you have already demonstrated some form of commitment to the values of the tribe.

Launch products and services that support the linking value, accompanied by marketing communications that favour tribal-friendly media

Instead of launching advertising campaigns in general media, sponsor activities, and events that have significance for the tribe, Cova and Cova discuss how Salomon supported events organized by the snowboarder tribe and advertised in their cult magazines.

A further emergent stage in the process is adoption of the tribal brand by the mainstream. However, in seeking to enjoy the commercial benefit of such an expanded market for the product, it is important to continue to support the tribal brand's authenticity by maintaining support for the tribal linking value.

Outline summary of the rest of the book

All of the above issues and approaches are explored in greater detail in the remainder of the book, beginning with Chapter 2, which begins with a reminder of the difference between tribal marketing and conventional marketing before reverting to a discussion of the reasons why tribes form, an initial discussion of some of the benefits of tribal marketing to the marketer, and a consideration of some of the possible reasons why tribal marketing has not been more widely adopted. The chapter concludes with some further thoughts on the differences between conventional marketing and tribal marketing (including a critique of social media marketing as currently implemented by many companies).

Chapter 3 then expands on the importance of a sense of imagined community, before elaborating on the tribal emergence process, the development of tribal linking value, and the establishment of tribal rituals that serve to perpetuate tribal identity and transcendent (or sacred) experience, via a detailed consideration of the Beamish tribe.

Chapters 4, 5, and 6 offer a more in-depth consideration of how to achieve entry to the tribe and how to begin to explore and construct a sympathetic understanding of tribal linking value.

Chapter 4 begins by introducing the ethno-marketing phase of tribal branding in more detail. It explains how to approach the challenge of what Robert Kozinets calls gaining 'cultural entrée' to the tribe and provides some additional case material that further illustrates the benefits to be gained from tribal marketing.

Chapter 5 elaborates on the methods and tactics necessary for collecting the sort of tribal data that is needed in order to gain an accurate understanding of tribal linking values. It discusses participant observation, fieldnote-taking, interview techniques, and netnography. It also provides some initial thoughts on how to begin to derive useful brand-related insights over a shorter time frame than what would normally be required for full-scale conventional ethnographic research.

Chapter 6 explains the process for analysing and interpreting the tribal data collected via the various approaches explained in Chapter 5. It provides a step-by-step, fully illustrated approach to initial coding of qualitative data, pattern identification, negative case analysis, corroboration of tribal themes, and development of overall interpretation of tribal values and identity so that insights for brand development can be ascertained.

Chapter 7 looks at a number of different cases of tribal brand development once linking value has been ascertained. It emphasizes tribal branding as an evolutionary process that continues over time rather than as a radical shift in brand identity post the completion of a full-scale conventional ethnography. This is a key point – tribal branding depends on implementing insight as it is derived and refining the brand as further understanding of the tribe is acquired. Tribal branding is really an ongoing process whereby a relationship with the tribe is built up and maintained over time. Also, while some of the cases in Chapter 7 provide exemplars of tribal branding at its best, other cases such as that of the *X Factor* tribe are discussed in order to help demonstrate the way in which tribes can emerge in response to marketer-led initiatives even without the implementation of conventional tribal marketing tactics. However, what is also important about the *X Factor* case is that it shows how when a tribe emerges in an unanticipated way that the marketer needs to adapt to this by embracing a tribal marketing approach, or the tribe may begin to fragment. The chapter concludes with another case that shows how the adoption of a tribal approach, once it becomes apparent that a tribe has emerged, can yield a rich dividend.

Chapter 8 offers a reflection on the ethics of tribal branding. This develops the idea of the tribe as brand stakeholders who, in keeping with normal stakeholder theory, should be regarded as legitimate stakeholders vis-à-vis the brand. The usefulness of such an approach means that it acknowledges the tribe as different from the conventional view of customer as stakeholder, it reinforces the need from the marketer's point of view to become sensitized to the tribe's view of the world, and finally it also formally recognizes that the tribe is just one of a number of stakeholders. This is a useful and important idea in practice, because it clarifies that while the interests of the tribe cannot be allowed to supersede the interests of other legitimate stakeholders in the brand that their interests still need to be respected. Such an approach should help to maintain good relations with the tribe even in situations where decisions that are inconsistent with some aspect of tribal linking value may need to be implemented.

Finally, Chapter 9 poses the question of where we might go to from here, in the further development and implementation of the tribal branding concept. It applies the tribal branding approach to sponsorship and social media, to demonstrate how the potential of both can be greatly enhanced once marketers take a tribal approach. It also borrows from the work of Schau, Muñiz, and Arnould (2009)[18] on brand community value creation to outline ways of facilitating and reinforcing ongoing co-creation of brand value, and it outlines how to take an integrated approach to all the principles and processes we are about to discuss.

2 What Is Tribal Marketing, and Why Hasn't It Been More Widely Implemented?

Introduction

To return to the question posed at the beginning of Chapter 1 – what is tribal marketing, and what makes it different from other, more conventional forms of consumer marketing? Tribal marketing seeks to establish what it is that holds meaning for consumers, and it seeks to support those things. It is about relationships, not coercion. It is about allowing people to post about your product or service on Facebook themselves, because they feel like it, not because they were solicited into e-granting permission for the brand to post as them.

Tribal marketing recognizes that if you simply seek to impose your brand and by extension your agenda on people, then you risk alienating yourself from them. Instead it supports the tribe's agenda and thus becomes part of the fabric of the tribe.

This in return means that the tribe co-creates the brand. It means they support one another in brand-related use. It means they are more brand-loyal and effectively spread the brand's message on your behalf. It sometimes means they engage in innovation and help with the development of new products. It means that they help to differentiate the brand. It represents a chance to shift from the monologue approach of conventional marketing, towards a more transparent and truly interactive relationship between brands and consumers.

In his recent autobiography, former Tour de France winner Stephen Roche describes having to follow instructions, early on in his career, to let his team leader win a race stage he felt he himself could win. Afterwards the manager explained that by letting the team leader win the stage, the Peugeot team would receive much greater coverage in French media, thereby reassuring the existing team sponsors and also potentially attracting new sponsors of the value of sponsoring the team. The truth was that positive headlines in Ireland concerning a win for Roche were commercially useless to the team. Roche's assertions that he felt strong enough to go on and win the race were pointless. It was the bottom line that mattered, and a victory for the team leader would bring in greater short-term benefits to the organization. Besides, it is implied – or at least, I think we can infer – that the ordinary punter was none the wiser and would assume that the team leader's victory was perfectly legitimate and worthy of celebration.

This is a useful story because it helps to clarify what tribal marketing is not. Conventional marketing says that it's all about the numbers, the awareness levels. Tribal marketing recognizes that contemporary consumers tend to be better informed, so there is a greater benefit to transparency than to obfuscation, not least because it builds trust.

What are the potential gains from such an alternative approach? Well, the potential of brand tribes has been highlighted by a rapidly growing number of different commentators.

Muñiz and O'Guinn's (2001)[1] introductory article on brand community was one of the first works to point to the potential of brand community for the fulfilment of commercial objectives. They were the first commentators to note that brand community affects all four dimensions of brand equity as originally defined by David Aaker in 1991. Members of brand tribes strongly affect each other's perceptions of brand quality, for instance. Things that might otherwise be perceived as problematic can instead turn into ways in which members of the tribe reinforce one another's loyalty to the brand – a Harley Davidson experiencing mechanical failure becomes an opportunity for members of the tribe to support each other in rectifying the problem, for example. This becomes the basis for believing that through owning a Harley Davidson you get to meet great people and become part of a social network. Someone pondering whether to buy a Mac instead of a PC comes across a friend's webpage or blog containing a passionate advocacy of all things Macintosh, and it persuades them to go with the Mac. A young person walking down a city centre street with their friends suddenly hears a chorus of car horns blaring and turns to see a cavalcade of colourful Mini Cooper cars approaching, drivers and passengers waving cheerfully at the passers-by. That's it, they suddenly know which car they just *have* to buy, once they can afford it. Very often, people can be drawn to brand tribes because they sense that by doing so they can experience a fulfilling sense of community. Their perception of the brand shifts so that it somehow personifies the link or emotional connection they feel to that community. So brand tribes can make brands more attractive to consumers and once consumers have joined the tribe, they remain loyal to the brand not only because the brand has become for them a symbol of that sought-after human connection, but because of the friendliness they experience and social connections they make through participating in brand-related activities. Brands thus integrated into social relationships will retain consumer loyalty even in the face of negative product experiences or high-pressure marketing communications from other brands.

Brand choice and collective identity

Contemporary consumers are inclined to express identity via consumption, so we tend to choose those consumption objects that help us to express our sense of identity. If you think that this seems to have an element of self-fulfilling prophecy about it, you are right. In what Susan Fournier and Lara Lee[2] have notably described as the turbulence of today's world, the search for meaning and a sense of purpose is ongoing, and is often expressed via products and brands. When we come across something that feels special or different, that feels authentic and meaningful, this can help to anchor us and affirm a sense of who we are. We increasingly define ourselves by means of 'those activities, objects, and relationships that give our lives meaning,' to use John Schouten and James McAlexander's memorable and insightful phrase. If you are passionate about something, it is through your passion for this object, that activity, that you choose to engage with other people, form relationships, and 'share meaning and mutual support' (see Schouten and McAlexander 1995[3]).

Furthermore, because contemporary consumers are also concerned with the demarcation of difference (in other words, the important principle that what I am is also understood by what I am not), we need to feel that the objects we engage with, or the ways we engage with them, are different to the ways in which others engage with their particular objects of devotion. Tribes need to feel that there is not only something authentic about what it is that they do, but that this is something distinct from and *superior to* the expressed preferences and choices of others. This sense of difference can even take place within the wider context of more loosely defined tribes. For instance, from the outside, the video gamer tribe might all seem the same, but, in practice, many PlayStation devotees tend to shun Xbox consoles (see Fournier and Lee 2009) and doubtless the opposite may also be the case. Each tribe tends to have its own specific sense of what makes their identity meaningful. Counterintuitive as it may sound, tribal marketers need to support this sense of distinction, while at the same time exploring ways of making the tribe accessible, so that potential members of the tribe do not feel excluded or discouraged from joining.

The second notion that will also seem counterintuitive at first is that *it is the tribe that creates the distinction and the marketer who simply supports it*. The basis for this sense of difference from others and connection with one another is called 'linking value' and is something that the members of the tribe will generate for themselves. The marketer simply aims to sympathetically support this process. The tribal marketer must primarily focus on supporting the tribe's initiatives. Even in cases where a tribe emerges in response to something a marketer has initiated, the marketer *must* remember that the basis for this social link may not be something they had anticipated, but instead could be something slightly or radically different. They need to patiently begin to explore the *tribe's* basis for linking together around the product or service, rather than assuming that the members of the tribe are acting solely out of motives that the marketer intended or anticipated.

Even in cases where the tribe seems to have emerged in an entirely predictable way, it is unwise to assume that their agenda is the one the marketer foresaw or intended. The audience for shows like *The X Factor* may be a case in point. A huge tribe emerges and members feel a connection to one another, via the emotional narratives and heightened sense of the dramatic apparently constructed by one charismatic leader, who at first seems to have his finger on the tribal pulse. However, the failure to understand and support the tribe's sense of linking value is potentially a huge factor in the slide in audience numbers, and none of the (allegedly) contrived rumours about behind-the-scenes romances, rows, or splits followed by emotional reunions can reverse this. Tribes crave a feeling of authenticity, and while they are willing to overlook some things, if the level of perceived inauthenticity becomes too much, then this seems to trigger a falling-away in tribal participation. Hence the kind of stunts that might initially attract attention will ultimately fail to hold it. So while a tribe may certainly begin to congregate around something a *marketer* has initiated, the marketer should certainly not assume that they know exactly why the tribe has done so. Instead they need to begin to explore the basis for tribal affiliation, using the sensitized approaches outlined in more detail later on in the book. However, for now, the question arises as to how tribes actually begin to 'crystallize', to use Martin Kornberger's[4] term, if not for those reasons planned or intended by the marketer?

So, how – and why – do tribes emerge? In other words –

Why do people join tribes, and why do tribes form around brands?

People join tribes, and tribes form around activities and brands, for a small and surprisingly simple number of reasons. Yes, people will affiliate around those things that give their lives meaning, as noted above. People will seek out social affirmation or validation of the meaningfulness and singularity of these things quite simply because it is gratifying to discover that someone else 'gets it' for the same reasons as you.

It might seem a little self-delusional to assume that buying a mass-produced commodity says something unique about you as an individual, until we consider the following idea. Simple as it admittedly sounds, buying a beautiful car or an electronic item like your first iPad can be perceived as a unique experience simply because it is the first time the meanings embodied in the brand have become in a sense physically accessible to you. You get to touch and feel the object, knowing that it is now yours. If it is an exotic food or drink, you get to taste it for the first time. Even not-so-exotic food or drink items can, if consumed in novel settings or novel circumstances, seem unique and special. This in some ways is not completely dissimilar to the experience of really enjoying the local wine when you are enjoying a foreign holiday. You might experience a sense of novelty, a sense of difference, a sense of unique experience that this bottle of the local wine somehow symbolizes or represents – although in this example, the feeling of epiphany may not last. In the case of brand tribes, that initial feeling that something special has happened when you experience the brand personally *is* kept alive – by the work that you and the other members of the tribe put into preserving it.

Think about how much easier it is for a Lady Gaga fan, for instance, to nurture and maintain their feeling that there is something inherently special and important about Lady Gaga, if they make contact with other fans and discover that these other fans find Lady Gaga wonderful, significant, and special for the same reasons that they do. Won't that give them a bond and help them to feel that they have something important in common? They see their like in one another, they see a reflection of self, they feel an affirmation that those things that they feel to be important are important. And increasingly, in many, many cases, this results in what Muñiz and O'Guinn have defined as consciousness of kind, whereby people feel a common bond. These bonds form the basis for the new communities of consumption, or as they are more commonly called, tribes.

Hence the motives for engaging in 'tribal' consumption include both the need to express the self *and* experience community. Postmodern consumers' 'desperate search' for social links (Cova 1997[5]) is thus fulfilled through feelings of affinity generated from shared emotions. It is perhaps more *compulsive*, more of a drive towards enjoyment of a particular activity in the company of like-minded people (via often-extrovert behaviours) than desperate, in the normal sense of the word. Hence, too, not only the willingness but the imperative to participate, including participation in the different forms of group narcissism as defined in Chapter 1 and further discussed later on. However, while we would thus expect people to actively participate in order to consider themselves to be part of the tribe, it is important to bear in mind that it may suffice for people to *imagine* themselves as participants. Hence the idea of imagined relationships helps to blur the boundary between those who are active members of the tribe and those who are not. This potentially widens the circle of those individuals whose consumer behaviour is influenced by the tribe.

It is equally important to bear in mind, as indicated earlier, that choosing to become loyal to a particular brand doesn't make you part of the tribe. Being a member of the tribe is not compulsory. If you *feel* you want to be part of the tribe, then, in effect, you are, and this will continue for as long as the tribe exists, provided you experience sufficient affirmation of your imagined engagement. It also follows that individual consumers can belong to as many tribes as they wish, although clearly they will self-exclude, or otherwise be excluded from, tribes that are regarded as representative of tastes and preferences that differ from specific tribal choices of theirs, as in for instance the PlayStation example.

Benefits from the marketer's perspective

A number of potential benefits to commercial organizations can derive from the existence of brand tribes.

In the first place, members of brand tribes are advocates for the brand. The brand is meaningful for and important to them, so they are predisposed towards spreading its message. In a way, they are similar to the notion of the opinion leader, whose recommendations count for more with consumers because they are perceived as independent of any commercial interest. However – and this is a critical difference – we used to assume that opinion leaders would relay brand messages to other consumers in a more or less unaltered way. The message marketers sought to spread would thereby move substantially unchanged from one consumer to the next.

This is not true of brand tribes. Idiosyncratic meanings emerge, are exchanged, and are altered as they circulate among the tribe. However, the overall effect is the mutual affirmation of positive feelings and attitudes towards the brand, and the spreading of the brand's message to 'newbies'. Because members of brand tribes tend to be passionate about the brand, they will encourage others to adopt it or to keep using it. This can be expressed in a variety of ways, including anything from recommending the brand to friends during informal conversation to the slightly more structured affirmation of brand adoption that takes place when consumers interact at a company-initiated 'brandfest' event, such as the Harley Davidson Posse Ride. Either way the brand message is relayed by what will be perceived as an authentic, unbiased, non-commercial source.

Another huge benefit of brand tribes is their tendency to generate user-led innovation. Such is the scale of this phenomenon that there are too many examples of it to cover in comprehensive detail here. However, I will briefly mention some of the examples referenced by Schau, Muñiz, and Arnould (2009) by way of partial illustration.

One such example is the StriVectin brand community. StriVectin is defined as a 'cosmeceutical', meaning that it is a cosmetic that also has pharmaceutical properties. It is used by its customers in the treatment of various skin blemishes.

StriVectin users tend to congregate online, both on the official manufacturer's forum and on other unofficial websites to share personal testimonies about their experiences and the efficacy of the product. StriVectin users also share information with each other on various aspects of product use, such as how to mix the product with other cosmetics, or how to store it to increase product longevity.

Incidentally, some of the many other examples discussed by Schau et al.[6] include the capacity of the Apple Newton brand community to 'tweak' their Newtons to achieve functionality completely unanticipated by the marketer, the customizing of camera components by members of the Lomography tribe in order to achieve a much greater range of photographic effects, and the sharing of product care guidelines by members of the 'Xena -Warrior Princess' community.

While such innovations can personalize and thereby deepen the connection that each member of the tribe feels with the brand, they also represent a stream of ideas in the potential generation of new products by the company. One of the prime examples of this is the successful appropriation of the 'chopper' style of Harley Davidson motorcycle by the Harley Davidson Corporation (see Schouten and McAlexander 1995 for a more detailed discussion). Brand tribes are thus a potential source of what has been referred to by some commentators as 'lead users' (Von Hippel 1986[7]), in other words those innovative, pioneering customers whose creativity and passion leads them to come up with new variations on the product, some of which may be successfully commercialized by the corporation. Hence another potential benefit to be derived from the achievement of closer ties with the members of a brand tribe.

An absolutely critical point in deriving benefit from the existence of brand tribes is to keep in mind that the tribe do *not* exist to generate benefits for you, the marketer. They exist as a collective to generate mutual *benefit for one another*. Again from a conventional marketing perspective this might seem counterintuitive, but if the marketer can exercise patience and restraint, through supporting the community you should see a return to the brand.

The case of Ducati (Mandelli 2004[8]) is a prime example of the benefit that can be derived if, as Fournier and Lee argue, the marketer can pursue an agenda of facilitating the community rather than pushing the brand.

Ducati and the setting up of Ducati.com

Ducati realized that through supporting the tribe, they could transform the fortunes of their brand. As Mandelli explains, Ducati's approach to developing the Ducati.com website was to begin by patiently exploring all existing manifestations of the brand online. In order to understand the needs of motorcyclists, they studied the online conversations that motorcyclists had with each other. In carrying out this research, the company focused not only on the 'Ducatisti', as the members of the Ducati tribe call themselves, but also devotees of other motorcycle brands, to help develop an overall understanding of what motorcycling means to its enthusiasts.

They found that motorcyclists posting online were exchanging advice on maintenance, comparing different brands, advising one another on what to buy, engaging in brand comparison, helping each other to organize events, sharing information on the history of different models of motorcycle and so on.

They also scrutinized their competitors' websites in order to see what sort of strategic variations were being implemented elsewhere. The new website would have to offer something different in order to strongly differentiate

Ducati from the existing alternatives. Simple as it now seems, the approach they adopted ticks so many key tribal marketing boxes that it could be argued that it was essentially the tribal approach that made it so successful. The website was designed to not only give free access to a wealth of content relevant to community interests, but also to allow members to upload their own content and interact with one another. To encourage participation in this online conversation, Ducati awarded points to contributors that could be redeemed in the website's online store. Ultimately the online store became successful because the website's emphasis was to act as a hub for members of the tribe to engage with one another. It became a virtual space for the tribe to assemble, and as a consequence buying items from the online store was simply a logical extension of this. Thus 'hotspots' in various locations around the website, with hyperlinks to specific offerings in the online store, helped to drive traffic to the store because the website had become a natural place for the tribe to gather.

While I think it is important to avoid getting sidetracked into the mechanics of online retailing and website design in a book intended to provide a more general guideline to the implementation of tribal branding, I do want to mention a small number of additional points before going on to the next section. Corporate websites that seek to support the tribe by providing an online location for the tribe to gather need to incorporate several principles. First, there needs to be interesting content *as defined by the tribe*. Second, members of the tribe need to be given some facility to not only interact but also upload their own content. This also generates a sort of virtuous circle whereby a stream of original content caters to the tribe's need for novelty (the need for novelty is more pronounced in some tribes than others, as Robin Canniford (2011)[9] has recently explained, but all tribes share a need for novelty to some extent). The presence of novel content gives the tribe something new to talk about, and the prospect of fresh content and fresh conversation lures members of the tribe back to the website for repeat visits. Over time, with the right sort of support, more and more members can be encouraged to join in the practice of uploading content and starting conversations which in turn generates more repeat visits from other members and so on. If the marketer is willing to facilitate authentic discourse then the website can potentially become a virtual home to the tribe and a differentiator of the brand that competitors will find very difficult to replicate.

Why tribal marketing hasn't been more widely adopted

When I first came across the whole idea of consumer tribes, I have to admit that I was really puzzled as to why the practice of tribal marketing wasn't being rolled out by far more organizations, when the potential benefits were so apparent. However, in hindsight, a number of cultural barriers mitigated against its wider adoption.

The way to successful tribal branding is to focus on the tribe. Of course, many tribes are utterly devoted to particular brands and engage in multiple practices that contribute to their success, but it doesn't automatically follow that those tribes will actively work towards the commercial success of those brands. Tribes may want brands to be successful, but their reasons for this, and the methods that they may choose to work for brand success, are complex and do not necessarily correspond neatly to the reasons and methods of corporate marketers. Hence marketers and members of a tribe may end up at odds with one another because of diverging objectives.

Another point about tribes is that they represent a shift from the normal brand communications process. Tribal marketing involves learning how to support product and consumption meanings as created by tribes, rather than carrying out market research, deciding on a brand personality and message, and aiming that message at a target audience. For this reason, it has often been referred to as an alternative paradigm for consumer marketing. Many commentators, including Canniford, Cova, Fournier and Lee, and Mitchell and Imrie (2011),[10] have defined it as such, but because adoption of this paradigm may have implications for control over the creation of brand meaning, this may have caused marketers to shy away from it. For instance, many marketers could not come to terms with the relinquishing of *any* level of control over a corporate asset. It was too much for most marketers to accept. In hindsight, it was simply too radical a proposal to take on board without at least some initial resistance to the idea.

Thus in some cases, consumer tribes even became the subject of legal proceedings, because they were engaging in behaviours that corporations found objectionable. This in retrospect seems incredible when we consider that, in many cases, these behaviours simply consisted of unauthorized online usage of copyright material, when all that these consumers wanted to do was share their passion for the brand in a positive way.

Also, in some of the admittedly more extreme cases of tribal appropriation of brand meaning, brand management could not help but feel legitimately alarmed by the effect that the behaviour of some of these tribes was having on the image of their brand. For instance, as Gil McWilliam (2000)[11] documents, the Harley Davidson Corporation were understandably apprehensive about how the behaviour of outlaw bikers was effectively bringing their brand's image into disrepute.

Thankfully for the future of the brand – and the future of tribal branding! – the company decided that the most effective way to address the problem would be to create its own brand tribe, or community, one whose image would be more positive. This was ultimately very successful, arguably because Harley Davidson willingly engaged in tribal branding, or brand co-creation with the tribe. They thus accepted the principle of consumer co-creation of meaning, and recognized that they were no longer the sole creators of brand identity. In practice, brand identity and brand meaning can be created anywhere that brand users come together to use the brand. When consumers deliberately engage in creation of alternative brand meanings, this is sometimes referred to as brand hijack.

This take one of two forms (see Cova and Pace 2006,[12] for a more detailed discussion of Wipperfürth's (2005) initial development of the concept). The first is serendipitous hijack, whereby the tribe appropriates the brand's 'ideology, use and persona'. This is usually 'unanticipated by (and independent of) the brand's marketing department'. The second form of hijack is 'co-created hijack, which is the act of inviting subcultures to co-create a brand's ideology, use and persona, and pave the road for adoption by the mainstream'. Cova and Shankar (2012)[13] believe that Harley Davidson's strategy represents an exemplar of co-created hijack, because it successfully established a symbiotic relationship with the community, resulting in the co-creation of brand meaning and the extension of the brand's appeal to the mainstream.

The idea that tribes tend to demand some level of autonomy can thus be alarming for marketers. However, we need to remember that very often tribal motives may be perfectly genuine. Hence through pursuing a deeper understanding of the reasons for tribal affiliation, we can learn how to build relationships with tribes, instead of being fearful of their apparent unpredictability. In learning how to go about this, several key principles must be kept in mind.

Tribes do not belong to the marketer

The tribe are their own masters. They are neither the property of nor an extension of the corporation. Their consent for and cooperation with any collaboration should be sought rather than assumed.

Tribes create their own meanings, rather than simply relaying brand meaning as developed by the marketer

Even when tribes come into being as a form of collective response to some action of the marketer's, it should never be assumed that they have done so for reasons anticipated by the marketer. The basis for tribal linking value should thus be explored in a sympathetic way, rather than assumed.

Tribes have their own basis for asserting distinction with regard to identity. This principle must be respected even where it has the potential to cause tension. It follows from the principle that tribes create their own linking value that they also create their own sense of distinction or difference with regard to that identity and sense of linking value. With many tribes, this sense of difference will be communicated through adoption of an oppositional demeanour to users of other brands and sometimes even the same brand. Members of some brand communities abhor those who buy into the right brand for the wrong reasons. Fournier and Lee argue that the marketer should accept the presence of such intra-community tensions, rather than seek to actively quell them.

It also follows that marketers should feel free to take decisions that some-times conflict with the linking values of one sub-tribe in order to facilitate another's. However, this should never be done without firstly being aware of the potential tension this might cause and secondly having some alternative tactic in mind to support the offended sub-tribe in some other way, albeit that this may be difficult to implement in practice. For example, while the Saab brand community's initial objections to the introduction of the Saab 9000 were overcome by subsequent efforts to involve the community more deeply in the design process, Porsche's efforts to persuade owners of the Porsche 911 to accept the introduction of the Porsche Cayenne SUV as a 'real' Porsche initially backfired. While it is not always possible or advisable to simply pander to the tribe's every whim, good relations are more likely to be maintained when efforts to affirm or reaffirm linking value are at least characterized by genuine interaction as well as transparency. In short, if the tribe perceive that the marketer seems to be acting out of a spirit of genuine custodianship of the brand, rather than just out of desire for short term com-mercial gain, then it is highly probable that any short-term tensions will be overcome.

Hence the corporate path to brand maintenance should be guided by an overall sense of what most of the tribe feel to be authentic. The company needs to be seen to live the brand values. This will help to retain the respect, if not the undying love, of the hard core brand devotees.

The other thing to bear in mind is that it is not undesirable to have a hard core of brand users whose linking value seems occasionally difficult to support. The presence and practices of a passionate tribe of brand devotees proclaims the authenticity of a brand in ways that corporate brand activities by themselves cannot replicate. This authenticity attracts other consumers, even if they do not necessarily understand the motives and values of the hard core. However, they are capable of *imagining* that they understand what is going on, and that is sufficient to attract them towards the brand meanings as portrayed by the hard-core devotees.

So from the corporate point of view it is important to remember that while it might not always be possible to have a completely symbiotic relationship with every cluster within the tribe, the presence of a hard core of devotees who want to do their own thing is ultimately something you may want to nurture rather than suppress. It may be far more appropriate to offer support for linking value to the degree that each cluster seems to desire it, than to try to offer the same level of support to everyone. The more idiosyncratic clusters should probably be given more freedom to generate a sense of authenticity around the brand in their own way.

Tribal marketing is not the same thing as social media marketing, as currently implemented by many organizations

An alternative explanation for the failure to properly adopt tribal market-ing is that because the philosophy of the new paradigm was so different, it was possible to misinterpret it. Having spoken to quite a few executives about this, I think many marketing practitioners assumed that tribal marketing was simply a different way of segmenting the market. Once you had identified this 'tribal' segment, you could then move through the usual marketing communications formula of developing a message and targeting them with it. However, the main flaw with this kind of thinking is that a tribe is not the same thing as a market segment. Market segments are so-called because the market has been segmented into aggregations of consumers who bear a homogenous resemblance to each other in respect of one or more characteristics of interest, such as age, income, or even attitudes towards the environment. However, they do not affiliate with one another in the passionate manner that a collective of otherwise heterogeneous consumers do, around an activity and/or brand.

Also while in the past it has been possible to target such homogenous segments with the same marketing communication, tribes cannot be 'targeted' in the same way. Tribes come together to create their own meanings around a brand. This makes it a little frustrating to see how so many brands use social media such as Facebook to essentially attempt to target consumers with a corporate rather than a co-created message. Similarly, Twitter could be used to much better effect than the manner of its current usage. Rather than recognize the potential of social media for meaning co-creation, many marketers still seem to use them to follow a conventional, broadcasting-style approach, or alternatively a 'customised' approach whereby an individual's behaviour is tracked and the messages on their page are adjusted accordingly. This may yield some return but it doesn't recognize the potential for consumer co-creation. The interactive nature of social media makes them ideal for the identification and support of tribal linking value and this is the approach that tribal branding needs to take.

Thus our next task is to clarify in more detail what identifying and supporting linking value actually involves. Hence Chapter 3 expands in more depth on the meaning of linking value and the importance of imagined community, while the rest of the book provides more detail on how to go about acquiring an understanding of it and then implementing its implications for tribal branding.

Concluding thoughts

This chapter has expanded on the differences between tribal branding and conventional marketing. It has discussed some of the benefits of tribal marketing to the marketer and considered some of the reasons why tribal marketing has not been more widely adopted. It has expanded on how to address the issues raised by some of these reasons for non-adoption and provided a critique of social media marketing as currently implemented by the many different organizations who have not grasped the potential of fully interactive media.

One final point to address is to clear up an issue of terminology. As indicated in Chapter 1, I am not going to make repeated distinctions between tribes, brand tribes and brand communities in this book. The main reason for this is that I see the key principles of tribal branding and brand community marketing as so closely related in practice that I do not want to cause unnecessary ambiguity by suggesting that the subtle differences between consumer tribes, brand communities, and other forms of contemporary consumer community necessitate large-scale differences in approach. Many of my colleagues in the academy quite rightly point to differences between consumer tribes, consumer subcultures, and brand communities. However, my purpose in writing this book is not to disrespect these differences, but to clarify how marketers should go about engaging with *any* form of consumer community.

The fundamental purpose of the marketer who seeks to engage with contemporary communities of consumption in whatever form is to identify and, where appropriate and possible, support the linking values that unite these communities, via products and services designed to do so. The exact manner of implementation of this task will vary from tribe to tribe and brand community to brand community, depending on the unique characteristics and practices of each one, but the underlying principles are the same.

It is only fair to point out that some commentators have suggested that contemporary consumer tribes are often too elusive to have their essence captured by means of the research approaches elaborated on in this book, but to that suggestion I can only respond that it is far more valid for marketers to at least attempt to immerse themselves in consumer communities, thereby capturing at least some of this co-creative essence, than to not attempt to do so at all. In any case, all tribes essentially emerge from wider cultures and subcultures. By using the methods of ethno-marketing to sensitize oneself to these wider social meanings, marketers can better position themselves to cultivate much richer insight into the phenomenon of consumer tribalism. Also in many, many cases, consumer communities can evolve into more enduring social structures that are best understood by means of the approaches discussed herein.

Overall, the tribal marketer's role will still be to identify and support linking value as defined by the community. The company's presence as part of the tribe will only be accepted for as long as the brand supports the tribe's agenda, even if this occasionally necessitates supporting activities where the benefit to the brand is not immediately apparent. If the brand is seen over time as an authentic supporter of community linking value, then it will ultimately reap the benefits of tribal branding.

The final point to mention is this. Of course in concluding that tribal marketing is interesting but not wholly relevant for them, some marketers will argue that they have NO choice, that the products they are trying to sell are relatively uninteresting, and that they simply have to get their message out there in the conventional traditional way, to raise awareness and so on. But I would suggest that the number of product categories capable of supporting linking value is higher than we might think. If we remain trapped by conventional thinking that puts the product ahead of the linking value, then for sure we won't get anywhere. It also makes very little sense to me to claim on the one hand that 'low involvement' products are inherently unsuitable for tribal marketing and then on the other hand devote significant resources to inappropriate usage of social media, for instance, when the same social media could be used to identify and support linking value via those very products. But if we make the product subservient to the linking value, suddenly the possibilities change. There are so many tribes in cyberspace where the potential exists for products to provide linking value that affirms the communal identity. As I write these words, 1,174,693 people currently 'like' Pampers nappies (diapers) on Facebook! Who'd have thought? Of course that is certainly not to say that all these people feel they are part of the same brand tribe, but it certainly suggests that some potential for a sense of social affiliation exists. People who buy diapers have a lot in common with one another. After all, diapers, or nappies, if you prefer, are part and parcel of a particular stage of parenting, so maybe we should not be all that surprised to see one of the better-known brands serve as a basis for some form of social affiliation. On the subject of parenting, we've already seen that one of the better-known contemporary tribes is Mumsnet (see www.mumsnet.com for more!). Judging by the level of advertising on this website, marketers at least seem to be aware of the potential return to be derived from targeting this tribe. Imagine the return to be derived from identifying and supporting their linking values though. Also, what about tribes for Dads? There are a huge number of them online. Suddenly the potential for so-called low involvement products to support linking value becomes far more apparent, if the marketer changes their approach and uses the product (such as childrens' skincare-related products, products that help to protect baby against nappy rash, or products related to nutrition issues) to support the linking value.

In short, there are no hard and fast rules, and if there were, the tribe would break them! But for now, instead of refusing to engage with tribal marketing, we should instead let the tribes decide where the boundaries are and what the linking values are. It is our role to identify and creatively support them. I hope the rest of this book helps you to do just that.

3   Tribal Origins and Idiosyncrasies – Why Brand Tribes Form and Why They Need to See Themselves as Unique

Introduction

Why do tribes coalesce around brands? It is an interesting question. Why should consumers self-initiate what might normally be seen as some sort of marketing initiative? As we've seen so far, the answer is that they don't engage in it from a marketing perspective. Consumers initiate brand tribes for their own reasons, not for marketing-related reasons. They do so because brands allow them to form social links and engage emotionally with one another.

What all this boils down to from a marketing perspective is that the tribal marketer simply needs to be patient and seek to gain an understanding of the basis for the tribe's sense of social link with one another and the way in which they (the members of the tribe) see the brand as a resource to express that link.

The other principle to keep in mind is that consumer tribes are inherently playful, in the sense that they will always engage in some form of group narcissism. There will always be an element of display, an element of spectacle, involved, whereby the tribe both participate and, literally as well as metaphorically, gaze at one another. The purpose of this is not only to enjoy the show, but to enjoy the emotional gratification that comes from seeing other people declare their devotion to the object(s) and/or activity you yourself are also devoted to. In some cases, this sense of shared devotion may be short-lived, but in others the social links become more strongly formed and the tribes develop into the sort of full-blown communities increasingly well-documented in the marketing literature.

One of the most interesting aspects of this is the question of how this entire process actually begins. What are the early stages of brand tribe development actually like? What chain of events leads to the emergence of a tribe around a brand? This chapter of the book will consider an interesting case of brand community emergence that sheds some light on these issues.

We know from the work of Bernard Cova (1997)[1] that members of consumer tribes do not just crave social linkages with others just for the sake of community membership. They only crave social links with people who feel excited, inspired, and stimulated by the same things as themselves. We have also known for some time that consumers willingly choose brands as a means to express the self and to affirm a sense of identity. If I want to have my identity as a fan of Formula 1 motor racing validated, I will seek to engage in social discourse with other fans. If I want to think of myself as a budding gourmet cook, I may buy cookery books published by celebrity chefs and inflict my subsequent culinary experiments on my friends in the hope that they will admire my cooking, but I might also find myself drawn to cookery websites where I can interact with other foodie enthusiasts. If I want to feel that I am the sort of person who cares about the environment, I will 'like' one or more related groups on Facebook, and engage in online conversations about sustainability and ethical consumption. Of course, during such conversations, products and brands will be discussed and may become useful reference points for the community, as a way of expressing the common ground people within the group feel with one another. So this is one way in which brands may become a resource for a consumer tribe.

At other times, consumers can have such strong feelings about a brand that they make the brand the focus of the group. Again it is imperative to remember that in these cases, the intent is not to engage in a marketing initiative. The intent is to express how you feel about the brand, and to engage with like-minded others who love the brand for the same reasons you do. In discovering a community of like-minded others, you can simultaneously satisfy your desire for community, for social relationship, for the social links and connectedness that everyone needs to feel. Contemporary consumers thus often express an extraordinary willingness to put themselves on show, to help speed up the social connection process and locate like-minded others. This is me in my favourite bar, these are the music acts I 'like', these are my holiday photos from last summer (isn't Corsica *amazing*). In revealing the self and willingly giving others something to gaze at, contemporary consumers are thereby initiating a process of reciprocity whereby others will reveal something of themselves in return.

Brands represent an extraordinarily useful resource in this process. Many brands have such clear symbolic, even iconic, meanings that by openly expressing one's feelings about a brand, consumers can by association proclaim and socially project desired aspects of their own personality, aspects they wish others to see in them, into the social milieu, as a way of initiating social linkages with like-minded people.

Some brands in particular are extremely well-suited for this purpose, because their perceived symbolic meanings can be so easily appropriated. Having a very positive brand-related experience can serve as a catalyst that drives you to have your feelings validated by other people who have gone through similar experiences.

What is surprising is the extent to which consumers are capable of imagining that those who share their passion for a particular brand or activity effectively resemble them in other important ways, whereby other values and personal characteristics are also shared. The basis for the ability to do this lies in the concept of imagined community.

Imagined community

The usual definition of imagined community in the literature on brand communities is the definition first coined by Benedict Anderson[2] in 1983. For Anderson, a sense of community does not depend on knowing other members of the community personally. For any community larger than a village, the sense of community relies on our human capacity to imagine that all members of the community are very much like us. We have mutual interests and thus share mutual values. We are concerned for one another's well-being and will come together to uphold the communal identity. It is fascinating to reflect that a book chiefly concerned with the origins and spread of nationalism has made such a contribution to our understanding of contemporary consumer community, but as we will see, the ability to extrapolate from one shared passion to a belief that other passions are shared as well is a key element in the make-up of brand tribes. Other elements are the nurturing, affirmation, and defence of the shared identity.

Anderson originally cited the example of newspaper reading to illustrate his point. It is a good image, because it is easy to grasp the notion that in reading your daily newspaper (for those of us who still do so) you can imagine others reading the same stories and reacting in the same way to the various events and opinions expressed therein. Of course, the moment we reach the level of national media, we have clearly transcended local geography and thus we are now firmly in the realm of 'knowing' others as a mental or imagined construct. We do not know all the other people reading the same stories as us. We just imagine we do, because sufficient bases exist for us to be able to imagine that we share the same interests and concerns.

As Martin Kornberger (2010)[3] clarifies, we can thus generate 'a national consciousness that allows people to be part of the same social and cultural events'. Just as someone reading the newspaper can imagine themselves reacting in the same way as their fellow readers to the various news items, consumers can and do imagine themselves responding in the same way to all other media. Communities of mutual interest can by the same token transcend national boundaries completely, hence Muñiz and O'Guinn's (2001)[4] assertion that brand communities are 'non-geographically bound'.

This sense of imagined community, or alternatively, 'consciousness of kind', to reference Muñiz and O'Guinn's term, means that consumers can readily imagine that other people who share their passion for particular must mean that they are all 'sort of like each other', even if they have never personally met. Of course, because of changes in technology and the advent of social media, consumers can readily converse online, compare notes, and support each other in brand-related practices and other activities that further affirm this sense of mutuality.

The other interesting 'twist in the plot' where brand tribes are concerned is that the brand-related meanings that consumers begin to share with one another may not have been anticipated in any way by the marketer. Similarly, the brand-related practices engaged in by the tribe might be entirely of their own making and thus be similarly unanticipated. This can lead to a perceived singularity of practices and related values that of course helps to affirm these communities in their belief that nobody else 'gets' the brand like they do.

In order to consider all these issues in more depth, we will take a look through what happened when one group of young consumers shared a brand-related epiphany and formed their own tribe around that brand (for the full version of the story, see O'Sullivan, Richardson, and Collins' (2011[5]) article in the *Journal of Marketing Management*). The brand in question is Beamish Stout, a beer brewed in Cork, Ireland. In documenting the emergence of this tribe, my colleagues and I drew from a landmark work on sacred consumption by Russ Belk, Melanie Wallendorf, and John Sherry (published in the *Journal of Consumer Research* in 1989),[6] to argue that brand communities effectively emerge from a communal conversion experience, whereby the brand becomes sacred to the community as the result of a transcendent experience that radically alters their perceptions of that brand.

This 'conversion experience' (Belk et al. 1989) both bonds the community to a particular brand and also serves as the basis whereby other devotees of that brand are viewed as members of a special collective who share a mutual understanding of the sacred qualities of the brand in question.

This experience is therefore closely related to the idea of transcendent consumer experience, or TCE, as proposed by John Schouten, James McAlexander, and Harold Koenig in 2007.[7] To construct this idea they drew inspiration from the concepts of peak experience as proposed by Abraham Maslow and flow as defined by Mihaly Csikszentmihalyi.[8]

Peak experiences, flow, and transcendent customer experience

Peak experiences, as the term suggests, are unusual. They have also been described as ephemeral, a word meaning short-lived. I think it is useful to mention at this point that the term 'ephemeral' has often been used to describe tribes, even though as we now know, many tribes evolve into long-term stable communities. The effects of peak experiences can vary – sometimes they leave long-lasting effects whereby someone's perspective on objects, events, or people is permanently changed. Not every emotional experience leaves such a lasting effect, which partially helps to explain why some group experiences result in the emergence of tribes that endure for the long term and others do not.

Peak experiences are characterized by feelings of awakening, epiphany, and novelty. They are also unexpected, in the sense that the depth of emotion accompanying the experience is unanticipated by the person. Even if you are looking forward to something and have some sense of how special a particular experience will be, it is therefore in a sense the element of surprise at just how much you are affected by it that helps to differentiate between peak experiences and other relatively enjoyable or emotional experiences. It is also impossible to guarantee that, all other things being equal, each person present on a given occasion will have a peak experience. For instance, not everyone who goes sky-diving for the first time will necessarily feel it was a life-changing experience that they can't wait to repeat. It follows that peak experiences cannot be imposed on people and that there is an element of subjectivity involved – although clearly a group can socially construct and affirm an experience for one another so that each individual's perception of that experience is shaped by the group dynamic.

A further aspect of peak experience that helps to differentiate it from flow is that it tends to be characterized by feelings of unity or oneness. People who have had peak experiences tend to report a feeling of oneness with humanity or nature, for example. So a profound, unprecedented, and potentially overwhelming sense of connectedness with nature, the divine, or a particular group of people can also form part of peak experience, and this can leave a strong and lasting effect on subsequent perceptions of the people, objects, and times associated with these experiences. The meanings attributed to the experience can also often be integrated into the identity of the individual, giving the moment an enduring legacy in their life.

Flow, on the other hand, while it too can be characterized by feelings of connectedness and unity, is not characterized by the same sense of epiphany. Flow is much more accessible, albeit that it comes about not through a conscious determination to experience it as such, but rather through focusing on and engaging with a particular activity. As many people have testified, flow comes about when you focus on the activity at hand and seek to master it. This of course requires concentration, and once you concentrate on the task at hand you tend to disengage from other thoughts, distractions, or anxieties that might otherwise upset you or disrupt your enjoyment of whatever it is you are doing. Hence the point that flow is something pleasant. Nor do you have to be engaged in anything outlandish to experience it. You can experience flow while sky-diving, but you can also experience it while making a jigsaw or playing chess. You can thus experience flow on your own or as part of a group. Given the often everyday nature of flow, it follows that flow experiences by themselves will not have the same potentially life-changing impact as peak experience. However, the gratifying nature of flow does mean that we will seek to repeat those experiences that produce this pleasant state.

Schouten et al. envisage that consumers will seek to repeat those experiences that either evoke a sense of flow, reaffirm the meaning associated with a peak experience, or both. The fact that both peak experience and flow are capable of generating a sense of transcendence, or altered consciousness, led to the idea that they could be combined in a marketing context to produce the notion of transcendent customer experience. Hence they define transcendent customer experience as flow and/or peak experience in a consumption context. Because transcendent customer experience is occasionally a combination of both peak experience and flow, it can therefore have the sort of profound, enduring effects initiated by peak experience and it can exercise a lasting influence on consumer behaviour.

What makes this idea of transcendent customer experience so interesting from a tribal branding perspective is the possibility that marketers can do something to facilitate these special experiences for consumers, and that people who have such experiences are likely to interpret them via the prism of not only the brand, but also the community of people with whom they have shared this special experience. This is therefore one of the ways in which brand tribes can be supported and affirmed by the marketer. What we have to keep in mind, though, is that you can't force someone to have such an experience. You can only facilitate it. Similarly, you can't force consumers to form a community or tribe. You can only provide the context – or more correctly, *a* context, whereby the formation and/or the maintenance of a tribal community is facilitated. The rest is up to the consumer. The Beamish case is an excellent example of the ability of tribes to appropriate brand-related resources and manage the TCE process for themselves, thereby reminding us that the entire process can be initiated by consumers without any prior planning or intent on our part as marketers.

In pondering the emergence of the Beamish tribe, as I've already mentioned, while my colleagues and I were interested in the relationship between brand community formation and transcendent customer experience as explained by Schouten et al, we ultimately found ourselves returning to the work of Russ Belk and his colleagues to see what they had to say about the kinds of things consumers do when they have had some kind of sacred experience. They explain that the need to retain a sense of the sacred can result in the emergence of a rich variety of what they term practices of sacralization maintenance.

We found this explanation very interesting and relevant to the emergence of the Beamish tribe. Consumers will often go to great trouble to 'keep that which is sacred, sacred'. While I am certainly not claiming that every single tribe or brand community originates via exactly the same process as that of the Beamish tribe, there are some very useful ideas to be gained from viewing its emergence via this theory of sacralization maintenance, alongside the notion of transcendent customer experience.

The emergence of the Beamish Tribe

In the case of the Beamish Community, the initial group experience occurred when a group of ten young men arranged to go on a tour of the Beamish and Crawford Brewery on Cork's South Main Street. While not everyone was known to each other, everyone present had mutual friends in the group. The mood was one of pleasant anticipation, rather than one of a unanimously positive predisposition towards Beamish beer in particular. Beamish is a little unusual in that as a dark beer, or stout, it is not typically considered to be a young person's drink. It is therefore not that surprising that prior to the emergence of the tribe only three of the group were loyal Beamish drinkers, although their enthusiasm for Beamish had doubtless been influential in selecting the setting for the outing. However, there was no intention whatsoever on anyone's part to use the trip as a means to establish a beer drinkers' club. What happened next changed all that. The group essentially underwent a form of transcendent customer experience that inspired them to set up a brand tribe to jointly celebrate all things Beamish-related.

Some things, more so than others, contributed to the singular nature of the whole experience. The brewery tour finished up in the visitors' bar, where each person was given the chance to skilfully 'create' their own pint. The task of pouring a pint of Beamish requires two separate stages and it takes a number of minutes to complete. This opportunity to enact the role of skilled barman and pour your own pint of Beamish in the traditional way had an unanticipated effect on the whole group. The fact that it is normally the sole responsibility of expert bar staff steeped in the best imagined traditions of stout-pouring conferred a sense of magic on the moment when the group finally had the chance to do this for themselves:

> It was a great feeling pouring your own pint, it's yours. I never worked in a bar, it was fun, the pint was lovely, and I can't wait to do it again.
>
> (From interview with Beamish tribe member 'Brian')

That first Beamish 'tour', as the group subsequently termed the occasions dedicated to venerating Beamish, concluded with a visit to several other pubs in the vicinity but it was the experience of those first few pints in the 'hallowed ground' of the Beamish brewery that was afterwards evoked as the standard by which all other pints would be measured:

> ... it has a special kind of feeling being there (in the Beamish Brewery), a buzz.
>
> (From interview with Beamish tribe member 'James')

What this designation of both pints and location as special points to is the idea of quintessence. In their article on sacred consumption, Belk et al. explain that when a consumer good is sacred, one of the key meanings to be inferred from this is that it is 'just right', so to speak. It is perfect, it should not be inappropriately altered, and it should not be treated with anything other than respect. Very often the consumption of such products is tied into particular locations in place and time that provide the perfect setting for their consumption. Douglas Holt gives an excellent further example of this in his (1995)[9] discussion of the consumption of hot dogs at baseball games. You can't improve on a hot dog and beer at the ball game. They are already the perfect accompaniment to the occasion and each other.

Getting back to our group of young Beamish converts, what happened next?

The conclusion that the group had effectively undergone a transcendent customer experience together is supported by the ways in which they began to engage in what Belk et al. would call sacralization maintenance. Not only did they try to retain the magical aspects of the experience they'd shared, but they also recognized in each other a bond arising directly from the experience. Their subsequent rituals, while intrinsically playful, therefore had the additional purpose of affirming tribal linking value. This desire to maintain and re-live the initial TCE is essentially what initiated the emergence of the brand tribe.

Sacralization maintenance and affirmation of tribal linking value in the Beamish Tribe

The first manifestation of sacralization maintenance among the members of the Beamish Tribe was an outburst of creative activity online. Social networking site Bebo was used by the group to keep in touch and reminisce about the experience. Photographs were uploaded and commented on, quizzes about the day's events were created, and members recounted brand-related incidents that had occurred on the day in order to playfully tease one another. This online interaction allowed consciousness of kind to remain intact until such time as the group could organize a follow-up 'tour'. At this stage, fate intervened in that the idea of visiting other stout-producing breweries was floated, but no opportunity to visit any alternative locations emerged.

In the end, the only available venue for a second outing for the newly formed tribe was the Beamish and Crawford brewery. The second tour proved so enjoyable that the group decided to keep repeating the 'Beamish Tour' on a regular basis. Since it was impractical to continue to visit the brewery, the notion of what constituted a 'Beamish Tour' was gradually redefined:

> Originally, we started in the brewery, but people can't make it on Thursdays and it's not open on Saturdays. So a tour now is just when we are all together drinking Beamish.
>
> (Interview with 'Brian')

The pubs visited on these tours are selected for their vintage qualities. They are thus old-style, traditional pubs that fit the group's image of an appropriate venue befitting the stereotypical (older) stout drinker. While the members of the brand tribe do visit trendier bars at other times, those times and occasions are kept apart from 'Beamish time'.

Another way of retaining the sense of novelty and magic surrounding the 'Beamish Tour' has been the introduction of new rituals. While on tour, the group do things that they would normally not do while out with their friends, to help differentiate between 'Beamish time' and non-Beamish time.

A typically idiosyncratic example of the collective marking of 'Beamish time' was the decision on one occasion to take snuff. This happened in every pub visited on the 2006 Christmas 'Tour.' Snuff, a form of tobacco that can be sniffed or inserted in pinches inside the upper lip, resembles Beamish in the strong association it evokes with the customs of older male consumers. This sort of playful appropriation of other resources in the devising of new ways to consume the brand is typical of brand tribes. It is exactly the kind of behaviour that in allowing them to construct their own idiosyncratic brand rituals, gratifies their desire for quasi-exhibitionistic behaviour, and allows them to believe that nobody else 'gets' the brand the way they do.

Another ritual typically practised by many brand tribes is the adoption of a playful title of some kind. As Muñiz and O'Guinn note in their 2001 article, brand communities tend to come up with strategies to differentiate between users of their brand and users of competing brands, as part of the processes around consciousness of kind. Brand tribe names like 'Saabers' and 'Ducatisti' help members of the tribe to self-construct as a distinct social category. Having a unique name helps the tribe to de-commodify their identity and separate it from the wider social universe outside their collective (de-commodification and de-commercialization also being important aspects of sacralization maintenance, according to Belk et al.). The members of the Beamish tribe have bestowed a number of different titles on themselves since their foundation. The purpose of names like 'The Beamish Society', 'The Beamish Appreciation Guild', the 'Beamish Brigade', 'Beam Beam Heads', 'The Band of Beamish', and the 'Beamish Appreciation Guild' is yet again to engage in mutual affirmation of linking value via the playful and quasi-narcissistic adoption of the Beamish brand to differentiate the tribe from others.

These names are added to and alternated while on 'tour' to maintain the sacredness of Beamish time, to help ensure that the group's identity as 'Beam Beam Heads' does not become mundane, but retains its distinctiveness and marks the tribe out as not only being up for the 'craic' but being simultaneously both playful and knowledgeable in their ability to differentiate between dominant beer brands and underdog brands representative of skill and tradition. So as it turns out, there is quite a lot in a name in this case.

The importance of virtual community

Another typical dynamic of brand tribes is the way in which they grow online. This is essential in order for brand tribes to be able to overcome geographic and temporal boundaries. In the case of the Beamish tribe, their establishment of a personal page for the brand allowed like-minded others to become affiliated to the community. This allows the celebration of all things brand-related to be further extended:

> *Go on the Beamish. Found a spot where they do it in London, but all the stout here is like tar. It doesn't do justice.*
>   ('Liam', posted on BeamishClub.Bebo.com; see O'Sullivan et al. 2011)

Another example of the playfulness that a dedicated online space can facilitate is the online issuing of instructions for correct implementation of brand rituals:

Recommendations for going on a beamish tour:

▷ Don't wear a light coloured top as there will be spillages
▷ Please research Beamish, as there will be lengthy conversations on Beamish
▷ Everybody try and look out for Barney, as he is prone to injuries. (nutter)
▷ Please learn the (Beamish) prayer off......impersonators will be dealt with
▷ Do not let Frank sucker you into an argument.
▷ Have a good meal prior to tour, as we may not have time to stop for food
▷ Have a song prepared (Brian exempt)
                    (BeamishClub.Bebo.com – see O'Sullivan et al. 2011)

The social reinforcement of linking value

The combined use of various different social media, including YouTube for the posting of brand tribe video clips, allows the tribe to maintain consciousness of kind in a non-geographically, non-temporally bound way. As illustrated by the above example, it also allows the tribe to come up with ways of socially reinforcing devotion to tribally approved ways of consuming the brand. This idea of rules applying to tribal behaviour is something of a departure from the original understanding of tribes as social domains free from rules, but I include it here nonetheless for a few related reasons.

In the first place, tribes that flare briefly into existence before dissipating again for whatever reason will fail to develop brand- or activity-related rules in part because they will not have had sufficient time to engage in their social construction. Second, tribal 'rules' are not the same as normal, compulsory social rules or laws. Normal rules apply to everyone and are not submitted to out of free choice. For tribes whose evolution reaches the point where social interaction becomes an established and ongoing act, social norms will evolve and informal rules of conduct will emerge. With some tribes, formal rules might even emerge earlier in the process.

Some commentators argue that the presence or absence of rules of conduct constitutes a categorical difference between tribes and brand communities. Brand communities will tend to have rules and tribes will not.

However, I think that many tribes will resort – and freely submit to – tribal rules, provided those rules uphold and affirm the tribal linking values that each member has effectively signed up to out of a sense of 'emotional free choice', to borrow Cova's (1997) phrase. As long as the rules affirm the tribe in their pursuit of spectacle and quasi-exhibitionistic behaviour, as long as they uphold rather than oppress the requirement for a hedonistic and liberatory ethos (Muñiz and O'Guinn 2001), there is every chance that they will be embraced. Without going off on a tangent into the admittedly very interesting and insightful theories of Johan Huizinga (1955)[10] on the nature and purpose of human play, without a set of rules by which to play the game, the game cannot continue. Human play is always accompanied by shared rules to hold the sense of playfulness together, so it follows that in the playful context of consumer tribes, some form of rule will apply.

The clearest manifestation of a set of tribal rules in the context of the Beamish tribe is the 'Beamish Constitution'.The Beamish Constitution is a very apt illustration of the way in which the membership of a tribe will readily submit to a set of rules, once those rules support the linking value and endorse the tribe's playfulness. The constitution is a mock-serious proclamation of the tribal requirement to practice full loyalty to Beamish Stout.

As with most if not all of tribal practices, the eventual emergence of the Beamish Constitution owed a good deal to serendipity. One night while the group were on 'tour' together, an empty cake box was appropriated for use as a mock-parchment, which was then signed by all present to pledge obedience to the Constitution's decrees. The decrees state that if a member enters a pub with the intention of consuming alcohol and the pub serves Beamish, then Beamish must be ordered. If the bar does not stock Beamish, another alcoholic beverage may be ordered only once the member has complained (to at least three people) regarding Beamish's absence. A breach of the decrees of the constitution is punishable by the sanction of having to buy Beamish for one or more members of the tribe. The Constitution is thus enforced in a gentle and capricious manner, but nonetheless this does amount to a form of what Algesheimer, Dholakia, and Herrmann (2005)[11] refer to as normative group pressure.

Ultimately, there is an acceptance of the rules because they maintain the tribal identity. Through their participation in tribes, consumers get to enact aspects of self that they are not normally at liberty to express. In the context of tribal participation, consumers can not only temporarily elude their everyday responsibilities but have this elusion affirmed by others, thereby simultaneously affirming the desire for social connectedness with like-minded others who have freely chosen to share in the same particular expression of liberatory hedonism as you.

Perhaps in the case of some tribes, the sharing of tribal identity may have as much to do with affirming one another in roles that are inherently less playful, and yet even here there is an escape, a safety valve, through the accessing of consciousness of kind and realizing that others are going through the same challenges as you. At the time of writing, I note that Weight Watchers' main page on Facebook has over one million 'likes'. Somewhere between a few semi-jocular 'decrees' written on the back of an empty cake box by a tribe of beer aficionados and the detailed prescriptions for achieving a healthier lifestyle shared by members of Weight Watchers lies the principle that tribal rules are welcomed because they allow you to express your chosen self in the company of your chosen tribe:

> *You are 'beaming' for a few days [after a Beamish Tour] – pardon the pun.*
>   ('John', interview, O'Sullivan et al. 2011)

Without at least a tacit agreement to share a set of rules, the shared identity would be unsustainable and the tribe would begin to dissipate. It is worth noting that Huizinga also originally asserted that failure to agree on a joint set of rules is a basic cause of fragmentation in various forms of play. When an innovation is introduced, those who wish to embrace it sometimes leave the original 'game' to set up their own organization. Hence rugby's split from association football for example. In the state of flux that characterizes emergent consumer tribes, who knows how often such splits occur? It is easy to understand why those consumer tribes who go on to become more firmly established will tend to manifest more complex sets of rules, as a means to further affirm and uphold the communal identity.

Thus another form of enforcement of social norms among brand tribes is what Muñiz and O'Guinn have termed oppositional brand loyalty. This is a frequent characteristic of brand tribes. As more time elapses, post the original transcendent customer experience and the formation of stronger bonds among members of the tribe, the practice of oppositional brand loyalty is a useful way for the tribe to reassure one another of the sacredness of their brand and by extension their collective identity. Oppositional brand loyalty was originally defined by Muñiz and O'Guinn as

> '… *another social process involved in perpetuating consciousness of kind. Through opposition to competing brands, brand community members derive an important aspect of their community experience, as well as an important component of the meaning of the brand. This serves to delineate what the brand is not, and who the brand community members are not.*'

As a quick perusal of Muñiz and O'Guinn's notes on the Apple Mac and Saab brand communities reveal, members of brand tribes tend to project all sorts of negativity on to competing brands, partly because this is such a quick, easy, and convenient way to differentiate between themselves and the sort of people they imagine use these other brands. So it is that only the most barbaric philistine would use a PC rather than a Mac, or only the most boring and staid individual would drive a Volvo rather than a Saab. According to members of the Saab community, Volvo 'don't make tractors for nothing'. (As a former Volvo owner who only parted company with my own Volvo S40 Sport due to a particular set of circumstances at the time, I've always been vaguely troubled by this latter idea!)

Oppositional brand loyalty is not inevitable, and in the case of tribes that are focused on an activity rather than a brand, it might be expressed as opposition to alternative products, rather than opposition towards specific brands. Many members of what Mitchell and Imrie (2011)[12] have termed the record collectors tribe still abhor all forms of recording other than vinyl records – the same principle is at work here. Record collectors often dismiss alternative product such as CDs as inferior, as part of the apparatus for justifying the idea that the tribe's object of devotion is superior. This should be seen for what it is – a way of singularizing the tribal identity, a way of holding onto the elusive feeling that the object(s) and practices that inspired the tribe's passion in the first place are still special, still superior to the alternative.

Oppositional brand loyalty was not apparent at first among the Beamish tribe but eventually manifested itself as tribal disparaging of rival stout brand, Guinness. The members of the Beamish tribe not only refuse to drink Guinness but some members readily admit to booing Guinness delivery lorries! The clearly playful, even juvenile nature of this behaviour should not distract us from the underlying significance of its intent. It is an important part of maintaining the tribal belief that there is something different, something special, something unique, about their brand. Some members of brand tribes can become quite vehement about the difference between their brand and the rival brand or brands:

> *I'm known as the Beamish guy in Limerick. People don't even know what Beamish is, I enjoy telling them all about it ... ... I hate when I'm drinking stout and people think it's Guinness. I correct them aggressively and make sure they remember I drink Beamish.*
>
> ('Frank', Interview, O'Sullivan et al. 2011)

Another issue clearly highlighted in this assertive statement by 'Frank' is that brand tribes will often feel very strongly that *they* are the real owners of the brand. By now, I've alluded a number of times to this idea. This can manifest itself in ways that might at times be viewed as problematic by the corporation behind the brand, due to the potential for public criticism of some aspect of brand strategy. In the case of the Beamish tribe, the tribe's feeling of ownership over the brand extended into the area of open criticism of the brand's advertising strategy and unfavourable comparison of brand messages with the advertisements for other brands, even Guinness:

> *Did you see the new Mossy O'Sullivan billboard ad [for Beamish]? It's terrible, they all are.*
>
> ('Brian', Field Notes, O'Sullivan et al. 2011)

The Guinness ads are brilliant. They are directed at young consumers and are a talking point. They are genius.

('Frank', Informal conversation, O'Sullivan et al. 2011)

I mention these things because companies do have to bear in mind when deciding as to whether they are willing to support a tribe that they might occasionally have to accept the sort of spontaneous criticism that sometimes emerges from a tribe of brand believers. Personally, I consider that the benefits to be derived from supporting brand tribes far outweigh any negative issues that might crop up. In any case, an organization that has taken the time to gain an insight into tribal linking value should find itself in a position to anticipate when actual or potential problems might occur and should be able to take appropriate action to address this. As the management of such issues is of such clear importance, it is addressed again in more detail later on in the book.

It is reasonably clear from all this that while people can have a transcendent experience, the extent to which they associate it specifically with one brand only may vary, and this is what makes the follow-up period, post the conversion experience, particularly important. In the Beamish case, there was no formal corporate follow-up to brewery tours as such. With brandfests, events designed to immerse invited customers in brand-related social activities, follow-up should be included as an important part of the process of supporting the tribe and encouraging new customers to interpret their conversion experience as related to your brand.

Schouten et al. therefore argue that while 'brandfest' events can trigger TCE experiences, follow-up is vital. Not only should marketers design events in a way that facilitates brand-specific conversion by provision of appropriate brand displays and resources, but this has to be followed through by facilitating subsequent interaction and repeat events in a clearly brand-related way.

As to how to go about implementing this, there needs to be a sensitivity towards group proclivities as to what level of brand presence is appropriate. The optimal way to assess the appropriate level of tribal facilitation is to implement the sort of respectful and humble approach to ethnomarketing outlined by Cova and Cova.[13] You can try to rush things and devote resources to brandfest events and brand Facebook pages, but to fine-tune these activities you really need to take a more patient approach. Ideally, tribal marketers should immerse themselves in a process of gaining insight into tribal sensibilities and sensitivities through the use of a range of participative research tactics first – before undertaking any promotional activity. Tribal marketers should first seek to understand the tribe's view of the world, before they begin to try to cater for it and support it, via brandfests, social media, or any other formal means of promotional activity.

Before beginning this more detailed consideration of what Cova and Cova refer to as ethno-marketing tactics, I therefore want to elaborate on another important idea – the notion of subcultural, or perhaps more specifically, tribal cultural capital.

Tribal cultural capital

As a general rule, tribes are inherently playful. People come together in tribes to express aspects of the self that are outgoing, capricious, emotional, quasi-exhibitionistic, and pleasurable. All these features can be seen in the Beamish tribe.

Further, to enter a tribe is to seek affirmation of these aspects of the self – *and to provide such affirmation for others.* This process of mutual affirmation also fulfils the desire, the need, the compulsion for social links, for community membership.

It also follows that fulfilling these desires via membership of specific tribes might or might not be a long-lived phenomenon. In some cases the tribes may well dissipate quickly, while in others, sufficient common ground is established for the tribe to continue to grow and continue to affirm one another.

Thus part of the point of being a member of a particular tribe is that it also affirms you in the belief that your particular object of devotion is special. That brand, product, or activity that you feel embodies or expresses some particular aspect of the self is also venerated by other people – by extension, this means that those people understand you. They 'get' you. Hence any objects of mutual devotion that symbolize this mutual understanding in some way become hugely significant as representations of the linking value that binds the tribe.

It also follows that anything that might undermine tribal linking value is a potential problem. If someone wishes to join the tribe but they are uncertain of the 'rules of the game' their violation of these 'rules' can sometimes provoke a backlash. On social media it can result in practices like 'flaming' where novice members are subject to verbal abuse.

One way the tribal marketer can address this is through trying to provide appropriate support to nurture 'novice' members of the tribe. However, it will be very difficult for the tribal marketer to act or react in a culturally appropriate way to any incident unless they are familiar with the tribe's system of cultural capital themselves. In fact without such an understanding the marketer runs the risk of violating tribal sensitivities themselves. Hence the need to gain an in-depth understanding of what tribal cultural capital actually means.

The question of what constitutes cultural capital, tribal capital, or subcultural capital sometimes tends to be a little bit elusive. While its importance is obvious, the problem arises, for instance, that as soon as it becomes apparent that a particular object is representative of some form of cultural capital, some tribes will jettison it and move on to something else. Alternatively they will mock those who try to appropriate the object and tell them they are using it the wrong way or have only bought it in order to be fashionable. Cova and Shankar (2012)[14] recently concluded that tribes are so elusive that by the time the marketer has caught up with them and gained an understanding of their motives for engaging in some practice or other, the tribe will have moved on to something else! In a similar vein, Robin Canniford (2011)[15] has recently argued that while methods like ethnography may be suitable for the study of brand communities that contemporary tribes move too quickly for their motives and identities to be accurately captured and interpreted by ethnographers. There is some truth in this but it is also something of an overly pessimistic conclusion in my view.

The reasons why I think it is worth trying to capture a sense of tribal capital are fourfold. First, I don't think anyone would deny the insight to be derived from it, it is more that it can be elusive, which makes it hard to pin down. Second, not all tribes are so ephemeral that their systems of tribal capital shift faster than tribal marketers can continue to track via ethno-marketing. Admittedly in asserting this I am again dissenting from the strict delineation that Canniford draws between tribes and brand communities. While I appreciate his reasons for making this distinction, I don't accept that these reasons invalidate the premise that ethnographic approaches are suitable for researching tribes. While it is in some ways easier to study a community whose identity and activities all revolve around one particular brand, communities whose devotion extends to an entire product class and/or activity are in my opinion just as accessible as their tribal logic can be explored via the same methods that apply to ethnographies of brand communities.

It is also important to remember that quite a few tribes tend to remain devoted to their tribal totems in a remarkably persistent way. Certainly if you look at a phenomenon like Lady Gaga's fans, the self-styled 'Little Monsters', they have been together as a tribe for more than enough time now for a sense of their tribal capital to have been gained, should anyone have wished to pursue this in the appropriate way.

Third, in acknowledging that some tribes do emerge, metamorphosize, and sometimes dissipate with great speed, it is important to remember that tribes usually emerge from some kind of parent culture or subculture. Tribes made up of young consumers usually evolve out of youth subculture for instance. Hence it follows that if you maintain some degree of ethnographic understanding of youth subculture and youth subcultural capital, you will be less shocked by sudden shifts in tribal identity and tribal capital.

Fourth, some level of understanding of the desire for distinction that informs all manifestations of tribal capital should at least help the tribal marketer to gain a sympathetic understanding of *why* a new form of tribal capital has emerged. Finally it is also worth remembering that by the time the instigators are moving on to something else, your just-acquired under-standing can help you to facilitate the growing body of 'wanna-be' members of the tribe to express themselves.

So what exactly do I mean by the term 'tribal capital'? The best way to explain the term is to take a quick look at its origins. The term 'cultural capital' as most widely understood in the marketing literature is derived from the work of French sociologist Pierre Bourdieu in his 1984 book,[16] *Distinction*. As the name of the book implies, one purpose of cultural capital is that it allows those 'in the know' to distinguish between themselves and those who do not understand how to engage with an object or practice. While Bourdieu's work is concerned with issues of social class and barriers to social mobility, the concept of cultural capital is applicable to any context whereby the insiders in a community can share knowledge and transmit values. If cultural capital is demonstrated through knowing how to hold a proper conversation on antiques, for example, then a consumer who is unable to describe their collection in this way, even though they are aware that such a proper way exists, may feel some degree of social anxiety and/or embarrassment for instance (see also Holt 1998[17] for further discussion of this). Of course, the acquisition of such specialist knowledge implies that one has had the opportunity and the time to acquire it.

The main issue is thus usually not one of being able to afford to buy the object of interest, but knowing the why, the when and the how of consuming it. While Bourdieu addressed the issue of members of the upper class having an unflappable sense of social ease and self-confidence arising from their innate knowledge of how to consume those things representative of their status, the broader application of the concept therefore addresses the way in which members of particular consumption communities possess a shared understanding of not only what to consume but how to consume it.

There is thus an intrinsic connection between tribal capital and tribal competence. Your status within the tribe will relate directly to your level of competence in the context. If you are serious about gaining credibility with the tribe you need to bear in mind that this will 'demand a high investment of cultural capital in the activity itself, in preparing, maintaining and using the equipment, and especially perhaps in verbalising the experiences' (Bourdieu 1984:220). This illustrates the essentially social nature of cultural capital. Possession of cultural capital confirms one's membership of the group. Possession of greater levels of cultural capital suggests an elevated position in the group's prevailing social hierarchy. You need to be able to demonstrate a commitment to the activity and an ability to articulate that commitment. It is also worth pointing out that this does *not* mean that a company's senior executives have to go out and 'live the brand' 24/7, a point I will elaborate on in Chapter 7.

What happens if you try to join the tribe, but in your eagerness to join, you get things wrong? You inadvertently make social, or in this case tribal, *faux pas* that reveal you to be an interloper rather than an authentic member of the group? Yet again it is worthwhile reverting to Bourdieu for a deeper understanding of the possibilities here.

Bourdieu invokes the metaphor of Leopold Bloom to convey the notion of unintentional self-exclusion from the upper class. Bloom, being both

Jewish and a member of the petit bourgeoisie, is 'doubly excluded' from the culture into which he seeks to be integrated ' . . . and therefore being doubly excluded, doubly anxious to be included, he bows, just in case, to everything which looks as if it might be culture and uncritically venerates the aristocratic traditions of the past' (1984:323).

This double anxiety leads, ironically, to self-exclusion – exposing oneself as an outsider through mistaken reverence for the wrong objects or excessive reverence for the right ones. This behaviour, born as it is out of a craving to belong, ' . . . exposes the petit bourgeois to cultural allodoxia, that is, all the mistaken identifications and false recognitions which betray the gap between acknowledgement and knowledge'; in the rush to acknowledge he acknowledges the wrong things and fails to acknowledge the right things or does not acknowledge them in the right way.

Another interesting argument of Bourdieu's is that such mistaken reverence for that which is not really legitimate effectively gave birth to a new cultural form, middlebrow culture (1984:327). Even if such a cultural form, as Bourdieu rather harshly suggests, is born out of allodoxia, it is real. It has taken on a life of its own, in that it has become recognizable as a form of culture. Hence the presence of forms of 'pop' culture that are close imitations of 'legitimate' art and culture, albeit that their consumption is far more widely adopted. While a particular cultural artefact, if appropriated by the wider population, can lose its legitimacy as a marker of cultural capital for the elite, it can become a legitimate marker of identity for a wider tribe. In many instances this entire process can take place without any of the awkwardness or self-consciousness that Bourdieu attributes to poor Leopold. The quasi-narcissistic nature of contemporary tribalism means that small clusters of consumers can self-affiliate to tribes in a way that embraces and celebrates self-consciousness rather than experiences it as awkward or embarrassing. The explosion of interest in football is a case in point. For a huge number of fans the identity consists of facepaint, official replica kits, the wearing of jester hats in team colours and participating in Mexican waves. These practices make the longer-term tribal participants cringe but the new arrivals are oblivious to this. Instead they imagine their practices as representative of the values they attribute to the best traditions of sports fandom, such as passion and loyalty to your team. What this all means is that tribal capital can evolve and take multiple forms, but it is imperative for the marketer to understand what it has evolved from, in order to be able to support all the variants of linking value that exist within the disparate constituencies that make up the wider tribe. In particular, it behoves the tribal marketer to understand the differences between how tribal capital operates among the 'hard core' devotees who in some respects may make up the most visible face of the tribe, and how it operates among the tribal mainstream, who sense that something authentic is taking place and who may simply want to feel a part of it without wanting to necessarily concern themselves with every single nuance. In this way tribal marketers can position themselves to achieve a balance between providing support for both constituencies without having their marketing efforts collapse. This might seem like a complex or even contradictory idea, but it is important for the tribal marketer to realize that the perceived authenticity of a brand or activity may derive primarily from the sheer visibility of the hard-core devotees. Hence the brand or activity will only continue to be perceived as authentic by the wider constituency for as long as the most passionate members of the tribe continue to devote themselves to it. The very simple implication to be derived from all this is that products and services aimed at the potentially profitable majority should not undermine the linking value felt by the hard core minority. If potential conflicts arise then some kind of remedial action should be taken to affirm the hard-core linking value in some other way. However, none of this will be effective unless the marketer understands the manner in which the system(s) of tribal capital actually work(s).

In trying to identify and distinguish between different forms of tribal capital, it is reassuring to note that the real purpose of any constituency within a tribe trying to make distinctions between themselves and others is to reassure themselves of their own authenticity.

Sarah Thornton (1997)[18] argues convincingly that the 'mainstream' is nothing more than something that is invoked by members of a subculture when they wish to make distinctions between their superior (collectively 'hip') 'ingroup' and some easily derogated 'other'. She describes rave culture as 'not a unitary culture but a cluster of subcultures ... (which) maintain their own dress codes, dance styles ... and catalogue of ... rituals'. Thus 'club cultures are taste cultures' (1997:200) whereby communal identities form around shared tastes that can be altered if necessary, to preserve social distinctions. For Thornton, while rave is (or was!) a youth subculture, the cultural consumption of the participants is not primarily defined in opposition to either the 'parent culture' or mainstream society in a general sense. It is instead defined in opposition to the alternative musical tastes that populate the wider youth subculture. There *is* a desire for distinction, and this distinction is achieved through shared taste and collectively knowing what is 'hip'. Thornton invokes Bourdieu's concept of cultural capital to propose that 'hipness' is in fact a form of subcultural capital:

> ... *subcultural capital can be objectified or embodied ... in the form of fashionable haircuts and carefully assembled record collections ... subcultural capital is embodied in the form of being 'in the know' regarding use of ... current slang and looking as if you were born to perform the latest dance styles.*
>
> (Thornton 1997:203)

Members of subcultures therefore utilize subcultural capital to practice resistance to alternative tastes, in order to affirm the superiority of their collective sense of identity over that of the 'mainstream'. Consumers can form subcultures that allow them to develop and maintain a positive (collective) sense of self, through collective forms of leisure consumption that simultaneously satisfies the need for community and identity through the means of shared taste. This is in some ways most readily achieved through the dismissal of alternative identities as being associated with allegedly inferior tastes.

It follows that if the tribal marketer can learn how to affirm each tribal constituency in their own particular perceived authenticity, then any tensions between so-called 'newbies' or 'wanna-bes' and those who see themselves as purists may be much easier to manage. However, this does imply an acquired sensitivity to the tribe and a commitment to the methods needed to acquire that sensitivity.

This application of the concept of subcultural capital to tribes, in the form of tribal capital, makes even more sense when we remind ourselves that the basis for tribal membership is shared passion. To participate as a member of the tribe, you must be able to share that passion in some way. Mitchell and Imrie's (2011)[19] analysis of the record collectors tribe is a perfect example of this. For Mitchell and Imrie, 'an understanding of the specific cultural capital of a tribe ... presents an avenue for marketers to reach tribal members and develop a collective, bonded loyalty'. In the case of the record collectors tribe, the tribal capital does not reside solely in the ownership of the collection itself but in the rather less tangible attributes of expert knowledge of and emotional devotion to the records and the work invested in their collection. Members of the tribe need to be able to find common ground with one another, to have their devotion mutually validated. Before they can be admitted to the tribe, would-be members must demonstrate that they share the tastes of the group. One of the most important markers of tribal identity is thus the ability to demonstrate a commitment to the belief that the sound quality of vinyl records is superior to that of any other recorded medium. This is not to say that it's advisable to attempt tribal entry (or cultural entrée as Robert Kozinets calls it) by means of adoption of a few simple clichés about the superiority of the medium. Members of tribes pride themselves on their knowledge of the activities and objects they devote themselves to, and just as they look up to those who know more about such things, they will look down on those who profess knowledge but who cannot back their claims up.

It follows that anyone who attempts to present themselves as a member of the tribe but who clearly lacks the requisite insider knowledge will come across as insincere and inauthentic. Marketers who make such an erroneous approach risk being dismissed out of hand as 'suits' who 'don't get it' and whose motivation is to rip people off, rather than support the tribe. Hence the need to gain access to some degree of understanding of what the system of tribal capital actually is, and the need to retain what Cova and Cova refer to as a humble attitude in the meantime. It behoves any aspiring member of the tribe to retain a humble demeanour until they have acquired and can demonstrate contextual competence in their own right. Once the marketer has acquired at least some of this competence, or at the very least shown willing to seek to acquire it, their efforts to support tribal linking value will begin to have credibility with the tribe.

Concluding thoughts

For a brand tribe to emerge and establish itself as an ongoing entity, a number of conditions need to be present.

First, some kind of unanticipated peak experience must be shared by a number of people. It must be kept in mind that these people need not be geographically co-present but might have responded in a similar way to a media event or a personal experience. Either way, the singular nature of the experience means that they found it personally meaningful and wish to share it with others who also found it meaningful, emotive, and special.

In the Beamish example, there was a prior willingness to engage in a particular form of youth subculture activity, but prior membership of a subculture is not necessary for someone to suddenly wish to affiliate to a tribe who seem to have shared your experience.

What makes tribal formation more likely is that if an experience is particularly profound, the desire to share it with like-minded others will be all the stronger. It might also be perceived as easier to be able to repeat or re-live the experience if other people can be persuaded to either listen to your accounts of how exciting or special something was, or better still, be persuaded to repeat the experience with you. Of course given the level of take-up of social media among contemporary consumers, it is all the easier to proffer some account of personal experience into cyberspace and have someone else respond to it, thereby initiating social contact among devotees who might have never even met prior to this.

In the Beamish case, joint efforts at re-living or maintaining the singularity of the experience (what Belk et al. would call sacralization maintenance) led the group to experiment briefly with alternatives before reverting to the brand associated with the initial experience. In other cases, special experiences might instead come to be associated with an activity rather than a specific brand, so it may be highly context-dependent. Football fans tend to subsequently project their initial enjoyment of live football onto one of the teams playing that day, rather than to the idea of simply being a fan of football in general, but this is clearly influenced by the cultural context whereby the norm is to channel your identity into support for one team. Surfers, on the other hand, become addicted to getting 'stoked' (O'Connor and Richardson 2006)[20] rather than immediately becoming devoted to one particular brand of surfboard.

Thus while it can help to have one particular object to focus on as a tribal talisman, it isn't absolutely necessary. From the tribal marketer's perspective, either experiential marketing events can be designed in order to make the brand a particularly prominent part of the experience or a careful and rigorous approach to tribal marketing can eventually bring about a robust connection between the brand and the tribe's sense of linking value, over a longer timeframe (further examples of this are discussed in Chapter 7). This connection between tribal activity and specific brand can even develop in cases where the tribe originally disliked a particular brand, something which speaks volumes for the validity of the tribal approach to branding.

For a tribe to make the jump from an ephemeral to a more long-lived existence, one or two additional phases seem important. Repeat experiences must be accessible within a reasonably compact timeframe, in order to reassure the tribe that the sense of transcendence and flow can be re-lived. In the Beamish case there was an element of serendipity involved, because the emergent tribe had access to other brands denied them, but managed to re-live their initial experience courtesy of the generous response by the company to their request for a repeat visit to the Brewery.

One further point related to this particular case was the absence of intent on the company's part to initiate a brand tribe. The tribe initiated this repeat visit themselves and their brand-related bond was reinforced as a result. Deliberate attempts by marketers to impose tribal membership on customers risk coming across as contrived by comparison, unless there is a deliberate, culturally well-informed co-participatory style taken to any attempt to initiate the formation of a brand tribe.

On a related note, while another factor in the emergence of more robust and enduring tribal connections is the emergence of social enforcement practices, the marketer should probably leave these to the tribe to develop for themselves. Overt attempts on the company's part to define tribal activity exclusively in terms of one brand could amount to a kiss of death for the corporation's perceived credibility. If a marketer jumps the gun, in a sense, and seeks to confine the tribe to consumption of their brand only, it might be extremely difficult to persuade the tribe that the corporation are any different to other commercial entities whose concern to achieve commercial objectives must be achieved no matter what.

There is a subtle but important difference between tribal acceptance of the need for a brand to be commercially viable, and tribal perceptions that a brand is aiming to achieve that commercial viability at the expense of tribal linking value. For related reasons, the development of oppositional brand loyalty as a further element of sacralization maintenance should be left in the hands of the tribe. The Ducati case from Chapter 2 is an obvious exemplar of the benefits of a non-coercive approach. Through facilitating the tribe in their desire to engage in discourse related to all brands of motorcycle, the Ducati corporation succeeded in creating a perception of their brand as an authentic embodiment of a shared passion for motorcycling in general – or rather, I should say that they succeeded in co-creating this perception with the tribe. This came directly from following the principle that the tribe's freedom to interact with each other online should be as unhindered as possible.

Thus what will make the transition to a more long-lived community more likely is tribal access to multiple forms of social media. Playful online interaction is an imperative in the emergence of contemporary brand tribes. A further point for tribal marketers to note is that while facilitating such interaction via for instance a brand Facebook page is thus an advantage, that unofficial web pages dedicated to the brand are a thing to be encouraged rather than discouraged. Some groups seem to prefer celebrating the brand in their own idiosyncratic way rather than via official brand media.

This brings us back to the point that marketers really need to focus on providing opportunities for consumers to have an experience that they can make their own. This allows the consumers to exercise a form of personal sovereignty (Holt 2002)[21] that helps to singularize the experience. In the Beamish case, having the opportunity to engage in the ritual of pulling one's own pint effectively initiated feelings of ownership. This was a fundamental component of tribal formation because it was so special that participants wanted to talk to each other about and verbally and visually re-live what had happened.

How does this compare to the TCEs experienced by attendees at Jeep brandfests as described by Schouten et al. (2007)? This sort of sophisticated approach to experiential marketing, whereby participants must perform challenging brand-related tasks together, such as helping each other to successfully negotiate cross-country obstacle courses, is an excellent way to ensure that participants will experience a sense of flow through high levels of emotional involvement in an activity. Further, the resulting sense of personal achievement tends to be shared with other participants with whom they can swap stories and experience consciousness of kind. Well-designed displays of brand heritage-related material at post-challenge barbeques help to reinforce the perception that it is the Jeep brand that really signifies what the tribe have in common with each other. This means that brandfest events can form a very useful part of the tribal approach to branding.

However, it is vital to reiterate the point made above that promotional events, even events like brandfests that can sometimes result in customers having TCE experiences, are not to be seen as the initial stage of implementing tribal marketing. Tribal marketing begins with seeking to understand the tribal identity, tribal linking value, and system of tribal capital, via implementation of the tactics of ethno-marketing as discussed in Chapters 4 to 6.

Furthermore, once an initial period of ethno-marketing has been implemented, there is far more to tribal branding than a few well-designed experiential marketing events that allow consumers to have what they will perceive as unique experiences. For brand tribes to survive and grow, it is not enough to provide experiences that will hopefully prove to be transcendent. It is necessary to follow up on these experiences by ensuring that consumers have the chance to re-live them through further interaction with one another. This interaction should be as spontaneous as possible. In the absence of freedom to innovate and develop their own rituals, their own rules, a community will fail to grow. Hence a dual approach of facilitating or at least benign tolerance of unofficial social media alongside operation of official social media for the brand seems best.

One of the main implications to draw from the Beamish case is that tribes tend to designate particular places and times as appropriate spaces for the enactment of tribal identities and participation in tribal rituals. And of course while there will be ways in which the marketer can support that, a key issue is to respect the tribe's freedom to maintain their own spaces, including online. Not all members of the tribe will want to take part in the 'official' gatherings, be they virtual or offline, even if the marketer seems to have some level of understanding of the tribe's system of cultural capital.

Another advantage of a policy of benign tolerance towards unofficial media is that it recognizes that brand tribes tend to originate from consumers rather than companies. Unofficial websites are by their nature at liberty to permit a wider range of behaviours than might be deemed seemly on a corporate website. There is also the advantage that the content of such websites is clearly at a distance from the corporation. However, the existence of such websites and brand-related enclaves is of great potential benefit to the corporation, because they are potentially representative of those hard-core brand constituencies whose basis for linking value may be slightly different to the majority of brand users. They are thus a potential source of user-related insight and user-created authenticity that the corporation would otherwise have to do without.

Ultimately you need the tribe to engage in affirming brand-related meaning for one another. You should not attempt to set yourself up as the sole provider or generator of brand-related meaning. That is not your role as a tribal marketer. You can certainly propose certain meanings via advertising campaigns and brandfests, for instance, but these proposals should be grounded in an understanding of tribal linking value and the prevailing system of tribal capital or they will lack credibility with the tribe. Also, in allowing the tribe to generate meanings for themselves, you need to give them the freedom to come up with their own ways of doing it. Your role is to identify and support the ways in which they choose to connect with one another, so that you can make brand-related offerings to them that support this meaning, this linking value. Hence the methodologies for gaining a sympathetic understanding of linking value as outlined in Chapters 4 to 6.

I'll briefly mention two final points. First – this feeling of being in a tribe does not necessarily have to be initiated by a full-blown peak experience in every case. With some consumers it may be that their initiation into the tribe is more gradual, hence the importance of support and facilitation of follow up experiences and interaction. It's also possible that for some reason even after some kind of peak experience that the members of a tribe may suddenly feel that the object or practice of desire has lost its inherent sacredness. Too many people have adopted it. It has become 'too commercial'. It no longer says something special or magical about the tribe because everyone else is using it too. So peak experience is no guarantee of the permanent establishment of a tribe. However, it is all in the follow-up, a complex mix of tribal opportunities to interact and a marketer's sensitivity in realizing that a tribe is presently emerging and may be open to marketer support.

Also, if the company acquires an understanding of linking value, they can set the pace through innovations that reflect tribal linking value in some way. Apple Macintosh are the illustration par excellence of this. They cultivate a sense of mystique around each product launch so that members of the tribe are agog with anticipation, riven with rumour, and so forth! When the new product comes out the tribe seize it as an embodiment of this collective sense of excitement.

Table 3.1　Tribal activity and marketer action

Conditions for/signs of tribal activity	Appropriate marketer action or initiative	Further ethno-marketing implications
Some form of peak and/or flow experience, either brand-related (Beamish community) or activity-related (surfers, snow boarders), or both	Willingness to explore customer-initiated experiences/customer adaptations of brand initiatives	Need to monitor environment for possible emergence of consumer tribes
Usually consumer-initiated rather than marketer-initiated	(Note that while transcendent customer experience can take place at brandfest type events or via other marketer-led initiatives, it can't be forced on consumers, it can only be facilitated.)	Need to approach tribes and attempt to gain **cultural entrée** as defined by Robert Kozinets – see Chapter 4)
Desire/compulsion to *share the perceived meanings of such experiences with others*, in order to perpetuate a sense of epiphany and/or transcendence	Interact with tribe, take part in tribal activity, begin to acquire insight into basis for shared passion and linking value	Use methods and tactics of ethno-marketing to gain insight into tribal perspectives, as a basis for facilitating interaction and designing or revamping brand events (see Chapters 4 to 6)
Development of further playful ways to repeat experience/reinforce linking value (development of Beamish 'constitution', emergence of oppositional brand loyalty, construction of additional shared practices and emergence of rules)	Facilitate tribal activities, *including online activity*, where appropriate, based on emergent understanding of tribal linking values	Continue to use ethno-marketing tactics to refine your understanding of and support for tribal linking value(s), via support for tribe *and* initiatives of your own
Emergence of system of *tribal cultural capital* as tribe's sense of distinction becomes more refined	Sensitize yourself to the way in which system of tribal cultural capital is used by the tribe to evaluate your custodianship of the brand	Continue to use ethno-marketing to assess degree to which variations in tribal cultural capital exist across different clusters within the tribe

The Harry Potter tribe constitutes another example. Each book launch became an opportunity for the tribe to express itself, so what was essentially a new commercial product launch effectively became a triumphant re-sacralization of the community, a well-managed facilitation of TCE for the tribe.

For Harry Potter fans, the launch of the final book in the series was an opportunity to dress up as witches and wizards and enjoy the limelight that this event bestowed on them. Of course JK Rowling herself was on hand to interact with the tribe. As it happens, such events are the perfect opportunity for participants to exercise their tribal capital. One fan responded to the news that the launch of the e-version of the Harry Potter books had 'exceeded expectations' by posting the comment 'congrats on scoring an E! (not the drug)' on *The Guardian* newspaper website article that had covered the story. This typifies what I mean by tribal capital, because it is a reference to the grade 'Exceeds Expectations' that young wizards and witches must achieve in their 'Ordinary Wizarding Level' exams in order to be admitted to senior classes to prepare for their N.E.W.T. (Nastily Exhausting Wizarding Tests) examinations.

These are the sort of things that a member of the tribe is expected to understand and be able to converse knowledgeably and passionately – or at least playfully – about. A tribal marketer simply has to understand these things, and this understanding is really only to be acquired by a sensitive and humble approach to the tactics now outlined in Chapters 4 to 6. These tactics are thus a prerequisite to any form of promotional activity, or the aspiring tribal marketer will be unable to connect with the tribe. Table 3.1 outlines a summary of the stages in tribal development and some of the corresponding appropriate actions on the part of the marketer.

(For further discussion of the Harry Potter tribe check out my blog post on Tribal Rituals at tribalbranding.com)

4 Understanding Tribal Dynamics: Beginning to Engage with the Art of Ethno-Marketing

Introduction

This chapter introduces the ethno-marketing phase of tribal branding in more detail. It explains the need to understand the tribe on their terms. It outlines in broad rather than specific detail how ethnographic techniques can be used to gain an understanding of tribal rituals and tribal values. It also takes a preliminary look at a limited number of case studies which show the benefits to be derived from cultivating such an understanding, including a review of some cases documented in the existing literature on Tribal Marketing.

The good news when it comes to trying to gain access to any tribe is its very accessibility. Anyone can join, and joining one tribe does not preclude you from joining other tribes. There are some exceptions to this, which incidentally is where the distinction between tribes on the one hand and brand communities on the other becomes more significant and useful, but generally speaking the principles for approaching all forms of consumer community are similar, in that a careful and respectful approach (as outlined herein) is best. As particular nuances of the tribal identity and value system become more apparent, then the approach can be refined accordingly to enhance the chances of gaining deeper access to the tribe.

An example will serve to illustrate. The members of a local Mini club initially warmly received a colleague who was interested in conducting research on the Mini Cooper brand community. At first things went well, but when it became apparent that he could not commit completely to the group identity by acquiring his own Mini, the welcome gradually faded and the study was ultimately abandoned. A tribal marketer is unlikely to be aware at first as to whether the community more closely resembles an informal, loosely structured non-hierarchical tribe, or a slightly more formal and zealous brand community, but it is important to adapt to the mores and values of the group as their idiosyncrasies emerge.

Not every brand community takes such an absolute view of the world. In the above example, the investigation foundered because the tribe in question weren't *car* enthusiasts, they were *mini* enthusiasts. Once a community's identity and sense of hierophany, for whatever reason, becomes exclusively tied into the symbolic meanings associated with one particular brand, then that's it. Anyone who fails to take this seriously will lose credibility. However, not all brand tribes take such an exclusive or restrictive view. When you look at brand tribes like that of Ducati where motorcycle enthusiasts who own other brands of motorbike are welcomed to the community, it becomes clear that we should not over-generalize about the specific values of every brand tribe. Some tribes will have stricter rules than others, some tribes will be more exclusively devoted to individual brands than others, and so on. I would go so far as to generalize that the longer a tribe has been in existence, then the more likely it is that some kind of social hierarchy will have formed and the collective values of the tribe will be more readily observed, but every tribe still needs to be treated on its own merits.

This helps to clarify Cova and Cova's argument that tribal marketing approach needs to be grounded in the ethno-sociological approach of Dibie (1998, as cited in Cova and Cova[1]). What are the things, what are the emotions, what are the ideas and feelings that cause people to feel connected to each other? Tribal marketing thus examines consumption at the micro-social level, where people gather together in communities and experience linkages to one another via sharing collectively constructed meanings. This is below the aggregated macro-social level at which entire cultures and societies operate, but it is above the level of the individual. It is therefore concerned with the level of everyday social interaction between members of the tribe and it is through immersing oneself into the tribe's lived experience and social interactions that the tribal marketer learns the rules of the game. Only by immersing yourself, collecting tribal data in the appropriate way, and interpreting the data properly can you as an aspiring tribal marketer begin to understand how to fit in.

Thus we now know that we need to focus on what actually links people together, rather than trying to promote products and services AT people whom we have artificially aggregated together in segments. So how do we begin to approach these people and how do we begin to go about trying to gain a sympathetic, or better yet, empathetic understanding of these links, so that we can begin to support them? In short, how do you begin your approach to the tribe?

Beginning your approach to the tribe – first question: Who do you observe, and where do you observe them?

In their 2002 discussion of tribal marketing, Cova and Cova provide a useful example of how to begin observing a tribe when the tribal boundaries are unclear. Taking the example of the Citroën 2CV tribe, they note that while there are many thousands of registered members of the 2CV clubs, there could be many multiples of this number who derive an idiosyncratic pleasure from owning a 2CV, even if they don't feel the need to join a 2CV club. Maybe the hardcore enthusiasts who take part in clubs are the ones doing the most to keep the profile of the 2CV publicly visible, but the other 2CV owners certainly form some part of a much wider social movement, albeit a movement that is quite loosely bound and certainly not confined to admiration for or even ownership of one type of retro car. We now suddenly realize that in a sense those people who are in love with vintage Volkswagen Beetles or Camper Vans may also be part of this wider social movement, and even if they do not all interact socially with each other, they might feel a connection or emotional link.

Therefore if you want to begin to observe this wider tribe, you may not have to travel very far. Some initial desk research might be a great help in beginning to map out why people are so fond of vintage cars of different sorts. You might even have a friend who owns one with whom you could arrange to have a cup of coffee or a glass of wine or beer, while you chat to them about how this fondness for their old Volkswagen or 2CV came about. Alternatively you could begin to check local media to see whether any vintage car shows were coming up, or whether there were any vintage car clubs in the locality. You could even go online and begin to search for vintage car discussion forums and websites – although by doing so you might feel a little bit intimidated by the sheer number of such online communities! While it is very interesting and informative to dip in and out of the different online communities established on Google Groups (see groups.google.com), for instance, in order to get more of a sense of the sheer diversity of different types of online community that exist, in practice, the tribal marketer needs to explore both online and offline for traces of tribal activity.

In the Citroën 2CV case, any social setting where two or more people come together to affirm each other in their mutual interest and love of vintage cars can serve as an initial observational space. By observing people in this space and reflecting on your observations, you can begin to learn something about this wider social movement that will help you to sensitize yourself and prepare for your approach to a more specific grouping such as the 2CV tribe.

In identifying sources or sites of tribal activity where more specific traces of tribal identity can be found, Cova and Cova's figure of the Tribal Clover helps us to distinguish between visible and invisible traces of tribal identity and feeling (Figure 4.1).

Physical traces of the tribe are to be found on the horizontal axis of the clover, the so-called 'axis of visibility' upon which are located the institutions (for example fan clubs, owners clubs, sports clubs) that represent some aspect of the tribe, and the occasions (festivals, exhibitions, competitions, concerts, sporting fixtures) when members of the tribe gather together. This is analogous to the sources of initial information we've already considered, such as car enthusiast clubs with formal memberships, and car shows which can also attract a much wider audience who may harbour an admiration for certain

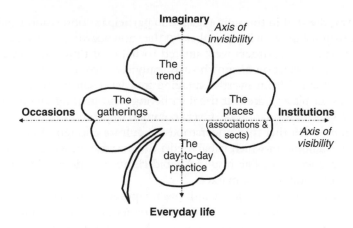

Figure 4.1 **The tribal clover**
Source: © Emerald Group Publishing. Reprinted with permission.

types of car but who do not necessarily wish to associate themselves with official clubs. As Cova and Cova also correctly point out, gatherings will take place in virtual space too. We usually think of virtual space as referring to the Internet but the notion of tribal space needs to be widened to consider other media and spaces both physical and virtual, such as the canteen, local bar, and TV or radio chat show where the DJ has asked people to call in to discuss that afternoon's football matches or the previous Saturday's contestants on a TV talent show like the *X Factor*.

The vertical axis of the clover, the so-called axis of invisibility, refers to trends that in one sense are invisible because we cannot observe exactly where they are going or even if they will all continue. Yet hints exist as to who the members of a tribe imagine themselves to be, or how they feel, so perhaps these feelings, whims, and fashions are not entirely invisible. In any event Cova and Cova advocate studying the daily lived practices and shared experiences of individual members of the tribe, in order to gain insight into the fantasies that might lie behind the visible behaviours. Thus while we might not be able to see their fantasies and imaginations with the naked eye, through observation and exploratory interviews we can begin to map out how the tribe express their invisible selves through their interactions with that which is visible and material, and in this way we begin to uncover and understand the invisible as well as the visible elements of the life of the tribe.

Cova and Cova then outline the case of Salomon as an exemplar of how to approach a tribe using tribal marketing. In both snowboarding and in-line skating Salomon took a similar approach. There was no immediate attempt to penetrate a market segment or segments. Instead there was a philosophy of humility and a desire to understand the activity from the perspective of the tribal members participating in it. Salomon set up a marketing unit dedicated to the snowboarding market but instead of engaging in promotional work right away, the staff in this unit engaged in participant observation and culti-vating relationships with key members of the snowboarding subculture. Over time, leading snowboarders were invited to help with product design until Salomon had a selection of snowboards ready for tribal use. Even then, they patiently refrained from overtly engaging in a hard sell of the new boards, instead just displaying them at tribal gatherings and inviting members of the tribe to try the new boards out. Overt commercial promotion was postponed until Salomon felt that they understood the culture enough to have an intu-itive understanding of which tribal media to advertise in, which tribal events to sponsor, and so on. The result? A rapid climb to suddenly becoming the number three brand in the market.

While Cova and Cova clearly indicate the potential benefits of a so-called humble approach, they refer to participant observation without fully unpack-ing the term for us. However, a couple of things are clear. It is obviously important to gain as deep an insight as possible into the ethno-sociological links between tribal members. It is imperative to put yourself in their shoes, or in the case of the in-line skaters, in their skates. What does the world look like from their perspective, and how do you gain that perspective? This is what the humility Cova and Cova refer to actually means – to bring yourself down to the level of the individual participant and to experience the activity and the brand through their eyes, instead of presuming that you, the marketer, already know what the activity is about or what the brand ought to mean. Only then can you begin to understand the nature of the tribal relationships and begin to understand how to support and facilitate those relationships.

Of course, while this advice is excellent, it still does not tell us everything we need to know about how to actually begin a participant observation. We now understand the need to be humble and we understand where to begin looking. However, how can we actually begin to participate and how can we be confident that the members of the tribe will accept our presence and engage sufficiently with us to admit us to the tribe thereby giving us potential access to the understanding that we seek?

What exactly is participant observation, and why do we need it?

It is worth mentioning that while the tribal marketing approach properly involves participant observation, that this does not mean the observation of participants. It means combining observation with actual participation. The correct term for uninvolved observation is, unsurprisingly, non-participant observation. I should also mention that not every commentator in this field would agree on the absolute necessity of participant observation as a part of tribal marketing and tribal branding. Cova and Cova themselves refer to several instances of tribal marketing activity that did not involve it at all – and I will discuss several cases of tribe/brand interaction in Chapter 6 that do not involve it either. However, I would have to say that by committing to participant observation, the tribal marketer is giving themselves the opportunity to gain a much greater level of understanding of tribal linking value and tribal culture. When this understanding is fed back into the brand, it in turn differentiates the brand far more strongly and makes it more difficult for competing brands to gain a foothold with the tribe. There is also a related risk that failure to gain this deeper level of understanding means that the marketer will commit the fallacy of prematurely engaging in promotional activity, trying to impose brand meanings that lack credibility with the tribe. Very often, given the typical structure of marketing career timeframes, brand managers might only spend 18 to 24 months or less working on a particular brand. Contrast this with the years of commitment that members of a brand tribe have given to a brand and suddenly the idea that we have something to learn from the tribe makes far more sense.

By actively participating, rather than observing, the marketer undergoes the experience of a novice or apprentice member of the culture, and consequently much deeper insight can be obtained – access is opened up to the kind of unspoken knowledge that distinguishes the insider from the outsider, the member from the non-member. As Alex Stewart puts it, 'the tacit knowledge that the novice acquires is . . . much more central to insider culture than is knowledge that can be transmitted explicitly' (Stewart 1998:24).[2] I accept that this has implications for how brand managers spend their time when they take over management of a brand, but as discussed elsewhere in the book, this need not be an insurmountable problem.

It's also worth noting that a preference for participant over non-participant observation is not universally accepted. It has been argued that people who are aware that they are being observed will not behave naturally and that the observational data collected is therefore diminished in usefulness. Some commentators therefore advocate undisclosed non-participant observation as a means of ensuring that the observational data thus collected is authentic. However, this automatically means that the opportunity to collect the deeper insights conferred by full participation is foregone.

This still leaves us with the problem of people who are conscious of being observed adapting their behaviour, either subconsciously or consciously, to portray themselves in a flattering light, to protect their privacy, or both. Either way, the criticism that it has now become more difficult to collect authentic data is a valid one. The situation is made even more complicated by the fact that the same issue also affects ethnographic interview data. So how do we get around this problem?

First we have to take note of the fact that the tribal marketer really has no choice but to resolve this problem. Tribal marketing depends on the achievement of at least some degree of tribal membership. Without this, the full efficacy of the approach will not be realized. Fortunately, there is a way around it.

The solution to the problem is this. Over the course of time, participant observers are more likely to achieve at least some degree of social acceptance by the group. Group members gradually become more relaxed and less guarded in their behaviour, so that over an extended period of time their behaviour in the presence of the researcher reverts to normal, natural behaviour for the group. This means that the resulting observational data is more reliable. This social acceptance also begins to result in social invitations of an informal nature being extended, thus conferring opportunities for access to the kind of rich, behind the scenes, data that ethnographers crave. As the level of social integration into the group increases, more and more opportunities will present themselves for capturing rich, natural, speech-in-action type data, in this ever more relaxed social setting.

Of course this greater level of integration into the group raises other issues. How can the observer continue to guarantee that they will be able to pursue their research agenda in an unbiased and objective way? Surely this kind of social integration makes subjectivity unavoidable? In fact, while this is a valid concern, there are ways of addressing it, but the best way to do so is to integrate those techniques into the more detailed discussion of data collection methods in Chapter 4. Also for this sort of approach to become possible presupposes that what Robert Kozinets (2010)[3] terms *cultural entrée* has been achieved. Hence the first step is to discuss how to go about achieving that.

Achieving cultural entrée

The achievement of cultural entrée is not necessarily easy but in some respects it is quite simple. Social acceptance into the group is dependent on the marketer's willingness to take an authentic interest in the group's activities. The researcher must show willing to take part and learn the ropes. Great patience may be required if the group's social hierarchy is particularly pronounced, as it will then take longer to achieve social status and credibility. Any attempt to rush things is inadvisable because it runs the risk of being perceived as insincere. If a perception develops that the marketer is not really interested in those things the group is passionate about, then the whole exercise risks being undermined.

Initially many groups may welcome a researcher's interest, for very understandable reasons. It is very gratifying when someone takes an interest in the things that you or I care about. There may even be an element of collective narcissism or normal, social exhibitionism involved in showing off the group identity and opening up to the newbie who has declared an interest. However, this will only take the researcher so far, and it is imperative that opportunities to roll up your sleeves and take part in a culturally appropriate way are seized as soon as they begin to present themselves.

While a short period of non-participant observation can help to shape the researcher's first impressions of how to behave, there is therefore no substitute for the sort of humble approach advocated by Cova and Cova and in practice taken by two leading consumer researchers in their achievement of cultural entrée to the Harley Davidson community. Marketers who are willing to adopt this approach really do have a much greater chance of being accepted by the tribe.

I'm therefore recounting the approach that John Schouten and his fellow researcher James McAlexander[4] took in approaching the Harley Davidson community, before reflecting on how this compares to the approach Lofland and Lofland (1995)[5] suggest for achieving the same goal in regard to other communities. I'll then explain how I adapted these strategies to achieve entrée myself into the die-hard culture of fervent football supporters. Finally, the chapter will conclude with a summary and brief reflection on all the tactics at the tribal marketer's disposal for the achievement of cultural entrée.

When Schouten and McAlexander decided to study what they termed the 'new bikers', their task was rendered less difficult by the decision to concentrate on Harley Davidson owners who were not affiliated to any of the notorious outlaw biker gangs often luridly associated with motorcycle subculture. Nonetheless they still had to prove their credentials in order to gain access to the sort of data they needed. Happily, they found that the more they proved their commitment, the greater the level of access they began to achieve to the sort of insider data that ethnography thrives on:

> ... as we deepened our ethnographic involvement our access to informants near the core of the subculture improved greatly. It was as though we were made to demonstrate our own commitment to the subculture before we could be taken into the full confidence of its adherents. Acculturation to the HDSC came gradually through attention to behavioral norms, through studies of scholarly and popular literature, and through information learned in the ongoing process of data collection. We also experienced periods of accelerated tutoring. When we first met the HOG chapter that we accompanied to two successive annual rallies, we were known as researchers working under the aegis of Harley Davidson. We were treated politely by some, standoffishly by others, and overly gregariously by others, but no one treated us as if we really belonged there. Our whole relationship with the HOG chapter changed dramatically less than 30 miles into our ride from Los Angeles to the Santa Maria rally site. One chapter member riding near the end of the procession of about two dozen bikes developed a mechanical problem and pulled off the road. One of us noticed and pulled over to render assistance. That act of consideration created an instant bond between us and two chapter members, who took us into their circle of riders and served for the remainder of the rally as our guides and tutors in the ways of HOG.

As the above passage demonstrates, authentic tribal marketing is predicated on the need for co-participation. This precludes the non-participant observation approach, because brand offerings from a non-participant are, ultimately, outsider offerings. Thus while there may be alternative levels of authentic co-participation, co-participation is a pre-requisite, and therefore cultural entrée must be attained. An aspiring tribal marketer, interested in cultivating a relationship with any tribe primarily because of the commercial opportunity they potentially represent, might not naturally find it easy to adopt a level of interest sufficient to be perceived by community members as sincere and authentic. However, without at least some level of authentic participation, the marketer will not be able to attain sufficient credibility to be perceived as one of the community. Without participating, the marketer risks being excluded, thereby failing to fulfil the potential of the tribal marketing approach. Hence the emphasis here on achieving cultural entrée via participant rather than non-participant observation as the key to successful ethno-marketing. Non-participant observation is certainly useful at the outset but it should only be used until sufficient findings have been generated to inform the cultural entrée attempt. Finally, it is also very reassuring to note the opinion of an expert and pioneer in the field, on the topic of whether participant observation causes excessive disruption. Robert Kozinets, the developer of the netnography method discussed in Chapter 5, says that any disruption to natural behaviour caused by the researcher disclosing their presence is in his opinion very small, but the potential understanding foregone by not participating fully is very large. He also says that while it is certainly possible to carry out non-disclosed netnography, he doesn't believe it is the optimal approach to take.

Additional perspectives on achieving cultural entrée – commencing social relationships

While Lofland and Lofland's book on analysing social spaces doesn't address tribal marketing per se, it does have some very useful insights to offer us. In particular what strikes me about their insight into approaching any group of people with a view to commencing a participatory study is the fact that what you are trying to do is effectively begin a social relationship with a number of people. In usual circumstances, we are more likely to begin social relationships with people out of mutual interest rather than out of a conflict of interest. Both for reasons of good ethical conduct and also in order to avoid problems later, therefore, it is better to disclose one's commercial identity as soon as possible. This should help to ensure that perceptions of intent to deceive do not arise later on. If any perception develops that initial interest in the identity or activity under study was simply feigned for alterior purposes, particularly commercial purposes, then it might be difficult or even impossible to regain the community's confidence. It is also worth bearing in mind that in normal social circumstances one might quite naturally disclose one's profession without it becoming a source of undue tension, so the act of identity disclosure on the part of the tribal marketer should not be allowed to artificially develop into a trepidation-filled experience.

Generally speaking, it should suffice to initially display a genuine interest in some way, while also taking the earliest possible naturally occurring opportunity to disclose one's identity and interests. A couple of additional factors are helpful, in my experience. Firstly, people are not necessarily particularly interested in a detailed explanation of who you are and what you do for a living, so you do not need to have an incredibly detailed and sophisticated explanation to hand. It is important to remember that the topic of mutual interest here is not your job, but rather it is whatever shared passion has brought the community together in the first place. That means that to embark on an elaborate explanation of who you are and what you do for a living would in all likelihood cause at least some degree of social awkwardness, even if your intentions were to sincerely disclose your identity. After all, the initial topic of conversation is more likely to revolve around the interests of the group. Hence initial engagement should be at that level, so that you are ready to discuss knitting, organic food, coffee, sport, or science fiction, to name but a few examples, in a way that demonstrates at least some level of interest in the topic at hand.

When an opportune moment to disclose one's identity as someone with a commercial interest actually arises, it is also important to keep in mind the need to have a simple and concise explanation to hand. Later on, if anyone has more detailed questions, it is preferable to take as naturalistic an approach as possible to answering these questions. Remember that most people will probably be more than happy with a very simple explanation of who you are, particularly if you yourself are relaxed about it and you have already managed to acquire and convey a sense of authentic interest in the community's activities. In my experience, the simpler the explanation, the better.

A further point to remember is that in any social clique, some of the participants may well have known one another for a considerable period of time and thus may spend a considerable amount of time engaged in social interaction and normal conversation with one another on all sorts of topics that seem at most peripheral to the group's main interest or activity. Just as it would be a bit on the crass side, socially, to impose oneself inappropriately on the conversation in any other context, it would be equally inappropriate as well as professionally insensitive to repeatedly attempt to artificially drag the conversation back to those things of direct interest to your research agenda. Patience and naturalistic behaviour are therefore key ingredients in the successful conduct of ethno-marketing. Remember that the people with whom you are seeking to engage are not there because you are paying them to take part in a focus group! They are there on their own terms and you, the ethnomarketer, must respect that.

In some respects, therefore, this is a slightly artificial and contrived situation. How can an aspiring ethno-marketer convince the people that they meet of an authentic interest in their activities, while simultaneously disclosing their identities and commercial agenda?

The answer is that a bespoke approach is necessary. Selection of the research team is important, but the required characteristics might vary on a case-to-case basis. The sort of person who works for a winter sports goods firm and gets on well socially with winter sports enthusiasts might seem ideal for a role as part of an ethno-marketing research team, but the question also arises as to whether they have the necessary observational skills and patience to take detailed fieldnotes?

Similarly, if someone has the ability to observe and take good fieldnotes, but cannot summon up the energy to engage wholeheartedly with, say, foodie enthusiasts on the subject of organic foods, recipes, and different styles of cooking, then they might not be suitable for a role as part of an ethno-marketing foodie research team. Ideally companies would therefore take a flexible approach to ethno-marketing team recruitment, and possibly put together small teams drawn from within and if necessary outside the organization. The emphasis needs to be on ensuring the right mix of social skills and research skills within the ethno-marketing team, to achieve both acceptance and the subsequent capture of the high-quality, rich data necessary in order for ethnographic insight to be derived.

It also makes sense that in practice not all members of the team can be expected to have a prior passion for the activity at hand. Given that situations might arise where it isn't possible to have a team member with a prior personal interest in the activity under study, it is also worth thinking about the approach to take in the event that a team, or for that matter, individual researchers have to try to achieve social acceptance or access when they are complete outsiders or novices without any prior knowledge of the community under study.

As explained by Lofland and Lofland, in these circumstances the 'learner' or even 'incompetent' role is something of a tried and tested approach to take. A genuine interest in learning about the activity will open doors into the community, provided you avoid the mistake of overdoing it by appearing to be excessively incompetent. A failure to ask reasonably competent questions can alienate rather than engage the very people you are seeking to establish a rapport with. This makes sense when you think of how a surfeit of inappropriate or superficial questions or behaviours can sometimes come across as indicative of a lack of interest.

You should also try to avoid interview questions that are designed to flatter your interviewee or pander excessively to their superior knowledge of different forms of tribal activity. Try also to ask questions that reflect at least some level of social competence in the context – although if you lack such basic competence it might be better to quietly admit it. It is fine to ask the sort of questions that someone who genuinely wants to learn more would ask, but it is dangerous and potentially counter-productive to ask questions that may infer an absolute lack of social competence in the particular context.

While from an orthodox marketing perspective it might seem more appropriate to ask questions that relate directly to the goods and services that members of a tribe buy, rather than ask questions about all the things that members of the tribe actually do, from an ethno-marketing perspective the objective is to acquire a deep understanding of tribal identity, so that you then understand how those goods and services fit in.

For instance, if you want to gain a deeper level of insight into the role and meaning of sports fan merchandise for members of particular sports fan tribes, you need to seek to gain an understanding of all aspects of fan identity, hence the validity of questions about ritual behaviours during the different stages of a football match or baseball game.

You need to probe the fans' self-appointed role as co-participants in determining the outcome of a game, in order to begin to understand how they use fan apparel and other forms of merchandise to achieve this. Hence merchandise such as team shirts can be seen as symbols of a co-participative identity. However, it is important to try to collect as much data as possible on participants' understandings of their roles, if you want to understand how they actually use fan merchandise – or any other resource – in order to perform these roles.

If you ask your sports fan interviewees directly about the importance of fan merchandise, they will be able to explain some aspects of its importance to you, but they will not be able to explain others. It is also worth noting at this stage that football fans will often say highly contradictory things about football merchandise, so without collecting observational data as well as interview data, it would prove far more difficult to understand the overall relationship. For instance, some fans will initially claim to have no interest in merchandise, but it often emerges that they have an extensive collection of football shirts and other memorabilia! Also, while they might not all wear team shirts to the match, their collection of team shirts at home may serve as an important resource in the affirmation of their understanding of what it really means to be a fan who supports their local team. So their behaviour inside the stadium may be an important driver of their behaviour in continuing to collect merchandise – even if they sometimes don't wear it and at first deny any interest in it.

What all this serves to illustrate is that we should not make over-simplified assumptions about the reasons why tribes do certain things, and we should ask questions in a sympathetic, interested and intelligent way – while bearing in mind that members of the tribe will quite often be unable to explain their own behaviour in response to a direct question. So tribal marketers need to go on patiently learning, observing, and questioning, in the knowledge that deeper insight continues to emerge over time, and comes from personal experience as well as observing and collecting interview data.

The research of Susan Fournier and her colleagues on ethno-marketing practices at Harley Davidson further demonstrates the way in which this works to deliver brand-related insight. For executives at the company, participation in the Harley Davidson Posse Ride allows them to access brand-related meanings that tap deeply into the tribe's core linking values. For ordinary members of the tribe, undertaking an arduous journey on your Harley is an initiation rite, a way of asserting that you too are truly a 'biker'. Sharing this experience allows executives to understand it from the tribe's point of view. Senior Harley Davidson executive Dave Storm explained it to Fournier and her colleagues like this:

> I'm a rider now... I am not a suit. I'm not an executive. The first Posse Ride I did... was to see if you could actually be upright on a bike for ten days straight, and make it cross country in all kinds of weather and conditions. So this – it's a quest like that.
>
> (Fournier et al. 2001)[6]

This level of personal commitment to participation in tribal rituals is echoed by (then) Business Development Vice President Clyde Fessler:

> One of the pleasures of (taking part)... is I get to be their guest and just play average Joe customer... riding a motorcycle just like our customers do. So, I arrive like everyone else, stand in line like everybody else, and that's part of our bonding with our customers... getting on a Harley and riding, experiencing what our customers feel as a first-hand experience, I can relate when we're designing our next type of motorcycle.
>
> (Fournier et al. 2001)

This has clear echoes of what ethnographers like Alex Stewart refer to as experiencing phenomena from the point of view of the participant rather than trying to evaluate it from gazing over their shoulders. That is not to imply in any way that going on a 'rolling rally' once a year can be regarded as some sort of substitute for a full ethnographic study of brand culture. Of course it can't, but that is not the point. The involvement of senior executives is complementary to and potentially highly valuable for the entire tribal branding project, but the point of including these anecdotes here is to introduce the point that what really matters is demonstrating to the tribe that you share their commitment to the tribal linking values.

Like them, you have been in the saddle for thousands of miles. You've pursued the 'quest' personally. This can sometimes matter far more than owning the very latest motorcycle or accessories – and in fact unless marketers grasp this important point, then they will never be able to develop a beneficial relationship with the tribe. For the tribe – for any tribe – the whole point is to share authentic experience and to share in tribal performance in an authentic way. Any marketer who tries to sell products and services to the tribe without sharing in tribal performance will not attain credibility or status within the tribe. If you cannot demonstrate enthusiasm for the activity the tribe are passionate about, if you do not participate personally, you risk being perceived as just another 'suit' trying to sell people stuff. That is not to say that tribes will never buy things from the 'suits' but it does mean giving up on the potential benefits of a closer relationship with the tribe. As the Posse Ride constitutes such an exemplar of good tribal branding practice, it is further discussed in Chapter 7. For now it is enough to note that if you can show a commitment to the tribe then you are far more likely to be accepted into the network of tribal relationships. You can then go on to use all the various tactics of ethnomarketing to gain insight and channel that insight back into your brand.

Other issues and challenges in achieving cultural entrée

It is worth noting that things can go badly wrong if online communities are not approached in the right way. Robert Kozinets details how one initial attempt at cultural entrée resulted in an online call from one of the leading members of the community to boycott the research! What is more useful about Kozinets' account of this experience is his subsequent elaboration on how his approach to the entire study should have differed.

He initiated an approach to one of the communities whom he had located via an Internet search for groups involved in consumer boycotts, without firstly informing himself as to that group's values, beliefs, and practices. He subsequently discovered that they had a very strong anti-establishment ethos, and that a request to them to cooperate with his study was an inappropriate course of action.

This corroborates the argument that you should not approach any group with a request for assistance with your research until you have undertaken sufficient initial research to gain at least some understanding of their identity. This is significant, because in practice it implies at least some degree of undisclosed observation. However, what makes this acceptable in my view is that the purpose of this initial work is not to carry out a study without the informed consent of the community, but rather to establish whether or not a full study can be carried out. Once it is clear that any initial findings are not to be used for any other purpose, or reported to any third party, or stored for any further use, there is no ethical issue that I can see.

The importance of approaching any online community with genuine humility is further emphasized by Kozinets' explanation of some of the other risks involved in taking an inappropriate approach. For example, the sheer number of research requests received by some communities means that community members have begun to equate such requests with spam. Even genuine requests asking people to contribute to a netnography and explaining that this is a new research methodology, completely dependent upon their cooperation and support, are no longer guaranteed a positive response. For community members who may well be highly educated and more than familiar with the fact that netnography as a research technique has been in existence for more than ten years, such approaches may seem very condescending, and, as Kozinets documents, may provoke a hostile response.

So what is to be done? For me, one part of the solution is to integrate offline ethnographic work with online approaches, so that community members whom you meet in offline, real-world contexts, can then take on the role of key informant and guide in online situations as well, thereby facilitating entrée for the researcher. However, this in no way precludes the usefulness of all aspects of Kozinets' recommendations for approaching online communities. It is just better in my view to use both, where and when possible.

There are several other preliminary stages that Kozinets recommends carrying out before initiating an approach to a particular community. Prior studies may give you very useful insights into the community's identity and ethos, insights that could prove invaluable in framing your own approach to the group. In general, a further preliminary step for any first-time student of tribes and tribal behaviour would of course be an immersion in the wider literature on the many idiosyncrasies of consumer tribes, to help give you an idea of what to expect. However, there is no substitute for community-specific insight, so any studies of communities of particular interest or relevance should be examined rigorously and religiously!

Incidentally – and this is extremely important – Kozinets also says that fieldnotes should be taken throughout this preliminary stage. (The techniques for taking such fieldnotes and analysing the resulting data are discussed in Chapters 5 and 6.)

A further point to be addressed prior to attempted cultural entrée is the need to familiarize oneself with any characteristics or idiosyncrasies of the particular community type in question. Again the point here is that it would be a huge mistake not to avail of the opportunity to gain as much initial understanding as possible of the type of community you hope to investigate, before you begin to investigate it. For example, blogging communities are more specialized in some ways than bulletin board-style community forums such as boards.ie or fan forums. In some respects 'newbies' on a blogging community, given its more specialized nature, might be more welcome than they are on a larger and less intimate bulletin board-style forum. While there is no one single hard and fast rule in relation to this, it can certainly help to alert you to what you might expect to find, and as to what is considered appropriate 'newbie' behaviour from one community type to the next. Initial perusal of the idiosyncrasies of particular community types, prior to an initial attempt at entrée, is therefore essential.

Finally, Kozinets advocates two additional stages prior to making the entrée attempt. Some study of any offline manifestations of the community is advisable, if such manifestations exist. This obviously makes sense, and is consistent with everything we have seen in the wider tribal literature to date. If offline versions of the community exist then they open up a much wider range of observational opportunities – while also confronting us with all the other issues already discussed. In any event, the tribal marketer fol-lowing the approach outlined to date in this book will have already devoted some time to identifying and beginning to scrutinize any such offline activity. The last stage prior to making the approach is to spend some time carefully mapping out a sufficient working knowledge of such aspects of community identity and practice as identification of the main topics of interest for the community, styles of community interaction, identity of those who seem to be the most active or regular contributors to online community life, and so on.

The moment of cultural entrée

It is well worth considering the imaginative approach that Kozinets actually took to formally approaching the *Star Trek* fan community. In this case he posted a question he felt would be of interest to community members, asking them to comment on the argument that *Star Trek* was a form of religion. He also posted a link to an article on the subject so that anyone who was interested in the topic could immediately read more about it. He then explained who he was, the sort of work he had carried out prior to now, and that he was hopeful of the community's help and support in helping him to investigate this and related questions in more detail.

Looking back at this approach, it is obvious that it was characterized by a couple of key attributes. Kozinets' preliminary work had given him a feel for both the style and the kind of topic or topics that the community would find interesting and appropriate in a forum post – the sort of thing that they would normally discuss with each other in the normal run of community events – so that in posting for the first time on a community forum, he was able to shape that post in a community-appropriate way. In posting something of potential interest to the community, he was also effectively not just introducing himself but also contributing something useful. The other key attribute of that post, as he himself emphasizes, is transparency. He gave community members ample information on who he was, and where to access samples of work he had previously carried out. His obvious feel for community preferences probably helped to counter or even remove any possible feeling of resentment or perception of intrusiveness on the part of community members. Their response to his request was receptive and the stage was thus set for his netnography to begin. Before I go any further myself, I should note that if it were not for Robert Kozinets' willingness to humbly and openly document his failures as well as his successes, I would have found it much more difficult to begin my own ethnographic research. Not only that, but a good netnography, in my experience, can also serve as the launch pad for successful completion of an offline ethnography. Nor would I ever recommend the maintenance of strict delineations or boundaries between the two. They are both non-linear and they should be allowed to overlap as interesting findings and patterns emerge. What this means for a tribal marketer who wants to achieve cultural entrée to a particular tribe is simple – move towards those places and social spaces where your tribe gathers, and don't place artificial distinctions on tribal boundaries. It is easier to go online to approach tribes because you don't even have to leave your desk – but if you don't go offline how do you expect to understand a tribe whose identity embraces both worlds?

Gaining entry to sports fan culture

The final example outlined here is included because it corroborates the usefulness of cultivating a sense of community norms before trying to gain cultural entrée.

In beginning the research for my PhD, although I was already a sports fan and sometime online participant in fan discourse, this did not give me carte blanche to enter an online fan community and begin to interact with the fans there. Instead I lurked on a small number of fan forums, honing my sense of what might be appropriate as a contribution to the conversation, before 'outing' myself as a researcher and asking for assistance with my research. In hindsight, I can see that my initial posts included a sufficient level of authentic fan comment on my part to qualify me in the community's eyes as a bona fide novice member. I would also suggest that my then naïve approach succeeded partly because of a highly benevolent attitude on the part of the fan communities concerned. In terms of an overall recommendation for approaching such communities, though, it is not enough to rely on goodwill, or to assume that participants will readily and eagerly take part in your research. It is best to be sincere and transparent in your approach, and to be willing to take 'no' for an answer.

It is also important to remember that you do not need to be accepted by everyone in the beginning. You may only need to establish a rapport with a small number of participants, with whom you can begin to establish closer ties, and over time they will introduce you to other people in their social circle.

In practice, if you can also begin to meet participants offline and have a friendly informal chat over a beer or a coffee, this accelerates the social acceptance process, again provided you take a respectful approach and you have a genuine interest in learning about their view of the world, and hearing about their experiences. By then you can also begin to use some of the qualitative interview techniques used by ethnographers and other researchers in an offline context, to help establish a rapport with your respondents and further facilitate the process of social acceptance. Once you have divulged the fact that you are present as a researcher, and they give their consent to the interview, this also helps to ensure compliance with appropriate ethical guidelines (as further detailed in Chapter 8).

Other tricks of the trade in attaining initial cultural competency

Earlier on in the chapter I mentioned how by reading up on an activity a certain amount of information can be acquired on the various doings and practices of different groups of enthusiasts. It should not be difficult to convert some of the information gathered via articles in the popular or academic press, into intelligent, culturally semi-competent questions that can be phrased in a sympathetic way in order to convey a sense of empathy to either the person you are interviewing or the community on whose forum you are divulging your identity as a researcher. If you combine this with Kozinets' careful, methodical approach to acquiring an understanding of the community's style of interaction, then your cultural entrée attempt is far more likely to succeed.

Overall, then, this points to the need for care in how you go about collecting your data, to both achieve acceptance *and maintain it* once the community has accepted your arrival. The next chapter thus elaborates in much richer detail on the various data collection techniques available to the ethno-marketer. It will also explain how to use these techniques in conjunction with each other in order to identify and reconcile the numerous contradictions that apparently arise at first. Only after reconciling these apparent contradictions between what consumers say and what we actually do while being observed in a naturalistic setting can we begin to gain proper insight into tribal value systems.

Hence the importance of addressing, as Lofland and Lofland observe, how to keep the data flow coming along as you continue to participate in the culture? Can you maintain the self-discipline to keep asking questions, to keep taking fieldnotes? Their notion of 'acceptable incompetence' is also useful – but more of this in Chapter 5.

Concluding thoughts

In the previous chapters we've looked at how tribes originate, why they exist, why they are so important to marketers, and what their key characteristics are. This chapter has begun to elaborate on how marketers should begin to approach tribes in order to begin a relationship with them.

In beginning your approach, the first questions are who – and where – do we begin to observe? Where do tribes gather? They gather in all sorts of spaces online and offline. Finding initial traces of tribal activity isn't difficult – Google Groups (groups.google.com) is just one of the ways to source online communities. However, instead of confining our search to the online realm we need to look for signs and traces of tribal activity offline as well as online. The short answer, therefore, is to be willing to travel to wherever the tribe themselves choose to gather.

Whether we can see members of tribes clad openly in tribal garb when they do gather is another question – hence the need to observe and interview people, *and* participate alongside them in tribal rituals, the better to infer how they imagine themselves and what they seek to express via participation in tribes. Because the insight we need takes a little time to acquire and is often tacit in nature, Cova and Cova thus argue for an ethno-sociological approach to acquire these insights. Hence the example of Salomon who accessed the snowboarding market through participating with the tribe and gaining insight over time instead of taking a more orthodox or conventional approach to this market.

This emphasis on participation is critical. Tribal marketing really involves both participation and observation, to make sure that when you move to support tribal linking values that you have correctly interpreted the tribe's shared sense of identity and their collective sense of emotion. Otherwise your products, services, and communications might not be seen as representative of tribal values and you are then just another marketer trying to sell people things they don't really want or care about.

In terms of participation, key to this is actually gaining access to the tribe, hence the importance of what Kozinets terms cultural entrée. Straightforward as it might sound, the most effective mindset to adopt here is sincerity. Take a genuine interest in tribal activity and try to participate. Demonstrate a commitment to tribal activity where possible and appropriate. In the early stages, when you are unfamiliar with the tribe's system of cultural capital, you may not be sure of what role to adopt or how you should behave, but if you show willing to learn, this will greatly enhance your chances of being accepted by the tribe.

At the risk of stating the obvious, another thing to remember here is that this is not the same thing as conducting a focus group! You can't afford to assume that in a tribal gathering, be it online or offline, these people are here to answer your questions and help you develop your strategy. They are together because they care about a mutual interest of *theirs*, be that knitting, cooking, motor-biking, or writing fan fiction. Your presence is acceptable as long as you remember to respect this difference.

The other thing you need to bear in mind is that a little bit of homework can go a long way to help avoid the sort of problems that can otherwise emerge if you approach a tribe prematurely – or if you inadvertently approach a tribe who may prove to be hostile to researchers. At least some initial period

Table 4.1   Beginning to observe and gain entry to tribes

Tribes gather in all sorts of spaces online and offline. It's important to be willing to go to where the tribe gather rather than just observe them virtually or from any other form of distance.
In order to gain proper insight into tribes, observation alone is inadequate. You need to use the appropriate ethno-marketing tactics of participation *and* observation.
Participation will only be possible if you approach the task of achieving cultural entrée in the right way. To do this you need to try to sensitize yourself to the tribe's communication style, show a willingness to learn about their identity and activities, and demonstrate some degree of sincerity rather than just pretending an interest.
Even in the preliminary stages of preparation for a cultural entrée attempt, be methodical about things like taking notes and reflecting on your impressions of the tribe. Kozinets advises that these notes and reflections are a huge help in the process of drafting something interesting and appropriate to say the first time you post online in a tribal forum. In short, don't assume that you can walk right in and know how to behave in the context, sensitize yourself first.
Remember at all times that these people are not gathered to either please you or to comply with your agenda. A meeting with them, online or offline, is not some kind of focus group situation whereby they are present for your benefit. You will be welcome for as long as you remember this and continue to demonstrate at least some form of commitment to the tribe.
Finally – remember not to rush things. The answers you seek will emerge over time and as they do you can begin to adapt product and brand communication strategies accordingly. In order to understand what products symbolize to a tribe, you need to understand the culture, the identity, the basis for shared linking value – an understanding of these things grows and is refined over time, not overnight. Once you have begun to gain insight into these things, you can begin to incorporate those meanings into your products and your brand communications so that they reflect tribal meaning and identity, and support tribal linking value.

of assessment of tribal ethos is advisable in order to better ascertain how to flavour or structure your initial approach so that it has a better chance of being accepted. In practice this need not be at all time-consuming – if you devote some time to immersing yourself in reading through some online tribal discussion threads, Facebook comments, blogs, and so on, this will help you to begin to cultivate a 'feel' for the tribe's approach to social interaction. Table 4.1 (before) provides a quick synopsis of these points as a final prelude to the detailed discussion of tribal data collection in Chapter 5.

5   Collecting Tribal Data

Introduction

The first thing to remember in reading this chapter is that it assumes that the sort of background information discussed in Chapter 4 has already been gathered and considered.

In short, if your objective is to try to gain an understanding of a tribe, how do you know what questions to ask when interviewing a member of that tribe, or what to look for when you are observing tribal interaction, either online or offline?

As explained earlier, you should begin by reading up on available material from different sources, in order to begin to build up a dossier of information. You can also start to note down and think about anything interesting you've noticed online or on TV and so on.

This preliminary stage is important because it will help you to identify things that you can bring up in conversation later on, when you begin to have informal conversations or even formal interviews with members of the tribe. It will allow you to develop specific questions that you can put to tribal participants. Often you can ask simple questions about activities, for instance 'I noticed activity "x" happens a lot. Can you tell me a bit about that?'

I would also very strongly advise that before beginning to ask questions, that you devote enough time to an initial observation phase, so that you feel that you have identified some interesting patterns and noted a number of interesting tribal behaviours so that you can cover a number of different categories when you begin to interview people. It would also be better if you can 'trial run' these categories via informal conversation, before you move on towards carrying out slightly more formal semi-structured interviews. As you begin to acquire more of an innate 'feel' for the tribe, you will also gradually acquire an understanding of the tribal system of cultural capital. It is also really important to remember that your understanding of this can only be acquired indirectly rather than through questioning people directly about it. Although it is tempting to think that you should be able to cultivate a sense of the tribe's system of cultural capital quickly and directly, you have to bear in mind that if you were to ask a member of the tribe to describe their system of cultural capital, they may or may not understand the terminology (it would be a bit condescending to assume they didn't) but even if they did, it is not the sort of thing that anyone can usually articulate directly.

If you instead asked someone to explain what they felt their group's values were, this might be a more accessible way to probe at least some aspects of the collective system of cultural capital but it is not really the right way to go about gaining the insight you need, not least because of a very understandable human tendency to give idealized rather than realistic answers to questions of this sort. In short, you can really only acquire the understanding you need by asking your questions and collecting your data in an ethnographic way. Fortunately, while this does require patience, it is usually an interesting and enjoyable way to carry out your research, and it is the best way to get the insights you need.

Ethnographic data collection

There are now a great variety of methods for collecting ethnographic data. They include ethnographic data collection as originally understood to mean real-world personal observation, netnography (which is but one of the terms used to denote online ethnography), videoethnography[1] and even telethnography[2] – the derivation of ethnographic insights into popular culture from the application of ethnographic technique to TV viewing. At the heart of all these methods is a small number of simple observational rules that help the novice to get started. By asking and answering the following questions, you can begin to collect ethnographic data. It really is this simple, though of course as you become more experienced and your approach to fieldnote-taking becomes slightly more sophisticated, you will capture more and more data.

Actually getting started

At the beginning of your first attempt at tribal observation, you might well find it hard to have a sense of what you are actually looking for. You might have your own theories about what is important, based on the information you've collected so far from your desk research, reading through various online and offline materials, and thus there is a tendency to focus on those things. Before you get started, therefore, one of the useful things you can do is take some time out to reflect on what these theories and prior opinions are. Take note of them and even consider writing out a short list of what you expect to see. The point of this exercise is not to compile a set of hypotheses, though. Instead it is to acknowledge your prejudices, by which I simply mean your prior conceptions, attitudes, and expectations, rather than a set of irrational dislikes.

Having thus reflected on what you expect to see and what you think it might mean, *try to put these prior expectations on hold* and, if at all possible, treat your first observation attempt as the chance to fill in a blank slate. Try to look at what is going on *as if everything you see may be of potential relevance,* rather than assuming that you will immediately have the ability to zone in on visual data that will point you towards a correct final interpretation of tribal culture. Try to take in as much as possible and begin to note what you can of it. Instead of assuming that the things you can see and hear will either turn out to have no significance or incredible significance, just take in what you can see, in as non-judgmental a way as possible, without trying to think for the moment of what it might mean or how it will subsequently help you to interpret tribal culture. Later on, as you go back over your fieldnotes, you can begin to look for patterns in your observational data, and as your study progresses, you can conduct further observational fieldtrips where you specifically look for corroboration or contradiction of these patterns, but that is another day's work. For the moment just relax and focus on taking in what you can see. While at first this will not come naturally, fortunately there are some simple guidelines to follow that I've always found very helpful in getting a new observation underway.

What to look for when taking fieldnotes for the first time

Lofland and Lofland[3] advocate beginning by asking yourself the following questions and taking note of the answers. Ask yourself who is here, how many people are here, what the place like – literally, what does it look like physically, is anything particularly noticeable? What are the sights, sounds, and smells that present themselves? What is being said and to whom? What are people doing?

How often are they doing it? What sort of body language can you observe in the people around you? If you can manage to suspend the normal human inclination to take your surroundings for granted, and you can continue to take in the answers to these questions, then you are on your way towards compiling your first set of ethnographic fieldnotes.

This is really a two-stage process. At the risk of grossly oversimplifying the whole art of fieldnote-taking, the first stage consists of jotting down your observations in bullet point form, and the second involves sitting down later on, whether that is in the car, at home, or in your office, and going back through these bullet points one by one, using them to jog your memory sufficiently so that you can write out what you observed in richer detail. It is this more detailed version that, strictly speaking, constitutes your set of fieldnotes. Obviously the temptation arises to prevaricate a little and put off writing out the full set of fieldnotes till the next day or even the following week but this is only going to lead to data loss as memory decays.

One useful trick of the trade if you are simply too tired to sit down at your laptop (for instance if it is late at night and your 'fieldtrip' has of necessity included socializing with the tribe) is to look back through your bullet points and elaborate on at least some of them onto a Dictaphone so that you won't be returning to them cold the next day. In practice, other things you may be able to do that facilitate recall are taking photos on a smartphone or digital camera so that you can look at them in conjunction with your bullet points, or even dictate extended observations onto your Dictaphone while carrying out your observational work. However, this has the obvious disadvantage that you will stick out in whichever environment you are trying to observe, and people will become self-conscious and start to behave in an artificial or contrived way. In practice the clear objective is to be as unobtrusive as possible, and in the current era of smartphones and texting, you can accomplish a huge amount without disturbing anyone. Some people might pine for the allegedly more authentic days of ethnographers hiding in strange places to surreptitiously jot down their notes, or the adrenaline rush of being confronted by someone who has just realized that you are observing them and who is feeling angry and suspicious of your motives, but personally I don't (incidentally there are clear ethical issues arising out of this sort of work so we will consider them in more detail later on).

None of this is to suggest that you refrain from writing out a longer note there and then if a particular thought strikes you, though you may wish to flag this in some way, maybe by using a different font or even opening a different note on your smartphone. It's best to jot things down, such as interesting phrases you've overheard, as you go along, and then elaborate on your points as soon as possible afterwards. If it is possible to mechanically record what's happening in some way then all to the good. While a video camera is ideal as a way of capturing both visual and aural data, even a Dictaphone recording can by itself be a great way to re-evoke not only the scene, but the feelings you had at the time. In some tribal contexts, emotional extremes are going to form an important part of the collective dynamic, so listening to the sound of a crowd of football fans reacting to a key moment can help you to recapture your sense of what the experience was like. Keeping a careful record of your emotions can also be very useful in terms of building up a set of topics to raise in conversation when interviewing members of the tribe, but more of this later.

Another question that presents itself at this stage, all this advice on note-taking notwithstanding, is how do you reconcile the detached act of taking fieldnotes while observing a group, with the kind of participation and interaction that tribal ethno-marketing is meant to involve? Wasn't it through getting on their own Harley Davidsons and taking part in tribal activities that Schouten and McAlexander finally gained cultural entrée (Chapter 4)? It's reassuring to consider the support in the ethnographic literature in favour of actual participation, rather than simply 'looking over the shoulder of the participant' as they engage in the activity. For instance, Alex Stewart states that 'it is not enough to witness a variety of performances – you also have to experience culture personally' (1998:25).[4] It makes sense to think, for example, that you will have a slightly different perspective on skydiving if you have gone skydiving yourself (see Celsi, Rose, and Leigh (1993)[5] for an interesting insight into combining participant and non participant observation in one study). Similarly it will be easier to converse with participants about an activity like white-water river rafting if they realize that you have shared similar experiences yourself (see Arnould and Price 1993[6]).

Getting caught up in the excitement and participating fully, even with your heart occasionally in your mouth if things get a bit too exciting, will enhance the quality of the research if you go about it in the right way. Emerson, Fretz, and Shaw (2001)[7] therefore recommend a dual approach, that is maximizing immersion occasionally, by virtue of full participation in the experience, while conducting other field visits with more of an emphasis on observation.

The argument occasionally used against this dual approach is that it makes it more likely that an ethnographer will have to disclose their identity to the group under study, or at least come up with a sophisticated cover story. The legitimate concern here is that once people are aware that they are under observation, they will behave in a self-conscious way, and the naturalistic data that you need will become unobtainable. Some ethnographers will argue that for this reason, non-participant observation is always preferable to participant observation.

However, the tribal marketer is in a slightly different position. Here, some form of disclosure of identity will of necessity have been made at the outset. The issue then becomes one of understanding how to gain the kind of superior insight that full participant observation ultimately gives over non-participant observation. In practice, what will happen if you conduct yourself in a natural way is that people's initial self-conscious response to your announcement of who you are and what you are doing will quickly dissipate, as they revert to natural behaviour and begin to include you in the group. You will also find that once you are a member of the group, you have access to the kind of 'behind the scenes' informal happenings and conversations that as a non-participant you would never even become aware of in the first place. This is discussed in more detail in Arnould and Wallendorf's 1994[8] article on market-oriented ethnography and its advantages are reiterated by Kozinets (2010)[9] and many other commentators. Over a prolonged period of time, as your membership of the group becomes a *fait accompli*, you might even have to overtly remind people of the fact that you are carrying out research, or ask them whether it is okay to record something they have said or use photographs of something they have done, so as to ensure that their consent to data collection is fully informed.

Netnography/carrying out your ethnography online

While participant observation is obviously therefore a highly attractive way to collect data, gain insight, and build relationships with your particular tribe, extending your ethnography into the online realm can generate a much wider and richer variety of insight than conventional offline research alone. This is not just because contemporary tribes are usually active online as well as offline, or in some cases only active online. It is also because even the most objective observer in the world cannot always manage to simultaneously observe and take in everything of importance in a detached way.

Ethnographers sometimes refer to the need to broaden the ethnographic gaze, partly as a way of acknowledging the limitations to one observer's capacity to notice things that might be important. It is not always possible in practice to pay attention to things other than those things you are personally interested in. It can be difficult, when trying to observe a group or tribe engaged in a particular activity, to avoid over-imposing your own agenda on the feast or even the overload of visual data that is all around you. Sometimes it is easier to be drawn towards the more obvious macro-rituals that some sub-groups within a tribe are engaged in, than to remember to pay attention to the rich detail of practices being engaged in by other less ostentatious members of the tribe.

While there are multiple potential benefits, therefore, to extending your ethnography into the realm of tribal online activity, one of the richest potential benefits of having an online dimension to your ethnographic research is the spontaneous introduction of data to your data set, in a way over which you as the researcher have very little control. In an online discussion forum, members of the tribe can introduce any topic they wish, usually without your being in a position to restrict them from so doing. Also, once initiated, that discussion is present in a format you can return to whenever is convenient, allowing you to broaden your gaze, so to speak, both temporally and spatially. You can take in more phenomena partly because they are not going to disappear on you while you pay attention to something else. In this way, a much more complete picture of the tribe's various interests can be collated. You have the time to look through and take note of things that might never have occurred to you to watch out for in an offline environment. This can lead to the kind of surprises that subsequently prove to be useful in gaining a deeper insight into the tribe's value system and collective identity.

For instance, in my online research on football fans, while I enjoyed the weekly discussion of what eventually became known as *Scran Today* (a weekly discussion on food preferences – on a football fan forum!), it took me a while to understand how this topic fitted into wider cultural identity patterns that prevailed across the entirety of the tribe. My prior expectations would have been that football fans gathering together online immediately prior to the weekend would be solely interested in collectively anticipating the outcome of the weekend's forthcoming football fixtures, or at most, planning the logistics of meeting up to watch the match and going to the pub afterwards. Instead they freely engaged in a variety of what seemed at first to be completely unrelated discussions.

Hence I was forced into considering the potential relevance of joint practices that I would have otherwise quite probably continued to overlook completely. Thankfully when there is an online dimension to tribal activity and you can engage in participant observation online, you can also begin to

adapt your offline data collection accordingly, as new things present themselves to you out of this spontaneous and wonderfully chaotic data set that
also has the benefit that it self-records. In short it is so useful that it is essential
to include it. The question is how, so here we will have a look once more at
what Robert Kozinets has to say on the subject.

In discussing netnography, I'm going to assume cultural entrée is achiev-
able. In mentioning cultural entrée again, it's worth repeating that if you have
the advantage of making contact with someone offline they can serve as a
point of reference for you online. Their friendly responses to your posts in an
online forum can help to secure the kind of acceptance into the community
that you need. Clearly some level of informed interest will help in achieving
acceptance as a member, but hopefully this should not be an insurmountable
obstacle for a marketer who is already involved in providing a product or
service that is of relevance or potential relevance to the community.

In short, all the points discussed in Chapter 4 about behaving in a
culturally sensitive way, and taking the trouble to be reasonably well-
informed about topics and issues of interest to the community, before you
try to establish yourself, very much apply. Kozinets also believes that it is
imperative to behave in a transparent way from the off. In declaring yourself
from the outset, he also suggests that you go about it in a way that demonstrates your own interest in something of concern to the community. Instead
of plunging headlong in, with a 'Hi, I'm new' type of post, it may be more
effective to hold back until you have had time to put some thought into how
to compose your first comment. Then if you accompany that first comment
with a link to an interesting article on the subject, you have done two things.
You have contributed something of potential value to the community and
also shown your own interest in it, thereby affirming and validating the community's interest in the topic. Although Kozinets refrains from mentioning
this in his book, one possible effect that you may succeed in generating as a
result of such an initial entry is a reciprocity of sorts. You have given to the
community and now the natural inclination (although there is no guarantee
of this) is to want to reciprocate by giving back to you. Hence now is a good
time to mention that you also have a professional interest in the subject, that
you are currently doing research on it, and that you would be interested in
any thoughts on it that anyone on the forum might care to express. It is
important to note as well that a disclosure of commercial interest is not the
kiss of death you might think! Marketers who declare themselves as such
but who can demonstrate authentic interest in tribal activities are in a much
stronger position than marketers whose cover is blown if a covert commercial interest is subsequently exposed. Incidentally I would recommend that
company staff post as individuals while declaring their dual interest, rather
than having a number of staff responsible for the same official company user
identity on an unofficial tribal website or discussion forum.

It's also important to bear in mind that you don't have to try to win the
entire community over. All you need is some level of social acceptance of your
presence, and you are far more likely to achieve this by demonstrating your

participatory credentials. (Kozinets provides a very good example of how in the context of an online ethnography you can still put yourself in the position of the cultural participants in his reference to the work of Muñiz and Schau (2005)[10] on the Apple Newton community. Rather than just collecting user data online, they went to the trouble of acquiring an Apple Newton and learning to use it, something which apparently was no easy task at first. This gave them an insight into community experience and community life that they would otherwise have completely lacked).

Another thing to remember in regard to netnography is to retain a willingness to be flexible when evaluating an online community for suitability for data collection. The main criterion is relevance to your interest, obviously, but of course it is not really enough for a particular website, Facebook page, or discussion forum to be relevant to your area of interest. It has to be active as well, by which we understand that there needs to be frequent communication. The forums you choose need to have high numbers of discussion threads and posts, so that there is plenty of data to collect and study. In terms of overall community size, while larger communities will often seem more suitable because of the volumes of data they can generate, small communities with plenty of interactivity can also be useful. Also while it is obviously desirable to choose a forum where the conversation is not dominated by a small number of individuals, it would not be sensible to rule out studying blogging communities as long as they are active and relevant to your area(s) of interest. However, in the case of blogging communities, it might be better to make sure that they are in addition to rather than the main focus of your netnographic work. In general it is better netnographic practice to have high numbers of posters as well as posts, and perhaps most important of all, to choose a site or sites where the interaction, as well as being frequent, is characterized by a rich depth as well as a reasonable degree of breadth. In other words, discussion forums where people expand on what they mean in rich and meaningful levels of detail are preferable to sites where they don't.

This is an interesting point because of course it suggests excluding Twitter, which intuitively seems an unwise thing to do in the current context. Also, incorporating Twitter into a netnographic study in some way would clearly be essential if it is something that the community makes frequent use of. In terms of collecting data from it, it would not only be important to devote time to analysing tribal Twitter activity in its own right but it would also be important to keep a record of the topics discussed on it so that further, more detailed discussion of those topics can be pursued elsewhere.

It is worth noting that while the above criteria for website/online community selection are not an exact match for those specified by Kozinets, I think they are faithful in the main to his advice.

One other point that Kozinets makes is that so-called off-topic posts should not necessarily be incorporated into your data collection process. Certainly, trying to incorporate every single off-topic thread into your analysis might result in your wasting a lot of time trying to understand different things that might eventually prove to not be related to your research at all. However, while the sheer number and variety of different topics on many online forums makes Kozinets' line of reasoning very easy to understand, you need to bear in mind the need to broaden your gaze, and you should at least occasionally reflect on possible relationships between different topics that at first glance are not related to your own particular interests. It might even be possible to use some netnographic software to analyse the different discussion threads and see whether any rudimentary patterns seem to emerge, or even whether some topics come up for discussion more than others. Anything that comes up for discussion on a fairly regular basis could well be a manifestation of some central characteristic of the collective identity, so it would be irresponsible to overlook it. At the very least, setting some time aside, on a regular basis, to ponder the possible meanings of some of the more frequently discussed off-topic topics will immerse you more deeply in the fabric and character of your community, and that is not a waste of time at all.

It is worth highlighting that this is also the first time that I've mentioned software, which in one way is unsurprising given that there has been no real discussion as yet of data analysis. However, there will not be any detailed discussion of software in Chapter 6 either, and here's why. Some researchers are very comfortable with making extensive use of software to both collect and analyse qualitative data, but I am not. There isn't much doubt that immersing yourself in your data manually is a more labour-intensive process, but the advantages for me outweigh the disadvantages, for the very simple reason that by doing it yourself, more analytical ideas will pop into your head and more research possibilities can be considered. By immersing yourself in the data rather than artificially distancing yourself from it, you are exposing yourself to more aspects of the data. Of course given the subjective nature of this, you will need to be as rigorous as possible in evaluating the thematic patterns you come up with, but this can be done too, if you patiently adhere to the right procedures.

There are a few other things that should be said about collecting netnographic data online, given the overwhelming volume of data that is literally out there in cyberspace. Incidentally, before going any further, the point is well made that not all the data you will be confronted with will be useful, relevant, or even inoffensive, and as Kozinets suggests, good practice dictates that you decide in advance how to deal with spam or even offensive content. This could include any inappropriate text or images that you were not expecting to see but that were posted out of context by other forum users. Keeping a log of what you intended to look for when going online, a note of why you felt a particular website would be useful to your research, and making a note of the circumstances in which anything particularly offensive or inappropriate suddenly appeared on the screen might also be a useful way of protecting your own integrity and character should the need ever arise.

Netnographic fieldnotes?

Just as in conventional offline observation, notes jotted down during observation do not constitute your set of fieldnotes proper. Instead, full fieldnotes can be written up afterwards. Also, netnography fieldnotes do not consist of the data you collect from the computer screen, but might be rather more reflective in nature than conventional offline fieldnotes. That is not to say that you don't collect data when you go online, and instead sit there simply jotting down the occasional reflection. It is important to collect relevant data and compile your own data records and archives from the data on-screen. However, there is no merit in trying to collect everything in an undiscriminatory way. Kozinets recommends that large-scale data sets should be examined for areas of specific interest, and only those areas should be saved. Smaller amounts of data, such as particularly relevant discussion threads, can be saved 'in their entirety' (Kozinets 2010:105).

While you are collecting your data in this way, make sure to keep some additional observational notes of your own. These will of necessity be more reflective and will consist of thoughts on the tone of interactions on particular discussion threads, any thoughts you may suddenly have on the character of the different posters on the thread, and in a more general sense, any reflections on the nature of the social performances being given. It can be very useful to devote some of your observational sessions to simply reading what you can see and jotting down your thoughts as they strike you, rather than setting yourself to both reflect and record in the same session. It can also be useful to allow yourself on occasion to simply engage in full participation mode and only reflect on it afterwards. However, for the most part, particularly in the earlier stages of your fieldwork, you should ensure that you are carefully archiving the data to go with your fieldnotes, even if this just consists of copying and pasting blocks of text into Microsoft word and saving them for more careful appraisal later on.

If you are going to persist with a fully immersed manual/ personal approach to analysis and interpretation, then Kozinets recommends that you download data more judiciously than if you intend to use software for data analysis (clearly, in the latter case, greater quantities of data can be downloaded, but this introduces the risk of creating an excessive degree of distance between you and your data and also seems particularly contrary to the notion of taking a participatory approach to tribal membership, for the marketer who seeks to establish an intuitive sense of connectedness to the tribe. Anything that has the potential to 'obscure the cultural experience of netnography (2010:105)' should be used with great caution and I would argue that from a tribal marketing perspective anything that reduces the capacity to attain a feeling of empathy with your tribe should not be used at all. If for some reason there is an insistence on the use of software then maybe that part of the research should be carried out separately by personnel not involved in any aspect of the tribal ethno-marketing activity, and the findings should only be discussed separately afterwards, to see how they compare with the findings generated by the ethno-marketing team).

Taking part in the online conversation

There are quite a few other very interesting things that Kozinets has to say about netnographic data collection and it is not really possible to do full justice to them all here. However, one of the more interesting points that he makes is that you do not have to be passive in your data collection techniques. You do not have to restrict yourself to simply reading and/or saving data based on discussion threads and other content. You should also take part in the conversation. Taking an active, fully immersed part in community discussion forums will give you much higher credibility with the community. Full participation can improve your status in the community, give you access to richer levels of cultural understanding, and open up more data collection opportunities, while making your research more enjoyable.

In fact if you confine yourself to asking questions that are directly related to your own interests, two things may happen. You may 'out' yourself as someone who is not really interested in the tribe, but who is only interested in their own agenda, and people may lose patience with you as a result. You are also thereby guilty of committing the basic error of intruding in an inappropriate way on the local culture. This is not how the native population behaves and it is inappropriate to impose yourself on the community in such a way. They are not there for your benefit and you need to remember that and conduct yourself in a more culturally sensitive way.

Kozinets also shows how you can take this a step further by setting up your own website to help both publicize your research and collect more data. With some thought and patience on your part, it might even be possible to design your web page in a way that makes it a useful resource to the community of interest to you. This works on several levels. It delivers on the criterion of transparency because you are openly explaining who you are and what you do. Such candour is often appreciated rather than scorned. It also allows you to portray your personal level of interest in and commitment to the activity in question, which can further assist with establishing your credibility as a member of the tribe. (This is not a completely risk-free strategy, because you may end up inadvertently portraying yourself as someone who doesn't understand the culture very well.)

Even providing links to research previously carried out on the tribe and/or tribal activities might prove to be of interest to members of the community and again this might make them more willing to respond to requests you post on your website for volunteers to participate in your research. Again, if you give the tribe something of value, it is natural that some people will wish to reciprocate by helping you with your work. This could extend into them agreeing to be interviewed online or even offline, an even better way in some respects to collect data because of the additional scope for various forms of non-verbal communication it offers. In practice though, most key features of the techniques for qualitative interviewing as described below can be adapted without particular difficulty for use in the online realm, so in the interest of brevity one discussion of them will suffice.

Incidentally there is now a (friendly) elephant in the room. Isn't all this beginning to look like something potentially very time-consuming? Well, yes, and cultural anthropologists have varied in their response to this issue of the amount of time ethnographic research can absorb. In fact, in Grant McCracken's case, his (1988)[11] development of the Long Interview technique arose directly out of his desire to develop a faster method for gaining insight without sacrificing too much quality compared to the insights derived from full ethnographic studies over longer timeframes. While there are important reasons why the tribal marketer should never substitute the long interview method for full ethno-marketing, McCracken's approach to interviewing has a number of merits as a data collection technique. In practice, I tend to favour a hybrid of McCracken's approach and one or two other techniques, hence I've incorporated some key features of a few different methods in the below approach to tribal interviewing.

Collecting tribal data via interview

The first thing to take note of is that collecting verbal data is never meant to be confined to the conducting of formal interviews. You should always be willing to take note of anything interesting that you either hear in conversation or have someone mention to you while engaged in participation. That said, the advantages of formally setting time aside to conduct interviews are numerous.

When you set aside the time to have a conversation with someone, it gives you and your respondent a chance to reflect on different aspects of the identity and activity in question. It also generates data that can provide a useful explanation for or sometimes even a contrast to many of the things you have observed.

One of the most useful things that you can accomplish through carrying out these interviews is that you can access certain aspects of individual or collective value systems more quickly than through observation alone. When people are being interviewed in this way, they usually do not manage to deliver accounts of their behaviour that are, in an absolute sense, objectively true. However, one of the main things to keep in mind is that the narratives they give you will often be *subjectively* true or consistent with their ideals. While it is not impossible that people will sometimes deliberately seek to mislead in an interview setting, it is usually more likely that they will describe the world – and their own behaviour – *as it ought to be* in their eyes. Thus the patterns and themes that subsequently emerge from an analysis of these interviews will offer an indication of their value system, if not necessarily their exact behaviour. An interesting example of this came up during

Wallendorf and Arnould's (1991)[12] research on Thanksgiving. People's verbal descriptions of the preparations for Thanksgiving emphasized how meals would be completely home-made, that is, fully prepared from fresh ingredients. However, the observational data collected during the study clearly showed that many elements of the meal made use of store-bought items sometimes with little or no preparation other than removal of the packaging. What was important, though, was that this discrepancy between statement and observation helped point to the underlying value system that prompted it. People's feelings about Thanksgiving were such that the renewal and celebration of family ties at the festival was *meant to be* marked by eating simple, home-prepared foods together, so the act of using store-bought goods was mentally reconstructed to fit this cultural imperative.

Therefore, as long as you remember at the analysis stage to not take verbal accounts literally, carrying out interviews alongside the collection of observational data will give you a series of points of difference that can serve to map out the underlying value system that you are trying to access.

The approach to take in carrying out these interviews is deceptively simple. Also, while there are a number of different approaches to qualitative interviewing, including a choice between semi-structured and unstructured approaches, in practice, the most important thing is to adhere to a small number of important principles. In outlining his Long Interview technique, Grant McCracken advocates a form of semi-structured approach, whereby in order to condense the time frame normally associated with a full ethnography, you begin by implementing a comprehensive desk research stage to your work. This involves both reviewing all available prior related research and your own prior knowledge and opinions on the phenomenon at hand, before drawing up a list of topics to be discussed with your respondents. Each of these topics is then drawn from during interviews, although what distinguishes McCracken's approach from other semi-structured approaches is that each topic is used to initiate a quasi-naturalistic discussion on that particular theme.

Thus McCracken's approach involves preparation of a comprehensive list of topics of interest but does not involve writing out a full set questions in advance, as this would detract from the natural flow the emergent dialogue should have. Instead you simply compose what McCracken refers to as an initial 'grand tour' question as a way of initiating discussion of each topic.

The key to conducting each of the ensuing mini-dialogues is to remember that you are to be guided by empathizing with your respondent. To a huge extent, the objective is to try to imagine what the world looks like if you accept what your respondent is saying as true. You need to assure each person that it is their take on things that matters and that you are not looking for the 'correct' answer, you just want to hear their answer.

As part of this empathy-based approach, the method requires that you watch for key terms as they emerge from the testimony and ask the respondent to elaborate on such terms as they come up. Hence the basis for follow-up questions to keep the conversation going is to tune in to what your respondent is saying and get them to elaborate on anything of interest.

Another important aspect of the technique is to establish empathy with their emotions. McCracken suggests that the use of phrases like ' "what I hear you saying is . . . " or "I hear anger in your voice" ' helps to 'play back' to them not only what they have said, but the emotion with which they have said it, and this should help to draw further answers out. It follows that your body language should be synchronized with what you say, so that the person feels that you are genuinely listening and not just feigning interest to further the needs of your own research agenda.

When the discussion of one particular topic on your list comes to a natural conclusion, you just move on to the next topic, and so on. While it is important not to exert excessive control over the dialogue, it is equally important to remember the need to retain some control, and ultimately to ensure that you get to discuss each topic of interest with your interviewee. In that sense it is often reassuring to have your list of topics to hand as a prop or even a form of security blanket to help you continue to legitimize your role as researcher and retain an appropriate level of overall control over the interview process.

Once you have interviewed an adequate number of participants and reached a stage where people's accounts and the emergent themes from these accounts have begun to corroborate rather than contradict one another, you can begin to be confident that you have collected enough data to compose an interpretation of the activity or phenomenon at hand. Hence the popularity of the method as a way of gaining some cultural insight over a shorter time frame than that required for a full ethnography, although clearly this approach by itself would not suffice for tribal marketing purposes.

Another interview technique that overlaps strongly with McCracken's in terms of its advocacy of naturalistic dialogue is the Existential Phenomenological approach developed by Thompson, Locander, and Pollio (1989).[13] Again the technique relies on establishing an empathy with the interviewee, assuring them that it is their answers, their perspectives, and their feelings that are important. This technique is significantly less structured than McCracken's, in that there is no prior list of grand tour questions or topics. The object of the exercise is to gain as pure an insight as possible into consumer perspectives on the phenomenon in question, by focusing solely on the consumer's account throughout, so once the conversation has been initiated by directing the respondent towards some aspect of the phenomenon at hand, the interview will take a fully unstructured approach.

This requires a specific approach to the wording of interview questions, because essentially the objective is to elicit stories or narratives. Questions should aim to generate descriptions of experiences and should be worded in a way that encourages respondents to share their feelings on those experiences. Also, once a particular narrative has begun, follow-up questions should begin with phrases like 'How did that feel' rather than 'Why did you . . .' so as to sustain and enrich the narrative rather than make anyone feel as if they are being called to account over their behaviour.

While it is clearly essential to avoid subjecting a respondent to inappropriate questioning, whether you are using an approach similar to the Long Interview method or something more closely related to the Existential Phenomenological technique, you still need to be sensitive to several possibilities. Someone might either engage in deliberate distortion and/or evasion of a question you have asked them, in which case it might be better to ask them whether the topic is something they would prefer not to discuss, or alternatively they may have genuinely misunderstood your question, in which case it is better to just clarify what was asked.

In practice many researchers usually construct their own bespoke approach to the interviews they carry out during ethnographic research. However, the two methods as briefly outlined here have the benefit that they are relatively straightforward and can be easily adapted to suit the needs of most ethnographic studies. In any case the research needs and objectives may vary from one stage of the ethnographic research to the next, so while at certain points in the research a semi-structured approach might be more appropriate, at other stages a less structured approach may be more useful. It is therefore better to retain the freedom to be flexible and vary your approach as required, rather than to confine yourself to one qualitative technique over another.

Concluding thoughts

We've just looked through the main data collection techniques for tribal marketers, including collecting observational data, netnographic data, and interview data. Additional questions that arise include such issues as how do you go about identifying who to interview, how do you decide how many people to interview, and how do you know how long you should keep carrying out the other forms of data collection that have just been discussed? The answers to all these questions are interlinked, because they will all depend on what comes out of your data analysis process. Analysis of your initial observational data will help you to identify both who to interview and what to ask them. Analysis of your interview data will provide you with themes and patterns to help you to continue to deepen your understanding of the tribe's identity and value system and will help you to refine what you are looking for in all forms of data collection. Hence (as Table 5.1 shows) different types of data play an important complementary role across all stages of the data collection process.

Ultimately as you begin to reconcile the different themes to one another, you will be able to decide whether the initial ethnographic study of the tribe is coming to a conclusion, and you can move on to other activities, or whether you still need to carry out some more fieldwork. Of course the role of the tribal marketer is different to that of the academic ethnographer because participation as a central aspect of ongoing tribal marketing will have to continue after the initial ethnographic interpretation has been finalized. Also the purpose of data collection will shift in emphasis over time. Once development

Table 5.1 Collecting tribal data

Remember that it takes time to access insight and the best insights are usually not acquired through direct questioning

You can really only acquire the understanding you need by asking your questions and collecting your data in an ethnographic way. Directly asking people to explain their behaviour or their values will result in idealized answers or even misleading information as people deliver verbal accounts at odds with their actual behaviour.

There are a great variety of methods for collecting ethnographic data

What matters is rather than trying to use every single method that you use a small number thoroughly, and that you collect both verbal data via interview and observational data both through observation of others and observation of and reflection on your own participation. By collecting both verbal accounts and observational data you should be in a position to identify interesting contrasts or 'disjunctures' between the two – these contrasts often prove particularly useful later on when building your interpretation of the tribe. It is also much better to mix periods of full participation, partial participation and full observation, than to skew your data collection activity too much towards participation, for instance.

Beginning to observe – what to look for

It's important to note what you think you are looking for in advance, as well as noting why you think it will prove to be important. However, it is even more important to keep an open mind and to assume that anything you see at this stage could prove to be useful later on. Hence the usefulness of basic observational principles – what's happening? Who is doing what? How many people are here? Are they all engaged in the same activities or are different people doing different things, and so on. This will help to broaden your perspective.

Divulge your identity

In the interest of good ethics and good future relations between company and tribe, make sure that you divulge your identity as part of the process of seeking to achieve cultural entrée. Once you've done so, any initial awkwardness people might feel towards you will soon dissipate as members of the tribe revert towards natural behaviour, and you will have access to a richer variety of insightful data.

Use methods like netnography to help broaden your 'gaze'

Even experienced observers can only do so much to avoid restricting their observations to those things that they have some kind of prior interest in. Immersing yourself in the scrutiny of online tribal discussion forums is a fantastic way to identify the sheer breadth of the range of topics of interest to the tribe, while simultaneously challenging your own preconceptions as to what they might or might not find important.

Be flexible when evaluating an online community for suitability for data collection

The classic criteria for site selection for netnography tend to emphasize numbers in some respects. How big is the community, how many people in total post on the forums, and so on. However, the criteria also emphasize *richness* – are the discussions meaningful and evocative? Do they have depth as well as breadth? If the answer is yes, then even a small forum might be suitable for your needs.

Don't procrastinate!

Write up full fieldnotes as soon as possible after a fieldtrip. Even though the contemporary tribal marketer has access to more kinds of digital technology than ever before to help capture data in multiple forms, write up your fieldnotes as soon as you can so that your observations are as fresh as possible. Video footage is a fantastic aide-memoire but it is a better one if you view it as soon as possible after the event.

Table 5.1   (Continued)

Do look for changes in behaviour at different times in the tribal 'calendar'

Don't assume that all aspects of tribal identity can be captured by even an intense devotion to observation over a short time frame. While insights can be derived and brand implications inferred from even the earlier stages of the process, it is important to pursue opportunities to observe the tribe at different events and times. In particular it is important to keep searching for observations that might challenge your initial conclusions, so that you can refine your emerging interpretation of the tribe till you're satisfied that your interpretation makes sense.

---

of an initial interpretation of tribal linking value is complete, the emphasis will shift towards monitoring for any changes or shifts in the tribal system of cultural capital for instance. However, it is still worth making a few key points about the duration of the initial data collection phase.

In order to be confident in the correctness of your interpretation, prolonged participant observation is important. The tribe will engage in different activities and different expressions of identity at different times and hence you need to develop an understanding of what these differences are by collecting data across entire cycles or calendars of tribal activity.

Collecting data at different stages of the tribal calendar means that you are more likely to obtain a fully rounded picture. For example, clearly at some stages of the tribal cycle members of the tribe may be more animated than others. Football supporters will be more keyed up towards the end of a season than they are in mid-season, for instance, provided that their team is in with a chance of winning a trophy. On the other hand, supporters of less successful teams might not be terribly excited if they seem certain to finish in mid-table, but they may be very animated at the start of a new season when nothing has happened as yet to undermine their hopes that this is their year. Hence a study that looks at fans across the entirety of a season is likely to gain a much deeper understanding of their behaviour.

Fans of TV shows like the *X Factor* will also behave differently at different stages of the series. It will take a while for them to decide which of the contestants to adopt or support, which of the contestants to take a dislike to, and so on. In order to carry out a full ethnography of the *X Factor* tribe it would also probably be necessary to observe the tribe in action at *X Factor* tour concerts post the conclusion of the season's TV broadcasts, and to repeat the observation process for another full series of the show, partly to see whether any new behaviours or rituals come up but also to verify whether your initial interpretation was correct.

If you want to understand the linking value that connects the Beer Pong Tribe you should not just go to Las Vegas to take part in the World Series of Beer Pong, you should also collect data at unglamorous satellite tournaments and from online tribal discourse before returning to Vegas the following year to see whether anything new is happening or whether what you observe just corroborates your findings from previous observations.

Finally it is important to remember that you should try not to jump to conclusions about your initial observations. In order to give yourself a better chance of ensuring that you have in fact gained a more accurate and authentic understanding of your tribe, you should test your initial conclusions by consciously checking them against data that may contradict them. Ethnographers usually refer to this process as searching for disconfirming observations or negative case analysis. Either term will do. The main thing is to retain a willingness to refine your understanding of the tribe, via ongoing analysis of your data, until you're satisfied that you've captured the key aspects of tribal culture and no new themes are emerging from your data. It can take a while to do this, and the exact approach to analysis is something we will discuss in more detail in Chapter 6.

Fortunately from a tribal marketing point of view, you don't need to wait until you have a fully refined interpretation before you begin to feed your findings back into brand-related activity, as some of the cases in Chapter 7 illustrate. However, you will need to keep collecting and analysing tribal data over time so that any shifts in the tribe's system of cultural capital can be detected as they occur. Hence whether you are carrying out your initial analysis or have shifted to monitoring for changes in tribal values, the analytic techniques in Chapter 6 are key to interpreting your data.

6   Interpreting Tribal Data: Analysing Ethnographic Data and Using It to Build and Maintain Tribal Brands

Introduction

This chapter explains the process of analysing the different data collected from participant observation, online and offline, and data collected from interviews. It looks at the steps involved in identifying patterns, checking for data that contradicts initial interpretations, and finally composing an integrated interpretation that allows the company to understand tribal values. The question of how to relate these values to brand development is subsequently discussed in Chapter 7. However, it is worth bearing in mind that because we are interested in developing a tribal marketing approach to analysis of the data, we can assume that the marketer is participating, collecting data and analysing it, and adapting their participation in the tribe accordingly, *in parallel with* ongoing work on development of an overall ethnographic interpretation of tribal identity, rather than waiting till a full-scale ethnography is completed before making even low-key changes.

Hence what this approach does not envisage is holding off for two years before finalizing your interpretation and then developing a strategy completely from scratch. So the emphasis here is on developing an approach to reflect the needs and the lived experience of the tribal marketer as you initiate and continue to express your own membership of the tribe. The only caveat to this is that as you get closer to concluding your overall interpretation of the tribe your overall insight will be stronger – so major decisions regarding product launches or radical changes in strategy are likely to be more successful if deferred till more insight has been obtained. In the meantime, adjustments should be tactical rather than strategic – and should be low-key and experimental until enough of an understanding has been achieved to have confidence that initiatives will be perceived as reflective of tribal linking value.

Analysing your data

The first thing to remember about the approach described here is that it requires that you treat your data, be it in the form of a fieldnote, an interview transcript, or a discussion thread from a web forum, as a whole. Gaining an understanding of your data derives in part from reading it in its entirety, and not assuming that answers to particular questions are only going to be found in particular subsections of the overall text. Instead, multiple instances of the same theme could turn up anywhere in the text, even in passages that at first glance might have appeared totally unrelated to each other.

One of the most important things to remember throughout is that the main objective here has to be gaining an understanding of tribal values and perspectives. How do the tribe collectively view the world and their place in it. As discussed earlier, the answer to those questions does not really come from putting them directly to members of the tribe, although you might get some interesting answers from occasionally taking that kind of direct approach. Instead your objective is to gain a more holistic perspective on the tribe. This perspective it built up by identifying patterns that recur in your data, and by carefully refining the underlying themes that are reflected in tribal practices and truisms.

As you participate and observe, you therefore need to begin to analyse the data you are generating. Fortunately, even though the different types of data you are collecting have come from different sources, the technique for analysis is the same.

Bear in mind that the following points do not have to be slavishly adhered to without any scope for adaptation or flexibility, but that they do form a very useful guide to the analysis of your data (Table 6.1):

Table 6.1 Beginning data analysis – a quick summary

- Read through the entire text at least once before starting to make notes
- Write down any overall thoughts, ideas, or impressions that you have
- It might be helpful to listen to the recording of an interview again, or watch a video recording all the way through, and make a brief note afterwards of those things that struck you as particularly interesting
- When you have carried out this initial immersion in your data, you can then proceed to a more systematic coding of the material.

Coding of tribal data

Remember that findings will *emerge* rather than be identified in a sequential way. Given that one objective might be to get an insight into the tribal value system, it is overwhelmingly tempting to think that when members of the tribe answers the question 'how would you describe this group's value system' that this will give most of the insight you need, there and then. Similarly, one observation session will not yield a tidy set of answers to research questions. It is only over time and via comparison across data that initial or interim 'answers' will emerge to the tribal marketer's questions. These interim answers, or more correctly, data *patterns*, can then be further scrutinized against each other and against existing and fresh data, in order to put together an overall interpretation of tribal identities, linking values, and systems of tribal capital. This notion of a comparative process is in fact central to the development of such an interpretation. Hence the following discussion of how to analyse tribal data will draw from what is often referred to as the constant comparative method first developed by Glaser and Strauss[1] but subsequently used by many leading interpretivist consumer researchers.

It is worth repeating the point that while this process is rigorous and systematic in nature, it is usually non-linear and iterative, in the sense that ideas that emerge from a reading of one paragraph of a fieldnote or perhaps one section of an interview are usually then used as a lens of sorts, through which to view other paragraphs of text, in a search for similar meanings. In practice, this iterative to-ing and fro-ing needs be documented in some way so that a record is kept of where ideas originated from and whether or not they have been tested against other available data. This can be done very easily, without any need for specialist software, and as has already been argued, engaging with this process manually gives you a better intuitive feel for the data. However, we still need to think in terms of coding of your tribal data, even though this is being implemented manually.

One of the most helpful and easily grasped explanations of how to code qualitative data is the account provided by Spiggle (1994).[2] The following explanation is thus inspired by her approach. The strength of the approach lies in how it acknowledges and makes use of subjective personal insight and perspectives while also subjecting such perspectives to a rigorous comparison process, to come up with an overall interpretation.

The first step in the process is therefore to be willing to engage with the data in a subjective way. A paragraph of fieldnotes, or section of interview transcript is read, and the tribal marketer then simply makes a note of what that passage means or seems to mean. A code can then be attributed to each of the apparent meanings, and the tribal marketer then proceeds to the next section of text, coding it in the same way. Spiggle refers to this as first order coding. So far, so subjective. Once an entire interview or fieldnote has been coded in this way, though, the next stage in the process is to scrutinize the codes, to see whether or not some of them are sufficiently related to one another in meaning to justify effectively merging two or more first-order codes into one second-order code. Before discussing second-order coding in any detail, though, it might be useful to actually try out some basic first-order coding to see how the process works. It is easier to grasp the principles involved by trying them out. Before you read the following fieldnote extract, grab a pen and paper, so that you are ready to start jotting down some first-order codes as they occur to you. Then go ahead and read the extract. Feel free to stop at any time that an idea strikes you as to the meaning of what you have just read, and make a note as to the title (i.e. code) and meaning of your idea. The key to getting started is to realize that an idea of this sort can strike you after just one sentence or even one clause. Sometimes one sentence or paragraph can generate several possible alternative meanings, and you should note them all. You should end up with a number of ideas, the titles of which are really your set of first-order codes. Don't hold back from allowing yourself to code the data in a spontaneous way, and similarly, don't restrict yourself to trying to figure out the 'right' or 'correct' codes. They don't actually exist, at least not yet! Just allow yourself to enjoy the process of reading the passage and recording your impressions and ideas – with titles to distinguish each idea/impression from the others.

The passage that follows is taken from a fieldnote written by a research student of mine while she was carrying out an ethnographic study of white water kayaking. It was written after a weekend away with her kayaking club. I won't say any more by way of introduction, because I think you will get more from this exercise if you just allow yourself to respond spontaneously to the text.

Friday Night

Upon arrival at the hostel (a converted church with no staff present), the freshers are told to store their gear in the large dormitory upstairs, while the 'oldies' (veteran members) and other current members stow their gear downstairs in the smaller dormitory rooms. In the kitchen, a game is begun which involves seeing how far a person can travel on a bread-board. No one escapes without trying, and as usual the person who falls or hurts themselves gets most points.

The party atmosphere continues until 3 am, when most freshers, most particularly the girls, go to bed, but everyone else waits downstairs. Once the freshers are asleep, all those awake promptly go upstairs to the main dorm and wake everyone up for a game of 'rafters racing'. The freshers, exhausted, look confused at this latest development. This game involves two competitors racing each other across bed bunks holding onto the roof rafters only. The beds are parallel to each other and the competitors must pass each other at some stage to finish the race. This involves biting, kicking and a lot of dirty tactics. The older club members start the game, with an 'oldie' called 'Shane' on commentary. The freshers enjoy the game, most look astonished and a little wary, but are quickly involved in it. One oldie falls off his bed and breaks a rib, yet there really is very little concern showed about this accident, and he retires back to his room. This game continues until 5 am when finally all races are completed. There are 40 people at Jacks so this takes some time. Finally, the freshers are allowed to sleep while the games are taken downstairs. One of the oldies decides that it would be fun to take a table and put four people on it and sail down the metal stairs. Screams of terror and pain reverberate around the hostel until 6.30 am when the last survivors crawl into their beds.

What are your thoughts? What have you written down? Are you wondering what on earth, if anything, can be learned from what you have just read? Does it seem a bit on the outlandish side or does it even leave you feeling that you have nothing in common with these people? If it does, that is absolutely fine, as long as you remain committed to attaining an insight into the tribe's mentality rather than judging them from the perspective of yours. The point of all this is not to continue to view the world through your own eyes, but to begin to learn to view it from the point of view of the tribal participant. Tribes have their own way of looking at things. The whole point of the research methods we are exploring here is to get an insight into their perspective, their worldview, and learn to suspend ours. At the heart of this approach is coding, so it is time to pay attention to the coding process.

In beginning to code this sample data extract, as suggested above, it is important to give yourself the freedom to react spontaneously to the data so that the codes you come up with capture the essence of your response. It's understandable to think that this might somehow not be the correct way to develop an interpretation of tribal behaviour, and that it is too subjective a way to analyse anything, but the thing to remember here is that this is actually just the first step. The eventual interpretation gradually becomes more sophisticated and insightful as more data is coded and the relationships between different codes are identified, but for now it is better to focus on the first step.

Looking back at the opening paragraph of the fieldnote, it is immediately apparent that we could use the term **'reckless behaviour'** to code the bread-board game that begins in the kitchen. Then the next sentence, where we are told that points in this game are accumulated through suffering injury, could be coded under a variety of ways, including for instance **'stupid behaviour'** or even **'rewarding of stupid behaviour'**. If you want to take an alternative approach, you could have even gone for a code along the lines of **'social reinforcement of reckless/stupid behaviour'** although this seems a little bit elaborate. However, what is interesting about this last alternative is that it is just as applicable as the first two, and it shows that there are three equally valid ways of coding the same short data extract. There may even be more than three, but that is enough for now.

As we proceed through the data, it becomes apparent that some of the codes we have already come up with could also apply to such behaviours as the rafters racing game that takes place at 3 am. The fact that someone falls and breaks a rib is testimony to the validity of the 'reckless behaviour' code as previously defined. However, if we just keep using the same codes over and over, then we run the risk of ending up with a very oversimplified understanding of the activity or activities we have observed. In order to gain deeper levels of insight, we should give ourselves the freedom to generate more codes every time we feel that something novel has been observed. Again it is important to reiterate that this is not about trying to guess what the 'correct' code is at this stage. Instead it is about generating fresh codes each time we feel we have noticed something novel. We don't need to worry about comparing those codes till later on. Instead what matters is capturing each novel phenomenon and assigning it a code of its own, even if this initially results in the generation of dozens of different codes. Eventually, we will be able to identify patterns across what we previously identified as separate phenomena, but that is a subsequent analytical stage, so for now we just carry on coding!

It is absolutely fine, incidentally, to take a term already written in the field-notes (or used in an interview) and use that as a code. In the above passage, **'biting and kicking'** could be used as a code, for instance. Alternatively, **'aggressive behaviour'** could be used, or some other term which denotes that this data not only merits designation with the code **'reckless behaviour'** but other codes as well.

It may yet prove to be the case that there are *multiple types* of **'reckless behaviour'** and the ability to distinguish between these types might prove to be important, so yet again we see the importance of avoiding an oversimplified approach to coding. In any case the guiding principle here is that if you feel the data should be coded not only with a code you have already come up with, but several other codes as well, code it under each. This necessitates appropriate documenting of the outcome, and normally part of the work of coding would include devoting a separate section per code in your analysis document, either with each extract included, or at least a reference to where in your data document each extract is located.

Jumping ahead to the rib-breaking incident, looking at this particular incident, again several alternative codes might suggest themselves. The term **'indifference'** springs to mind, for instance! Normally if someone falls and breaks a rib, people might react by going to their aid, making a fuss of them, or even calling an ambulance. In this case, the researcher notes that the victim has to make his way back to his bedroom alone and unaided. However, one piece of data by itself is no guide whatsoever to ascertaining whether or not this is truly a culture where indifference prevails, and we may subsequently find that this code will either have to be revised or even eliminated from our interpretation. Again though, those analytic decisions do not kick in until later in the process. Another possible code for some of the remaining data could include 'endurance test' which evokes the notion of sticking at these activities all night when most ordinary people need to get some rest, and 'feel the fear and do it anyway' may be one way of coding the apparently terrifying practice of tobogganing down a metal stairway on an upturned table. Of course this last activity could equally be coded under the term 'crazy prank' which in hindsight could also apply to the breadboard game mentioned earlier on in the extract.

There may well be other codes and other ways of coding the above data sample. It is also noteworthy that the above codes do not capture every aspect of the experience of the first night of the kayaking club weekend. This highlights the need to take a comprehensive approach to coding the data – this, naturally, does not guarantee that you will capture everything that there is to be captured, but at least if you make a determined effort to code every novel variant in the data then you are at least giving yourself a chance to make your analysis more meaningful. Other codes that might have emerged from a more thorough coding of the above data could have included **fun, group bonding, crazy people**, or possibly even **typical college students,** if you had been made aware that this study was carried out while the researcher was a member of a university kayaking club. However, this last code again might require revision or even elimination before the end of the analysis, given that there may be a difference between the sort of relatively safe pranks that many college students enjoy and the pursuit of white water river kayaking that this group devote themselves to.

You may also have noticed that the terminology used thus far in coding any of the data has been simple and straightforward. It is equally valid to use more complex terminology, provided that the basic principle of using each term once, to denote an idiosyncratic feature of the data, is adhered to. Hence academic terminology such as the names of particular paradigms or theories can be used as codes, whereby the data extract is seen as corresponding in meaning to a particular theoretical idea. This is not to say that such codes are exempt from the same subsequent scrutiny as other codes, but simply to note that if something strikes you, you can use it as a code.

At this stage, it is premature to impose the codes gleaned from one observation on the data from a second observation. As the analysis progresses, you will gradually begin to look through any fresh data specifically for instances that either confirm or even contradict codes that you have already developed, but this really applies to a later stage of your analysis. For now, grab a pen and paper again and try to give yourself the freedom to code the following fieldnote extract without imposing too many restrictions on yourself as to what you expect to find. You will never manage to liberate yourself completely from the perceptual boundaries that your preconceptions impose, but you should at least discipline yourself sufficiently to try to code each novel event or phenomenon separately:

Saturday

Bright and early at 9 am its time to wake up. People are tired, some are still drunk, and there are two twisted ankles, one broken rib and many much bruised paddlers and one broken table from the stairs antics. There is a new cooker in the kitchen and the designated chef of the club can't turn it on. People admit defeat and skip breakfast or get a lift into Killarney for breakfast. Then it's onto the bus again and off to the river. The club has a buddy system, consisting of one strong and one weak paddler paddling together for the whole duration of the river. When we arrive, a safety talk is given on how to avoid rocks and following the warm up, nervous freshers are given pep talks from their designated buddy. Some are jumping up and down nervously, teeth are chattering despite the sunny day, and there is a lot of tugging buoyancy straps needlessly. This may be because freshers are constantly being fixed by their buddies, as a loose buoyancy could cause serious problems. To see a buddy fixing their younger friend's gear looks like a parent sending a child off on a journey.

The buddy system works well, as some freshers wobble dangerously; their buddy immediately is at their side to right them at once. There is enormous trust placed in the senior buddy by the fresher and I notice that if the senior buddy wanders over to help someone else, or drifts away, there are a few panicked expressions on the faces of the beginners. They are obviously very dependent on their buddies and even seem to suffer almost from separation anxiety. Once the buddy is back at their sides they look relaxed once more.

...

We make our way downstream ... the rest of the river is uneventful; there is however a 'sandwich' event, where (first) a fresher gets caught up against a rock, then his buddy gets caught too and then 'Denis' gets involved. 'Denis', known as one of Irelands top river runners, quickly manages to free the buddy and then the fresher. The fresher, red faced, breathes a sigh of relief. The take-out, where all paddlers get out of the river, appears quickly, and many freshers express their disappointment at this. They have had great fun and learnt a lot in just two hours, such as seeing a 'v' in the water means there a rock directly underneath. Many freshers hug their buddies in delight and gratitude.

Right away we can see that in the aftermath of the night before that some of the previous codes might usefully be used to classify the new data. However, we can also see the possible usefulness of new codes such as **anticipation** or even **apprehension** that may serve to capture the feelings experienced by the freshers now that the time has come to finally take to the river in earnest. We can also see that some of the terms used in the fieldnotes might again make useful codes as is. **Buddy system** is one, and **separation anxiety** might be another. If the extract was longer there would doubtless be others, particularly now that the action has shifted towards a more dramatic setting that is in some respects more central to the activity in question. Interestingly, we can also see that the **indifference** code mentioned earlier may require some reconsideration, as the freshers are anything but indifferent to the presence or absence of their mentors, or senior 'buddies', and the buddies in their turn are clearly devoted to the safety of their junior partners. **Group Bonding** is another possible code that we might have jotted down as a way of coding the numerous instances of apparently close relationships manifested in the data, such as the careful, almost parental devotion of the senior buddy to their junior partner before the junior takes to the river, and the clear need the junior buddy has to remain almost surgically attached to their mentor while on the water (of course **mentor/mentoring** is another possible code here, but this is not meant to be an exhaustive list, just an illustrative one).

Follow-up stages in developing your analysis

We can derive several new points about the analysis process now that we've considered this second data extract. To begin with, codes derived from analysis from a second (or any subsequent) data extract might prove to be useful as means to revisit earlier data sets. If we re-read the initial 'Friday night' passage now, looking for possible instances of '**group bonding**', for example, we might begin to see multiple examples of this code in the data. Games like 'rafters racing' are ways to break the ice and are very much part of the bonding process. While this is a very obvious example of what you can find once you begin to take this kind of iterative, or to-and-fro approach to analysing your data, it helps to illustrate how this approach is a really useful way of making sense of and picking up on things you might have missed out on first time round. That brings us to another point – should, or will, everything make sense, or prove possible to code, first time round? And should you worry if it doesn't? 'No' and 'no' are the answers here. More meanings emerge as you re-immerse yourself. It will take a while before you are able to look at your data and expect to be able to interpret every single piece of it.

This is also important because it illustrates how the longer we immerse ourselves the more we see, and the more we can have our eyes opened to reconsider our first impressions of those things we saw earlier on in our first forays into the tribe's culture. This is how we begin to move from what might initially have been a completely subjective reaction to a more balanced view of the tribe's identity. This can happen either via revisiting of earlier data in light of new codes or correction of earlier codes in light of new data. Several of the codes derived from the first analysis of the 'Friday Night' passage now seem less insightful – and this means that we need to either revise them or discard them completely. 'Indifference', for instance, no longer seems to explain what's going on, while 'reckless behaviour' might also require either revision or elimination from our emerging interpretation, at least based on the evidence of our second fieldnote passage. Contrary to what we understood earlier by the code 'reckless behaviour', the group demonstrate *responsible behaviour* in many ways, such as the various safety drills and procedures they adhere to. So what does this mean for the code we developed earlier? Do we get rid of it right away – or take note that there are exceptions which contradict it, and that it may need to be revised?

In practice, it is inadvisable to regard one contradictory piece of data as sufficient to discard an entire emergent theme. Over a longer period of time initial observations and preliminary conclusions can be specifically assessed against observations of other kinds of behaviour that seem to potentially contradict them. This is called searching for *disconfirming observations*, to ensure that we don't draw incorrect conclusions about the tribe. However, overt searches for disconfirming observations are often deferred until the later stages of an ethnographic enquiry.

In the interest of clarity I'll jump ahead a little at this point and reveal that, perhaps unsurprisingly, one of the key findings from this ethnography was not so much that the relationships between group members were very strong, but that being part of such a tightly-knit community has an effect on people's perceptions of risk. Members of the group develop a strong bond with one another and one of the effects of this bond is a sharing of perceptions including a normalization of risk. In short, what seems extremely risky – or even reckless! – to non-enthusiasts gradually becomes less and less intimidating to members of the group. So 'reckless behaviour' might still be important as a theme in the eventual interpretation but our understanding of its dimensions as a possible element of tribal linking value will probably change as we refine it in the light of both freshly collected data and reconsideration of previously collected fieldnotes, interview data, and so on.

At this point in an ethnographic study, when a number of codes have been identified, the next step is to scrutinize the codes to identify possible relationships. As we've seen from the above examples, it is not that hard to imagine that some of them will be very closely related and can be merged with one another to form higher order, or what Spiggle calls second order, codes.

Later on, you will be more concerned with evaluating your second-order codes and as these codes in their turn are merged into themes, your emergent themes will in turn be assessed against data that might even have been collected specifically in order to see whether it is possible to contradict or disprove them (i.e. searching for disconfirming observations).

However, in the earlier stages of your analysis it is more appropriate to hold on to, rather than discard codes. For instance, once you have accumulated your first four or five sets of fieldnotes it would be very useful to set aside the time to immerse yourself quite deeply in the data, by being very restrictive in terms of elimination of any of your initial codes.

In this relatively early phase of interpretation development, you should be extremely slow to remove any code while it still seems to have any idiosyncratic characteristics, however small or apparently unimportant. In other words...

IDENTIFY WHAT'S <u>THERE</u>, NOT WHAT <u>YOU</u> WANT TO BE THERE.

I mention this now because a key issue for the tribal marketer is the need to tune into what the data will reveal to you *if you are willing to listen to it.* You should assume, at least for the moment, that *every* pattern is of potential importance in unlocking, or breaking, the overall tribal code. So instead of prematurely zoning in on those things that seem to be of obvious commercial relevance, be patient!

Try to assume that each pattern, each relationship, can potentially shed light on the underlying, uniting themes that, when developed, will reveal to you what makes the tribe tick. If you can genuinely do that, you are halfway towards becoming a real tribal marketer. Gradually, as you collect and analyse more data, and compare the codes from one analysis to the next, the relationships across these initial patterns and themes will begin to become clear.

Another useful, perhaps even essential, and certainly hugely beneficial, safeguard you can build in to this process is to have someone else look at the same data, generate their own codes, and then compare codes and themes

Table 6.2   Quick recap: The iterative nature of the process

Given that you should engage with each 'text' in its own right, it naturally follows that some things will strike you when coding a second, third, or fourth fieldnote (or interview) that result in new codes being developed. When this happens, it is important to revisit earlier texts and scrutinize them for possible examples of the same phenomenon. In this way, you are also ensuring that any potential themes that only strike you later on in the analytical process can be evaluated against earlier data sets, to help establish the extent to which you have identified a pattern or theme that prevails across all your data. This is partly what we mean when we talk about the iterative nature of the entire analytical process, a sort of to-ing and fro-ing across your data.

Two further points are worth mentioning at this stage. There is nothing wrong with taking a code developed from interview data and deliberately scrutinizing other data types to see whether instances of that code seem to be present, a point I'll elaborate on later. Similarly, if a particular theory or paradigm strikes you as relevant when analysing a particular fieldnote then it is important to treat this as you would any other potential pattern, and make sure to revisit earlier data of all types for additional instances of relevance and possible further insight.

with you. Ideally this kind of peer debrief should take place on a regular basis throughout the entire ethnomarketing phase (Table 6.2).

Broadening the ethnographer's gaze

As we now know, Spiggle defines coding as identifying a piece of data as representative of a particular phenomenon and labelling it accordingly. Each fieldnote, discussion thread from a web forum, and interview transcript therefore has to be read as a text in its own right, and every piece of data has to be considered as possibly representative of an interesting phenomenon.

It's important to remember that this process in no way guarantees the capture of all phenomena of interest. It only provides for analysis of the data as gathered. The data itself is limited by the boundaries of your 'gaze' as a researcher. All that any ethnographer or tribal marketer can hope to do is cast her or his gaze as widely as is practically possible. As discussed earlier, the use of complementary data-gathering methodologies that allow different types of data to be captured and a wider range of phenomena identified for consideration helps to broaden the scope of that gaze (for a more detailed discussion, see De Chartonay, Drury, and Segal-Horn (2005),[3] or Paul (1996)[4]).

Interview data, for instance, is co-produced, and will yield data that is dependent on the joint perspectives of interviewer and respondent. Observational data is subject to the boundaries of that which the ethnographer decides to focus on. However, in producing an overall ethnographic interpretation, the two methods can complement each other, in that issues that emerge from observational data can widen the perspective that the ethnographer brings to bear when conducting interviews, and vice versa. Therefore you can proceed with your analysis in good faith, provided that this strategy of complementarity is being followed and a reflective and sceptical attitude is retained towards emergent themes until they have been verified by consideration against all the available data.

To revert briefly to considering how this 'broadening of the ethnographer's gaze' might work vis-à-vis the kayakers we have just been looking at, this is why it helps to observe as many performances of tribal identity as you can (until you reach the point where you feel no new themes are coming up). By exposing yourself to different performances and seeing for instance how a group of extreme sports enthusiasts switch from what was previously termed 'recklessness' to what could be termed 'safety-oriented behaviour' alerts us to the need to reconsider our earlier views and points towards an overall interpretation of tribal identity as one that constructs a *shared approach to the consumption of risk*. This shared approach requires a wholehearted engagement in the activity, without which social acceptance may not be achieved, *and* a commitment to a strictly enforced social hierarchy whereby the authority of the senior members of the group is accepted absolutely – in risky situations on a white-water river, immediate deference to commands from senior members of the group can make all the difference between exhilarating experience on the one hand or serious injury on the other. Of course, the more we continue to observe, the more we may realize that occasional indulgence in relatively reckless behaviours may fulfil specific functions for the group.

What can also be extremely helpful about having different sets of similar data that can then be compared to the codes from other types of data is that it gives you more to benchmark what you've seen or recorded against. What you see or notice on one occasion might be very noticeable and important, but the more you can compare it to other observations or even issues that have arisen in interviews, the better you can place it in an overall context. It helps, when observing tribal performances, to ask yourself how exceptional the behaviour you're observing might actually be.

This is why interview data as well as observational data is important. You need to view the participation of actors from several different angles, in order to get a deeper insight into and understanding of the meanings of their actions. For instance, the significance of the behaviours of a group of football fans travelling to Lisbon for a match between Liverpool and Benfica for fan behaviour overall cannot be established from what is observed on that particular trip. Some aspects of tribal behaviour will be heightened on a trip like that and others will be suppressed. Before any final conclusions can be drawn, there is a need to systematically review the findings from that trip against other data for comparative purposes. The following extract from fieldnotes taken while attending a Champions League game in Lisbon in 2006 should help to illustrate the point:

> *The sheer passion of the Liverpool supporters was fantastic. Every song and chant was being roared out. This was more like it. Ordinary matches at Anfield just do not seem to have this sense of occasion, this feeling of passion, this degree of participation. The phrase 'You get the real fans on the away trips' was brought to life all around me.*

The point of this extract is not to argue for or against the truism that 'real fans' are the ones who go on the 'away trips'. What was more useful about this particular fieldtrip was the opportunity to corroborate patterns derived from prior interview data. What is also important to bear in mind is that although overwhelming, this was just one type of fan performance. You therefore have to balance observations of the spectacular against observations of the mundane before forming a final opinion. What is also of huge potential importance for the tribal marketer is to keep in mind that there can sometimes be an inverse relationship between tribal role-play and any compulsion to display products that should, you would think, strongly symbolize tribal linking value.

It was very noticeable on the above fieldtrip that the wearing of that season's up to date replica team shirts held no value for these fans. Many of them wore some form of team-related clothing, such as polo shirts with a club crest on the breast, but such items looked very much as if they had been worn a great many times before. Yet to deduce from such an observation that merchandise was a very low priority for these fans would have been a mistake. Merchandise can be very important for the more demonstrative members of a tribe, but the manner in which they make use of it might vary from the way in which other members of the tribe do so. Similarly, it would be misleading to assume that only those fans who wear their hearts on their sleeves and who sing and roar for almost the entire duration of a football match are completely committed to the cause. Within tribes, there are many different roles and it would be mistaken to overlook the less overt performances. You also need to look for the kinds of performances that other categories of fan will mount and explore the ways in which they express their identities as fans, before you can form a judgement as to whether they are more or less committed. This can all take time, but the good news here is that you can begin to get insight quite quickly and then refine it (via such processes as searching for disconfirming observations) as you go along.

The other issue here is that trying to capture all this by yourself is inadvisable. Some kind of peer debrief is imperative – it is obviously a huge help to have one or two colleagues involved in this entire process, because not only might they spot things you missed, but they will have their own perspectives on what the data means. They can also help you to question yours – and vice versa. By comparing insights and perspectives you can generate richer insights together. Ideally you should not try to move from second-order coding to development of overall cultural themes without such a comparative exercise with a colleague or colleagues. This should help to guard against coming up with overall interpretations that have been excessively affected by the impact of spectacular experiences. It should also help in the identification of different types of tribal member, the different roles they enact, and – again very importantly for the tribal marketer seeking to identify opportunities to provide products and services to the tribe – the different ways in which they relate to and use products that embody tribal linking value in some way (Table 6.3).

Table 6.3   Recap: Broadening the ethnographer's gaze

The data is limited by the boundaries of your 'gaze' as a researcher
Don't begin by assuming that only some phenomena will be important – try to take note of all the things that seem of interest to the *tribe*, rather than the things that are of immediate interest to you.
Cast your gaze as widely as practically possible, for instance via the use of complementary data-gathering methodologies (non participant as well as participant observation, netnography data as well as interview data…)
Within each data type, try to expose yourself to contrasting phenomena, giving yourself the chance to notice things you haven't noticed before (how do the tribe behave across slightly different contexts? How do members of the tribe behave at different times of the year?)
Try to ensure that you balance observations of spectacular tribal behaviours against observations of less spectacular, even mundane behaviours before forming a final opinion
In a similar vein, try not to overlook less spectacular roles adopted by less demonstrative members of the tribe
Compare notes with colleagues on your team – what have you missed that they noticed *and* vice versa
Finally, remember to retain a reflective and sceptical attitude towards *all* emergent themes until they've been verified. Keep looking for data that challenges your perceptions

Progressing from first-order coding to second-order coding

To revert to the question of progression from first-order coding to second-order coding in a bit more detail, while I am again going to refer to research carried on sports fans, the underlying principles here are the same no matter what type of tribal context you might find yourself immersed in.

Interviews with individual members of any tribe can sometimes generate a list of first-order codes longer than the original interview, particularly in the earlier stages of research. For instance, from one interview with 'Allan', a fan of Cork City Football Club, I eventually produced a list of first-order codes that ran to 43 pages of single-spaced text, in contrast to the 17 pages of the interview transcript itself. This might seem excessive but with any interview that comes early on in your research, it is better to err on the side of detail rather than risk omitting anything that might subsequently be important or useful. Later on, the number of codes you have to deal with is reduced through the implementation of second-order coding. This essentially involves assessing the extent to which first-order codes can be clustered together on the basis of any shared features. These clusters or groups can then be labelled to identify the new abstractions clearly as second-order codes. Each second-order code can be given a new label, or title, or one of the original first-order code titles can be retained as a second-order code.

It is worth reiterating that this entire process is in itself quite abstract for any novice tribal researcher until you have collected and analysed some of your own data. However, once you've reflected on your data on a few different occasions, a more meaningful analysis becomes possible. For example, one first-order code from the interview with 'Allan' was **'It's better than the telly'**. In short, 'Allan' felt that going to a live football match was preferable to watching football on TV. When you consider data for the first time, you are likely to find yourself coding it on its own merits as an isolated statement. You might sense that it is important, particularly when you consider how emphatically your interviewee has stated their preference (body language being an important cue when collecting data, incidentally!). Initially, you might not even be sure what something means, or whether it will subsequently prove to have any wider significance. In this case, it was apparent that the interviewee literally thought going to a match was a qualitatively more enjoyable experience than watching it on TV, but it remained to be seen whether that would or could be linked to other first-order data to form a meaningful pattern.

Instead of trying to impose second-order codes as you go along, though, just continue to code your data in the normal way. If you are studying a tribe that engages in spectacular behaviour you will probably come up with some quite colourful codes. Another first-order code from the interview with 'Allan', for instance, was **'The Call of the Wild'**. This reflected Allan's enjoyment of the opportunities that arise at a football match to behave in a manner that seemed rather wild compared to how he or I might normally behave in public, and as sports fans often get over-excited at sports fixtures, this was not all that surprising.

In contrast to this, what did come as a surprise was the extent to which 'Allan' had very strong opinions about other categories of football fan. He articulated a strong distaste for fans who professed support for more than one team. I coded this as **'Antipathy towards soccer meanderers'**, using Allan's own term of 'meanderers' as part of the label for this particular theme. He also professed a strong distaste for fans who did not support their local team. I coded this in an uncomplicated way as **'Support your local team'**. Overall, what every tribal marketer needs to do in the first instance is just code the data 'as is'. It might take a while before connections *across* your codes begin to occur to you, and you might even find that the process of second-order coding becomes much more productive once you've carried out first-order coding across a number of interviews, rather than trying to generate a full set of second-order codes after one interview. It might be much easier to understand why an individual fan might manifest **'antipathy towards soccer meanderers'** if you are patient and wait till you have collected and considered data from other members of the tribe before trying to come to a deeper level of insight via higher levels of abstraction.

In short, considering how data across a number of interviews might be related to first-order codes from one interview may prove the key to getting your second-order coding underway.

In the current example, it was far easier to note the relationship between the code 'It's better than the Telly' from the first interview and data from subsequent interviews with other football fans, than to progress to the

Table 6.4   Recap: Progressing from first-order to second-order coding

Remember – as with initial coding, this can all seem quite abstract till you have collected and analysed your own data.
Also remember that second-order coding helps to reduce the number of codes and identify patterns more clearly – sometimes the number of codes from first-order coding can feel a little overwhelming but you should persist with generating codes, particularly in the early stages of tribal analysis.
Second-order codes can be labelled using fresh terms or using one of the original first order codes – whatever term you feel suits all the associated data
Remember that it might take a while for connections *across* codes to occur to you – but once they begin to occur to you, you'll find the process easier to manage. It often helps, particularly in the earlier stages of a tribal analysis, to look at first-order codes from several different data sets and see whether common themes emerge

generation of second-order codes based solely on the interview with 'Allan'. I gained the intuition that there was a relationship between the first-order codes **'It's better than the Telly'** and **'Support your local team'** after noticing that the members of the tribe all tended to emphasize the necessity of supporting one's local team by going to the stadium instead of just watching football on TV. Ultimately, the first-order codes were linked by a second-order code of ***authentic fan identity***, which dictated that authentic fans by necessity must ***support your (their) local team in person***. Incidentally, this also amounted to what Spiggle describes as having a sudden sense of realization that a thematic pattern was present.

It is also important – maybe even more so! – at this stage to remember to follow Spiggle's guidelines on refutation, by going back through all your interview data to see whether any of it contradicts the emerging themes identified via this second-order coding. Some of your data might suggest that not all members of the tribe feel a burning necessity to comply with a particular value – if this is so, then you may have begun to find evidence that your tribe is split into clusters or sub-tribes with slight variations in linking value and so on. To revert again to the current example, I found that not all members of the wider tribe of Cork City fans subscribe to the notion that it is imperative to support their local team in person, but I was able to conclude that such a value system certainly existed among what I collectively termed the hard-core supporters.

In practice, once you begin to look for the linkages across second-order codes, you are well on your way to constructing an overall interpretation of your tribe's identity (Table 6.4).

From second-order codes to overall themes

Once you begin to generate second-order codes, possible *overall themes* will also begin to suggest themselves to you. You will begin to notice possible relationships across the second-order codes – so again simply record and label each emergent relationship, noting and refining its characteristics. If your feeling is correct and you have identified an overall theme, then it should provide a good fit to multiple instances in the data, so you should test your theme's overall truthfulness to assess it.

Once you have been immersed in the tribe for long enough to identify a comprehensive number of overall themes, you can confirm the veracity, or overall truthfulness, of your interpretation of your tribe's underlying value system, by spending some time assessing it against different types of data. For instance, you should spend some time downloading and reading web forum discussion threads on different topics, to verify that your interpretation provides a good overall 'fit' to your data. You should be able to look at video footage of tribal activity and be able to interpret what you see in light of the overall themes you've identified. Entire interviews should make sense, rather than still containing passages that are beyond your comprehension. When the relationship between pieces of data that previously seemed discrete suddenly becomes apparent, when multiple examples of the thematic relationship suddenly become obvious in the text, and once this happens consistently across different data, you have achieved the 'massive overdetermination of pattern' as Stewart (1998:29) calls it, that is necessary in order to have confidence in your interpretation.

It is also worth noting that just as the relationship between codes at earlier stages of your analysis can become clearer when you look at different data sets, overall tribal themes can often emerge much more clearly when you have begun to compare codes across different tribal data categories. Hence the further you are into your tribal analysis, the richer the levels of thematic insight you should be able to generate into the meanings the tribe derive from their use of consumer goods and tribal merchandise, because you will have a variety of both verbal accounts and observed behaviours to draw from.

For instance, to refer again to the analysis of the interview with 'Allan', I had originally noted a small number of first-order codes relating to football fan merchandise. These were very simplistic codes such as '**Wearing the team shirt**' or '**Wearing a football scarf**'. However, I had also noted an '**antipathy towards official fan merchandise**' on more than one online tribal forum. This was interesting and would have been more than a little surprising if I had not already come across Anthony King's (1997,[5] 1998[6]) analysis of the distaste for official fan merchandise among hard-core Manchester United fans. What really intrigued me about the behaviour of the tribe I was studying was when I realized that their *verbal professions* of distaste for official merchandise were not consistently matched by their *behaviour* in relation to it. In another moment of illumination, I came up with the higher order theme of '*downplayed consumption*'. Fans were declaring an aversion for merchandise, but were in fact buying a considerable quantity of it! However, the significance of these purchases was being verbally downplayed, hence the theme 'downplayed consumption'. Having identified this theme, I again followed the procedure of subjecting it to rigorous scrutiny against all available interview data. It was very gratifying to realize that the pattern presented itself again and again across almost all the interviews I'd carried out, confirming that I'd identified another important cultural theme that would help me to unlock the code to gaining an overall understanding of the tribe.

In short, what I eventually realized was that many of the higher order tribal themes were clearly related to each other. Fans were constantly engaged in attempting to distance their identity from the official fan marketplace. The theme of downplayed consumption illustrated how merchandise could not be unproblematically purchased. The theme of antipathy towards marketized fan identities further illustrated the underlying higher order theme that football fan identity had to be understood as an identity that resided primarily within the jurisdiction of the tribe and outside the control of the marketers.

When you get to the stage where you have identified some overall themes, it can also be very helpful to turn to conceptual frameworks that give you more of an insight into what these themes might mean. I finally resolved the question of how fans could verbally engage in a discourse of negativity towards the range of official merchandise provided by marketers while continuing to partially engage with it. This required a lot of iteration between the patterns in my data and the conceptual literature on consumer resistance, cultural capital, and sacred consumption (as discussed earlier). I realized that because the members of the tribe were primarily concerned with sacralization maintenance (as per Belk, Wallendorf and Sherry's 1989[7] definition as discussed in Chapter 3) and not anti-market resistance *per se*, goods that delivered on themes of sacredness, goods that constituted appropriate examples of fan identity and the team's glorious past, for example, could be accepted by the tribe. By the same token, any marketing initiatives that threatened to undermine the tribe's sense of distinction would be resisted. Hence the combining of the higher order codes into a set of overall themes that fitted consistently with the data eventually helped to comprehensively explain the consumer behaviour of an entire tribe of football fans (Table 6.5).

Incidentally, the question also remains as to whether the interpretation I came up with sheds a definitive light on *all* football fans. The answer is no. Many football fans happily regard all sorts of merchandise as sacred. However, I had gained an insight into how the tribe I had studied viewed the world, and *this is what matters* from a tribal marketing point of view.

There are a few different things we can learn from all this. One is that the analytical process, while non-linear, is extremely thorough. The second thing is that it is absolutely vital to keep clear records of all your codes, so that you know what each code means, where it originated from, and whether you have compared your codes against all available data. This brings us back to another point – the question of *purposive sampling*. Once the patterns in your data have begun to indicate that there are possible qualitative differences between the consumers in a particular tribe, even consumers who all seem on the surface to be members of the same tribe, this indicates that you should make sure to collect adequate data on all the relevant tribal categories as they emerge. In practice, in order to be in a position to evaluate the veracity

Table 6.5   Recap: From early analysis to development of overall themes

To extrapolate from the example of thematic development in the case of the football fan tribe in a way that allows us to develop a set of principles that apply to all tribes is very straightforward.

- You need to allow yourself the time to immerse yourself fully in analysis of tribal data. Primary data that might not make sense early on will make sense later when you have generated codes that can be used as lenses to revisit and interpret it. In a similar way first-order codes that might seem hard to relate to one another in the earlier stages of analysis will lend themselves to pattern identification more easily later. Be patient and don't expect everything to make sense immediately.
- When you have spent enough time collecting and analysing your data, higher order codes and themes will start to occur to you much more readily. In order to make sure that your emergent interpretation is meaningful, use it to try to make sense of large chunks of tribal data, such as entire discussion threads on tribal web forums, full videos of tribal activities, full interview transcripts and so on. If you have achieved 'overdetermination of pattern' then you won't keep coming across data that contradicts your themes.
- Strong overall interpretations also have the capacity to explain and reconcile the apparent contradictions identified at earlier stages in the analysis. Good tribal ethnographies both identify contradictions and provide meaningful and interesting interpretations of them, rather than trying to whitewash them away or pretend they don't exist. As shown in the above case of the football fan tribe, use should be made of different types of data *and* conceptual interpretations from previous research – where available – to help finalize the interpretation of your tribe.
- Last but not least, in finalizing your interpretation, you should be able to understand how the overall cultural themes are reconciled to one another. If some of your themes still seem to clash with or contradict each other, you still have a little bit of interpretive work left to do, and possibly even some further data collection and analysis to carry out.

---

of the insights you gain into tribal culture, interviewees whom you deem representative of each of the different cultural categories you have identified should be approached and interviewed, and the resulting data analysed until you are confident that you have incorporated all the relevant tribal categories, sub-tribes, or clusters, into your interpretation.

Third, while making the leap from lower level to higher level codes is often exciting and sometimes even euphoric (it is kind of exciting when you identify something that helps you to spot relationships across different data sets, after all) that does not entitle you to drop the requirement to be sceptical of your emergent themes.

In short, you need to test your themes. You need to revisit old data to see if they stand up against that, and you need to go out of your way to collect new data that will serve to test these emergent themes. Eventually, once a number of higher order themes have been identified, the emphasis in data collection and analysis will shift completely, from gathering data and looking for first order codes, to gathering data purely for the purpose of rigorously scrutinizing and even trying to contradict the themes as identified. It is inadvisable to try to impose a specific time frame in advance on this process, because it is dependent on generating the higher order themes in the first place. However, it is not unreasonable to assume that once you begin to see the same themes emerging each time you collect and analyse data, you are beginning to enter the final phases of developing your initial tribal interpretation.

To revert to my study of the football fan tribe, I knew that when I attended football games, for instance, and my observations conformed to patterns previously observed and the themes that had emerged from my analysis, rather than being at odds with them, my interpretation was an insightful one. Similarly, the (now refined) emergent themes were also reflected in relation to other data categories, such as online data.

When you have reached this point in your initial ethnomarketing phase, and developed and refined your interpretation, then your focus as a tribal marketer changes. From a data collection and analysis perspective, it is time to switch the emphasis towards monitoring the tribal value system to see whether it is evolving in any way, for instance, rather than having to constantly collect large volumes of new data. This of course implies that you will continue to be immersed in the tribe in some way, but that your brief is now one of trying to ensure that you continue to understand the tribal culture rather than trying to gain an initial understanding of it.

You can also begin to develop, or co-produce, products and services that fit in with the tribe's value system, and you can develop tribal communications messages with a reasonable degree of confidence that these messages are supporting tribal linking value and helping the tribe to perceive your brand as such.

On a related note, you can also assess the degree to which you may need to reassure the tribe in some way if some other marketing tactic you need to implement represents a potential contradiction of some kind to the tribal value system.

Last but not least, you should not assume that other categories of consumer outside your particular tribe will be motivated by the same values as your tribe. You shouldn't generalize or base marketing decisions on the findings from one ethnomarketing study. If you think other tribes potentially resemble yours, then that might help in your initial approach to those tribes, but it is important to be cautious in how you draw inferences from your work.

A final point here is that yes, there is a little bit of an elephant in the room. The above does seem potentially very time-consuming, and thus somewhat at odds with commercial imperatives. While it would be very superficial to try to address this in detail in what remains of this chapter, two points can be made. The first is that gaining this level of understanding and rapport with a tribe potentially gives the marketer a relationship with the tribe that should enable them to dislodge other marketers from the tribe's affections, and subsequently maintain this preferred position. It would seem a shame, therefore, to not be patient and devote an adequate amount of time to gaining this level of understanding and rapport in the first place. The second point is that while the literature on this question certainly refers to cases where the initial ethnomarketing phase may have taken as long as 18 months or longer, there doesn't seem to be any reason why insights gained from this sort of rigorous approach to ethnomarketing could not be applied to help refine the marketer's approach as soon as they begin to come on stream. Why not? If some initial higher order themes have been corroborated against available data after the first few months of ethnomarketing work, then it may be possible to use them to begin to refine the marketer's approach. As further insight becomes available, the marketer's approach can be refined further. The main caveat is probably that large-scale strategic decisions should await

Table 6.6   Checklist of activities for tribal analysis and interpretation

- Immerse yourself gradually and thoroughly in the data. Don't just plunge right into coding, but instead give yourself some time and space to allow initial impressions to form, whether by watching video footage, listening to an interview all the way through, or reading a transcript and allowing yourself to react to it, rather than trying to immediately scrutinize it for answers to specific questions you might have
- When you begin to code the data, remember to treat *every* piece of data as potentially representative of an interesting phenomenon
- Individual data extracts may easily prove to be representative of a *number* of interesting phenomena, so don't hesitate to assign more than one code to a piece of data
- Document *everything*, every single first order code, thoroughly. Don't be put off by the number of codes this generates, or the length of your analysis. At first you may find yourself generating a lot of material but as you get more experienced your ability to code in a more concise way will improve
- As you proceed through your analysis and insights begin to accumulate, you will increasingly recognize instances of phenomena already documented – and you will also become more adept at recognizing exceptions to these 'rules' – you can also consider beginning to develop some initial ways of refining current marketing tactics although any major decisions should wait till your interpretation is complete
- Try to work with at least one colleague with whom you can compare notes and review codes – an alternative perspective on things can be invaluable in interpreting what's going on
- Try to avoid the temptation to leave this work to software packages – there is NO substitute for immersing yourself in your data and gaining a personal 'feel' for what it means to be a member of the tribe in question
- Take a fully iterative approach to code development – look back as well as forwards through your data, and compare codes across data types as well, to generate further insights
- Remember that just because 'breakthrough' moments, when you suddenly feel you have unlocked the code to a theme, feel so good doesn't mean that your theme is the definitive optimal insight! Be patient and retain a sceptical outlook
- Make sure to search thoroughly for disconfirming observations and try to avoid drawing conclusions until you and your colleague(s) feel that 'overdetermination of pattern' has been achieved
- Once you have begun to generate insights based on over-determination of pattern, then it should be ok to start feeding these insights into the process of refining products, marketing communications and so on, in conjunction with the tribe.
- If you still have a number of themes that seem to strongly contradict one another you may still have to collect and analyse some more data, till you have managed to refine and reconcile your themes within an overall integrated interpretation of your tribe's culture
- Finally, the analytical emphasis can begin to shift towards maintaining understanding, while continuing to participate in the life of the tribe

the conclusion of full interpretation development, but the potential benefits of this arguably make it worth the wait.

The next step in getting more of an understanding of the entire tribal marketing approach is to consider how different marketers have taken a variety of approaches to developing their relationship with different tribes. What makes this particularly interesting is that, as the cases we examine in Chapter 7 will demonstrate, it seems possible to practice forms of tribal marketing that don't necessarily comply with all aspects of the thorough approach we have been following so far.

Concluding thoughts

This chapter has covered a lot of territory that might be new to most marketers. Some of the ideas, be they about coding, or about what to look for when collecting and analysing data, might even seem counter-intuitive at first. A lot of the ideas and principles might also seem very abstract to begin with. However, this approach really does become clear once you begin to engage with it, and it really does deliver insight into a tribe's view of the world in a way that you can then feed back into your brand. It is also vital to remember that while you as a marketer have questions you want answered and commercial/related objectives you want to achieve, that the answers will not emerge directly from specific stages of the analytic process. To become a tribal marketer, you need to allow the data to reveal its own story to you. Learn to look for what is there, rather than what you want to be there. In particular, resist the temptation to look for 'quick fixes' to help you derive immediate sales-oriented solutions focusing directly on product use. Instead, cultivate your ability to develop meaningful insight into the tribe's view of the world and their place in it – and then you will be perfectly placed to support them. Finally, in looking at the checklist in Table 6.6, remember that this is an iterative and not a sequential process! The 'checklist' will work best if you treat it as a set of guiding principles to inform your approach, rather than a set of sequential steps to be dutifully adhered to. As we will see from the cases in Chapter 7, tribes don't 'do' sequential and neither should you.

7 Meet the Tribes

Introduction

So far the focus in this book has been on how to collect and analyse tribal data in order to gain an understanding of tribal linking value and tribal cultural capital.

The next stage is to look at how to leverage this knowledge and this membership of the tribe to refine your approach to brand development, so that the brand comes to be seen by the tribe as symbolic of their identity and supportive of their values. In this way the link between the tribe and the brand becomes more firmly established and the brand can even become permanently embedded in the tribe's identity, with ensuing implications for loyalty to and advocacy of the brand.

The first two cases in this chapter therefore illustrate how the companies involved moved from collecting data via ethno-marketing to implementing changes to brand development so that the brand could be perceived as genuinely embodying tribal linking value. If marketing effort is diverted into supporting the tribe and allowing the tribe to exercise their own creativity, instead of attempting to impose brand meaning on them via conventional approaches to advertising and so on, then the tribe will be able to bond with the brand.

The other cases in the chapter serve to remind us that the marketer needs to remember that tribal marketing is ultimately about supporting the tribe. The *X Factor* case shows how a tribe can spontaneously emerge if the marketer's initial offering is sufficiently attractive, but that if the marketer does not commit to supporting linking value the tribe may begin to decline. The Red Bull case shows how spectacular growth can be sustained when the marketer continues to support tribal linking value, even if this is not necessarily implemented according to all the principles of ethno-marketing as described so far. The Cheffactor case continues this theme of marketer facilitation of tribal linking value and serves to illustrate how a tribe will respond passionately to a brand that recognizes the importance of facilitating the tribe's own creativity.

Salomon and the snowboarding tribe

In Chapter 4 we saw how in relation to both snowboarding and in-line skating, Salomon took a similar approach. There was a philosophy of humility and a desire to understand the activity from the perspective of the tribal members participating in it. Formal marketing communications of a promotional nature were not established until after the initial period of ethno-marketing mentioned earlier.

As already noted in Chapter 4, Salomon set up a marketing unit dedicated to the snowboarding market but the staff in this unit engaged in participant observation and cultivating relationships with key members of the snowboarding subculture. Over time, members of the tribe were invited to help with product design until Salomon had a selection of snowboards ready for tribal use. Even then, rather than overtly engage in a 'hard sell' of the new product range, the company displayed them at tribal gatherings and invited members of the tribe to try the new boards out. Overt promotion was postponed until Salomon felt that they understood the culture enough to have an intuitive understanding of which tribal media to advertise in, which tribal events to sponsor, and so on. In the end, when they did launch, they rapidly gained a significant market share – because the brand was seen as representative of tribal values.

In their discussion of this case, while Cova and Cova clearly indicate the potential benefits of a so-called humble approach, they refer to participant observation without fully unpacking the term for us. However, a couple of things are clear. It is obviously important to gain as deep an insight as possible into the ethno-sociological links between tribal members. It is imperative to put yourself in their shoes, or in the case of the in-line skaters, in their skates. What does the world look like from their perspective, and how do you gain that perspective? This is what the humility Cova and Cova refer to actually means – to acknowledge that it is not your prowess or power as a marketer that matters, but the perspective of the tribe. You as an aspiring tribal marketer must bring yourself down to the level of the individual participant and experience the activity and the brand through their eyes.

What makes the case of Salomon and the snowboarder tribe all the more interesting is that the snowboarders hadn't appropriated the brand at the outset of Salomon's initiation of a tribal approach, but in fact they specifically distanced themselves from it. For them, it represented a negative reference group, whereby it was a brand for their parents' generation, a brand for conservative people, certainly not a brand that possessed any linking value for them, other than as a way of understanding and communicating what they were not. It was also a skier's brand and they were not skiers, they were snowboarders. It may seem like a very subtle distinction, after all they are both winter sports involving snow, but for tribes, these distinctions are everything. If you do not have a joint basis for asserting your difference from other identities, you are not a tribe. And as a general rule, identities tend to position themselves against those identities that are closest to them in terms of social and geographic proximity. Mac versus PC. Snowboarders versus skiers. Liverpool versus Manchester United, and so on.

This did not bode well for Salomon. They had been considered by the tribe, but instead of being appropriated, they had been rejected. They seemed to be representative of the antithesis of the tribe's linking value, rather than epitomizing it. So how did they go about trying to address the situation?

Of necessity, I'm going to refer extensively again to Cova and Cova's summary of what happened. Owing perhaps to the situation the brand found itself in, the company took an unusual approach. They decided to listen and learn from the tribe and slowly build a relationship between themselves and the snowboarders, not via the usual approach of formal marketing communications or loyalty schemes, but by participation. When they set up a dedicated marketing unit to develop the relationship with the tribe, they recruited members of the snowboarding tribe to staff it. When they decided to support 'a team of good snowboarders' they did not try to force them to use Salomon branded snowboards but instead equipped them with non-Salomon boards. When they began to design Salomon snowboards, they recruited members of the tribe to help with the design project.

This unconventional approach continued through the launch phase of the new brand of Salomon snowboards. The new boards were introduced via snowboarders' pro-shops rather than the traditional winter sports retail outlets. This approach was also taken at exhibition, whereby the new snowboard range was not presented at the Salomon stand but at the pro-shop stand only. So far, this may not seem very unusual – it often makes sense to distribute your brand via the channels where your customers are, rather than expecting your customers to come directly to you. However, by taking such an approach, Salomon was also acknowledging how the tribe collectively felt about itself. They were not winter sports 'traditionalists', so why should they be expected to shop at traditional winter sport outlets?

This in itself was accompanied by another inspired tactic. The company refrained from advertising the launch. This seems at first counter-intuitive and counterproductive. How do you achieve awareness of your new product without formally communicating its existence? How do you communicate its unique attributes and differentiate it from competing products, if not through advertising? Yet in hindsight, Salomon's decision was inspired. By taking a low-key approach, the tribe's right to decide for themselves whether or not to adopt the new brand was respected. Instead of a marketer coming along and insisting that they knew and understood what snowboarding was all about, and that their new product encapsulated this knowledge, the company deferred to the knowledge and values of the tribe. This was certainly an unorthodox approach but it was completely consistent with everything that Salomon had done so far.

By 1997, however, it was time. Salomon branded boards were made available on a wide scale for snowboarders to trial them without any obligation to purchase. Having identified those places the tribe considered theirs, and having identified appropriate tribal media, Salomon finally launched their advertising campaign and also rolled out a support programme for tribal events. Within two years they had achieved the third-largest share of the French snowboarding market (Cova and Cova 2002:18).[1]

How did this happen? In hindsight, and extrapolating a little from Cova and Cova's analysis, it seems that through participant observation, Salomon gradually built up an understanding of what snowboarding meant to the tribe. Their humble approach, when accompanied by a genuine desire to learn from the tribe and to gain an understanding of what snowboarding was all about, meant that the tribe's perception of the brand was over time radically altered. It became a brand that was representative of the values and identity of the tribe. The fact that the new brand was launched without advertising must have also been perceived as significant. Instead of a hyped-up sales pitch, this was the brand whose staff were actually snowboarders themselves. The idea of boards designed by snowboarders, for snowboarders, sounds like the hoariest of advertising clichés but in this case it was actually true – and the company weren't trying to ram it down the tribe's throats. Instead they were just asking them if they wanted to try the new boards out.

As Cova and Cova also report, Salomon followed a form of tribal ethno-marketing in relation to the in-line skaters tribe. Again, rather than trying to simply cash in on a trend by launching a new product to exploit the demand for a popular activity, the company committed themselves to a period of participant observation of the tribe and a full analysis of tribal rituals. Post this initial period, the company moved on to a design phase which again involved securing the cooperation and participation of members of the tribe in the product design and testing stages. Finally by the time the product was launched Salomon was effectively a member of the tribe, so the brand could be perceived as representative of tribal values.

It is notable that Salomon took a long-term approach to successfully achieving their position in the in-line skating tribe. They displayed the same patience that had characterized their approach to the snowboarding tribe. By using the sort of methods outlined in the previous chapters of this book, they gained invaluable insight into tribal values. By participating in tribal activities themselves, they were also able to demonstrate a commitment to these values. They built a relationship with the tribe that was founded on participation and understanding. That ensured that both tribes came to see the brand as authentic and representative of themselves. Thus one of the most important lessons we can infer from Salomon's approach is the value of participation in ensuring that your brand will be perceived as an authentic reflection of tribal identity. When formal communications with the tribe are grounded in actual participation in tribal activities, they are far more likely to be accepted as an authentic reflection of tribal values than orthodox marketing communications. We will now have a look at what I consider to be an outstanding example of best practice in relation to tribal marketing and tribal branding.

The Harley Davidson approach

For me, Harley Davidson constitutes another fantastic exemplar of the participative approach to tribal brand development. Even though their approach seems to have evolved over something of a longer timeframe than Salomon's, and at times may have owed quite a lot to serendipity, there is a huge amount to be learned from it. Also, in the examples we will consider, we will see some of the other benefits that can accrue from paying attention to the activities of the brand tribe.

Harley Davidson's legacy as a brand is much fêted for various reasons. One aspect of its legacy that I've always found particularly interesting is the way in which participant observation has contributed to the brand over the years. Brand meaning as developed by members of the brand subculture has been fed back into the brand again and again. It is an outstanding example of the potential that exists when a brand is truly co-created.

This degree of brand co-creation was not achieved overnight. Yet again, an understanding of community perceptions of the brand was built up over time using ethnographic observation of, and participation in, community rituals. As layer upon layer of understanding was added, this was incorporated into brand communication strategies. The establishment of the Harley Owner Group was a recognition of the social dimension of the brand. Owning a Harley was not something you did in isolation, it was something you bought into to become part of a tribe. *Hog Tales*, the Harley owners' magazine, was established to facilitate the sharing of brand stories and to give members of the tribe an outlet for mutual expression of group narcissism. Harley Davidson supported tribal events, often including events not exclusive to the Harley Davidson brand, an interesting choice reminiscent of Ducati's approach to online community development as discussed earlier. However, for now we will look at one particular tribal development tactic used by Harley Davidson to support the tribe in a way that focused solely on Harley Davidson motorcycles. This is the Harley Davidson Posse Ride.

The Posse Ride

In their account of how the Harley Davidson Posse Ride successfully contributed to the further building of the brand community, Susan Fournier and her colleagues highlight a number of points, all of which have something useful to tell us about tribal branding. The first is that the event catered to a brand-related meaning that emanates directly from what the brand means to the tribe. Unlike the stationary 'destination' rallies (the most famous of which is the multi-brand 'Bike Week' in Daytona, Florida), 'Rolling Rallies' such as the Posse Ride are all about 'being in the saddle'. For the tribe, owning a Harley Davidson is about the freedom of the open road and the motorcycle as a means of accessing the pioneering spirit of the American West. It can also be about a spirit of independence that for some crosses over into rebelliousness and the outright flouting of normal social convention, but strangely enough, the behaviour of those on the margin can draw others to the tribe even if they have no intention of flouting convention themselves. Riding a Harley allows you to imagine yourself giving the finger to the Country Club set, even if in reality you would never dream of doing such a rude thing! So this facilitation of a group experience of riding Harley Davidsons cross-country is something that taps directly into the tribal desire to show off to one another and to others, via brand-related behaviours. As Lisa, one of the bikers quoted in the Posse Ride case, notes:

> *my kids were really embarrassed when I started riding ... Now of course the kids think it's cool! ... Everyone wants to talk to you if you ride a Harley and you get to know so many more people than you normally would. Harley is a real social facilitator. I don't see people going up to Honda riders and saying 'Hey I've always wanted to ride a Honda!'.*

(Fournier et al. 2001)[2]

Organizing an event like the Posse Ride gives Lisa and her fellow bikers an opportunity to enjoy the social affirmation they can access through the brand. Also (as discussed in Chapter 4), the event allows company executives to tap into tribal linking values for themselves – to pursue the same quest and to live the brand in the same way as their customers, while the insight thereby acquired, when fed back into the brand, helps to ensure that the brand retains credibility as a symbol of authentic passion for motorcycling.

This idea of brands as symbols of authenticity is fundamental to tribal branding. To revert briefly to the example of Ducati as discussed in Chapter 2, in their case, the decision to keep the Ducati forum open to all motorcyclists eventually paid a huge dividend. Instead of using the website as a narrow promotional channel to sell the Ducati range, it became instead a virtual home for all motorcycle enthusiasts to share their passion. By association, the Ducati brand came to represent a passion for motorcycling instead of simply another commercial brand. Hence tribal branding's capacity to differentiate brands in a way that other approaches cannot replicate.

Another key point in tribal brand development is that the marketer's role should not be confined to observing, facilitating, interpreting, and participating in rituals. A key element in facilitation of the tribe is the frequent introduction of novel brand-related possibilities that the tribe can then decide for themselves on how to use. For example, the Posse Ride begins by swearing members in and giving them their 'passports'. The ritual taking of the Posse Ride oath was introduced by Harley Davidson without any particular purpose or intent as to how it might evolve, but the members of the tribe began to take it seriously and it grew in significance to the point where members prided themselves on adhering to things like the 'no whining' clause.

While this might seem trivial, the underlying principle is hugely important. As Martin Kornberger explains in his excellent book *Brand Society*[3], the brand's role is not to present everything to the tribe as a fait accompli, but to provide inspiration via the provision of 'ghost scripts... and props' that allow the tribe 'to express (a shared)... creativity' (2010:140). Granted, the organizing of as detailed an event as the Posse Ride in many ways provides the tribe with something far more than just a 'ghost script' for the tribe to appropriate and expand on. Many aspects of the experience are indeed pre-planned. However, perhaps the important point is not so much whether the initial product or service is highly detailed, but whether or not it provides the inspiration for creativity on the part of the tribe, so that they have the free-dom to expand on and make their own of it. In relation to the Posse Ride, while each day's destination is specified in advance, the route is not, so mem-bers must plan their own routes to that night's destination. In the evenings, sometimes entertainment is organized, but often nothing is formally planned other than loosely organized storytelling sessions where members have the opportunity to share brand-related experiences with one another. In terms of mementoes of the trip, the company usually provides commemorative mer-chandise, including t-shirts, to participants, but members always improvise and add their own such as 'Route 66' tattoos to commemorate that par-ticular ride. The company also sometimes change the range of mementoes provided. Why provide a pin set one year and not the next? The answer to this question is that the spirit of the brand is supposed to be about a willing-ness to adapt to novel circumstances. Even the practice of having some basic mementoes that don't change but others that are new helps. It will continue to engage members' minds by introducing novel ways of celebrating and commemorating their Posse Ride experience. This helps to meet the tribe's experiential needs and gives them something new to appropriate. All these mementoes matter, because they are symbolic of something each individual Posse Rider accomplishes personally. The key for the marketer lies in doing enough to facilitate the marking of these accomplishments, without trying to over-prescribe for their marking. In short, what the marketer needs to do is adopt what Schau, Muniz, and Arnould[4] term 'seeding practices', an idea we will return to in more detail in Chapter 9.

One last point on this, at the risk of repetition, is that there is all the difference in the world between sharing mementoes with someone who has participated in the same experiences as you, and hence whose levels of tribal capital are potentially on a par with yours, and simply buying souvenirs.

In order to understand how to go about facilitating tribal experiences properly, it is therefore fairly obvious that you first need to carry out the sort of tribal research we looked at in the previous chapters, so that you have a proper insight into the values of the tribe and you know what it is you are trying to support. Salomon and Harley Davidson are clear exemplars of this approach.

While this does have clear implications in terms of the amount of time needed to carry out initial tribal research and plan approaches for tribal facil-itation, the question definitely arises as to whether alternative forms of tribal marketing can achieve success without being preceded by a long-term period of ethnographic immersion. In looking at a case that addresses this issue, I also want to acknowledge a potentially misleading impression that the previous case may have given. This is the idea that tribal marketing means your senior executives and maybe even your chief executive have to be out there 'living the brand' 24/7. The short answer to this is that they do not. To consider all these questions in more depth, let's take a look at the Red Bull approach to tribal marketing.

Red Bull

By now, Red Bull has become such an iconic brand, its message ubiquitously spread via heavy advertising and sponsorship, it is hard in some ways to conceive of it as a humble tribal marketer who simply invites people to invest and project their own meanings onto the brand. However, if we take a look at how the brand emerged, the process reveals many elements of tribal marketing.

Tribal marketers, we have thus far suggested, don't engage in a 'hard sell'. They seek instead to make their brand available 'should people wish' so to speak. It is also characteristic of tribal marketers that they go out to the places where the tribe are congregated and seek to facilitate them there. Red Bull did exactly this, even if it was sometimes lacking in subtlety!

They just had student reps driving round, going to places where people needed energy. They had their student reps hand out cans of Red Bull at campus parties so that the drinks were received from people living the same high-octane student lifestyle as the market Red Bull were targeting. Of course the question might arise as to whether university students always lead a high octane lifestyle but this shouldn't distract us from one of the main points of joining a tribe, or more correctly, imagining oneself, as part of a tribe. The disparity between high energy and students staying in bed all morning, getting up late, and missing lectures is an obvious one, even though there are clearly other times of the day or night when students want energy to go clubbing or to stay awake to study for exams they have neglected to prepare for earlier. Again though this isn't really the point. Very often the point of tribal membership is to imagine yourself as part of a particular group, even if it is just temporarily. While this can be enjoyable at an individual level, it is at a collective level that it can become particularly gratifying, through mutual affirmation of the experience.

So what did Red Bull do, to create meanings that consumers could use to re-imagine the self? In a way not all that dissimilar from some of the cases identified by Cova and Cova, such as Tatoo pagers and Helly Hansen outdoor gear, they implied an association between the brand and certain possibilities, and allowed the consumer to make the final choice. These disparate meanings included 'self as daredevil', 'self as DJ', 'self as persona with street cred', and so on. Through such things as the supportive, authentic nature of the Red Bull Music Academy, and the communicating of other symbolic possibilities through leaving empty Red Bull cans in the restrooms of fashionable nightclubs, they managed to consistently yet subtly convey the symbolic possibility that 'these cool, sexy, alternative, people drink Red Bull'. Postmodern consumers, eager to convey something (to themselves at least as much as to anyone else) about who they were, about the possibilities of becoming the exciting or alternative person they would ideally be, felt free to choose Red Bull as a way of incorporating these meanings into their sense of Self.

Ultimately such desired meanings for the self are better experienced through collective affirmation – and Red Bull kept organizing opportunities for people to express this identity and have it mutually and playfully affirmed via events such as the Red Bull 'Flugtag'. In another echo of the tribal practices engaged in by companies like Salomon, Red Bull did not commence heavy advertising of the brand until these meanings were established among the tribe. The tribe identified with the brand because it supported their linking value, not because of saturation advertising. That is what causes me to conclude that the success of the brand was ultimately down to tribal marketing, albeit of a sort that doesn't necessarily comply with all aspects of the template we've assembled so far.

Of course as we all know, Red Bull's strategy and evolution as a brand owes a lot to serendipity and notoriety, but this doesn't change the fact that many of the things they did that contributed significantly to the development of the brand were absolutely in keeping with the key principles of tribal marketing. Their subsequent success is all the more useful to us as an indicator that the key element for tribal branding to succeed is not whether a marketer commits significant resources to an initial phase of ethno-marketing, but whether or not a tribe emerges around a brand and decides to make it their own. It is the tribe, in the end, that makes its own rules and determines its own linking values. The marketer can only make offerings and try to facilitate the linking values, once identified. Thus even in those cases where there is a spectacular success even without an initial period of ethno-marketing, there is still a compelling argument to begin to use it later on, to make sure that you understand what the tribe's linking values are and how to support them. This in turn might help to prolong the longevity of the tribe. This is highly relevant for the next case we are going to look at, where the failure to adopt an ethno-marketing approach to identification and support of the linking value may help to explain the apparent demise of the tribe.

The *X Factor* – a tribe in decline?

Seth Godin[5] observes that companies worry too much about numbers; how many clicks, how many customers in total, how many views of the ad, that kind of thing. This is particularly relevant to the next context to which I'm going to apply the tribal model. For me, the *X Factor* represents another fascinating scenario whereby even without an adherence to the recommended practice of ethno-marketing, there has been something of a spectacular tribal success. At a time when TV audiences in the United Kingdom have been fragmenting, this reality talent contest, nominally based on the notion of uncovering the best 'unknown' singer in the country and awarding them with a recording contract, has consistently pulled in millions of viewers every Saturday night. Yet for me this success is now at risk because of an insistence on attempting to continue to drive the numbers – in this case audience numbers – instead of a focus on identifying and supporting linking values.

The right things will happen if you create a climate that allows people to retain their passion for what all this is about, and you retain an authentic passion for it yourself. Pursue authenticity, authentically. If I was to apply this to the *X Factor*, I'd say that this should not be about constantly trying to drum up enthusiasm for a stagnant format, through staged rows and PR stunts, and instead it should involve trying to find better ways of unearthing raw talent and bringing it to the fore. Not the pursuit of novelty for novelty's sake, but the pursuit of talent for authenticity's sake. The novelty and spontaneity will flow from this. The mini-epiphanies that the tribe must experience to stay together have to be grounded in something real and not something contrived, or tribal linking value will be undermined. So instead of staging mock-rows between judges, or between contestants, or between judges and contestants, if the marketer in this case wants to reinvigorate the tribe's passion for the brand, then they should consider things like setting up a School of the Performing Arts and giving some of the graduates wild-card entries into the TV contest every year. The point is that whatever you do must be perceived as authentic by the tribe.

Also, in looking at the *X Factor* audience as a form of tribe, we are reminded that you can join a tribe without leaving your armchair, and that tribes can form even in situations where the marketer had no prior intent of doing anything other than create an audience in the ordinary sense.

The argument that the *X Factor* audience effectively constitutes a form of tribe marketing is given credence by a number of factors. The *X Factor*'s initial success in attracting an audience owes a debt to the way in which talent competitions of this nature facilitate the desire to indulge in group narcissism. In this case, group narcissism manifests itself via the shared fantasy of discovery and celebrity status. Su Holmes (2010)[6] suggests that shows like Britain's *Got Talent* and the *X Factor* appeal to us because they allow us to imagine that we too have what it takes, and it is only by accident that we have not been discovered. It follows that this fantasy becomes all the more enjoyable when it is shared.

When we look at it, there are multiple ways in which the *X Factor* is effectively a communal or even tribal experience. The annual auditions process draws thousands of hopefuls towards acting out the fantasy as depicted on the show every week. By gathering together in such huge numbers to queue for a chance to audition, the show's fans really do take on the identity of a contemporary tribe engaged in group narcissism. Not only that, but the live audience inside the audition venues willingly continue this theme, putting themselves on show, so that they can be part of both the show and the audience.

Also, in what I would argue amounts to a form of tribal participation, Simon Cowell and the other judges constantly behave in ways that mimic tribal behaviour. After all, the tribe is not just here to sit quietly and watch the show. Absolutely not. Where would the self-importance be in that? The audience are there to judge the contestants, not just to daydream about being contestants themselves.

I would also suggest that the behaviour of the judges more or less amounts to a form of tribal participation. Their frequent displays of emotion mimic the reactions of the tribe to the emotional – or unintentionally hilarious – narratives unfolding on stage. The participative approach continues in the interactive *Xtra Factor* phone-in show that follows each broadcast of the *X Factor*. There is also the 'boot camp' part of the series, when the contestants stay in one of the judges' holiday homes, to consider. Thus we, the TV audience, get to vicariously live inside Simon's home. This feeling whereby Simon can be imagined as similar to ourselves and thus very much part of our tribe is sustained by the sheer familiarity generated by Simon's ubiquitous presence in the tabloids and other celebrity gossip media. Participation in social media and/or attendance at *X Factor* Tour concerts arguably provides further social affirmation of these tribal narratives.

It might not be clear where the audience ends and the tribe begins, or vice versa, but this is an audience with at least some tribal characteristics. We can see group narcissism, high levels of interactivity, and if we researched it we would probably find a strong sense of linking value. All of this adds up to the possibility that a form of tribal marketing has in a sense been used, to successfully create a tribe. This is really interesting because again it reminds us that it is tribes themselves who decide whether or not to form, and if someone offers consumers something interesting and novel they may decide to congregate around it and form a tribe, irrespective of whether we've embarked on some sort of elaborate ethno-marketing process to help us identify and support tribal linking values. However, when we start to take a closer look at whether other critical elements of tribal marketing are present or absent, we begin to spot a few potential problems.

Let's think back to what we know about tribes and tribal marketing so far. Tribes themselves decide whether or not to 'crystallise', as Martin Kornberger says, around an interesting brand. This doesn't preclude marketers from proffering interesting brands, whatever form they are in, in the hope that a tribe will embrace them. If something seems interesting and authentic and has the potential for linking value, it would seem to have a good chance of being adopted as the basis for tribal formation. What may have happened in this case is the marketer has hit on a format that appeals to an audience and because the narrative offers potential linking value, a tribe has emerged. However, if we begin to think about the other things that matter to a tribe, then we start to spot the gaps that can emerge if marketers refuse to acknowledge the tribe's need for authenticity and auton-omy. Tribes don't want the whole story, they just want enough to get started, and they want their role to be meaningful. They also want the narrative to be real, or at least have enough weight for them to be able to imagine it as real.

Enjoyment of the *X Factor* narratives was initially facilitated through the provision of participant biographies, the participatory approach adopted by the judges and presenter, and so on. But what if the biographies become too contrived? What if contestant after contestant has their bio edited using the same narrative devices, so that tales of a loved one to whom they owe absolutely everything, are over-used? What if the audience begins to believe that the judges are just trying to manipulate them to vote in a certain way, rather than vote for the contestant with the most natural talent?

For the *X Factor*'s success to be attributed to tribal marketing, we would expect to find evidence of an interactive, participatory approach by the marketer and a low-key, soft sell approach to formal marketing communi-cations, or at least a perception of the sales pitch as a call to participation rather than a call to purchase. Part of the resemblance to tribal marketing in this case thus lies in the perceived lack of an overt sales pitch from someone who is not a member of the tribe. The call to pass judgement (via premium-pay phone line) is not perceived as a hard sell. How could it be? Simon isn't a slick snake oil peddler, he is just an extension of ourselves. The in-your-face style of the frequent calls to vote may not even be perceived as coercive, but as affirmations of tribal identity. So why not become part of the tribe, enjoy the ride, and allow yourself to be persuaded to dial the premium pay phone number to vote for those upon whom you wish to bestow the *X Factor*?

An interesting study by Papacharissi and Mendelson (2007)[7] found that reality TV audiences may be aware of the relatively contrived nature of reality TV programming, but the enjoyable narratives actively facilitate suspension of disbelief, at least initially. However, as we know, tribes need to feel a sense of at least some autonomy and at least some level of authenticity. If the audi-ence begin to believe that they are being manipulated, or that they are not really being given a proper say in determining the outcome, this could be problematic and might even lead to the demise of the tribe and also of course the audience. Unfortunately there is some evidence to suggest that talent contest shows are still going the route of trying to control things to drive the audience figures, rather than support the linking values that help to perpetuate the tribe.

Kjus' (2009)[8] analysis of Norway's version of *Pop Idol* demonstrates such a case. For instance, by the time the television audience are presented with images of massive crowds queuing to audition for the show, huge numbers of applications have already been discarded by the producers. Some of those retained are only allowed to audition for their comic value. Only contestants who are seen as having potential to command strong audience figures receive favourable editing, in an attempt to sway the public vote to make sure that they get through the audition process:

> *Producers routinely select a number of promising candidates about whom they pro-duce a report in advance, and these are shown just before (the candidate) goes in to the audition. These people always have a commendable story to tell – for example, how they transcend a handicap, devote all of their time to an amateur choir, or entertain their local community… these candidates are presented as brave and positive, with a dream that Idol might, in fact, help them to achieve, and they often receive many votes and do well in the contest.*
>
> (Kjus 2009)

The live TV broadcasts of the semi-finals and final involve even more control, this time of the studio audience:

> *The producers of Idol therefore instruct their studio audience to act as fans in dif-ferent ways… (b)efore each broadcast, the audience is drilled on how to cheer loudly and wave posters supporting their favorites and on how to boo when the judges are being negative.*
>
> (Kjus 2009)

Thus even the acts of apparently spontaneous tribal narcissism in the studio were initiated and controlled in this case by the show's producers. Of course this does not mean that the producers of the *X Factor* are engaged in the same production practices and values as the producers of Norwegian *Pop Idol*. However, the plethora of allegations surrounding all forms of reality talent show may render it more difficult for members of the *X Factor* tribe to continue to perceive their particular show as authentic. For example, the con-troversy that erupted in relation to *X Factor* USA when allegations emerged that the results were 'rigged' (Cortez 2011),[9] arguably makes it far more dif-ficult for a fan community to sustain a collective belief in both the narrative and their role in co-creating it. Similarly if the tribe begin to believe that media stories about rifts between celebrity judges or any of the contestants are just a device to try to stir up interest in the show, this apparent inauthen-ticity, in undermining the basis for shared linking value, will eventually have the opposite effect to what was intended. The decline in audience numbers suggests that there may be some truth in the possibility that the undermining of linking value is causing the show's fans to simply leave the tribe (Sweney 2011).[10] The failure to allow for the possible presence of a tribe who demand authenticity and a little more creative autonomy may have begun to catch up with the brand.

Fans need to not only feel acknowledged but also to have their sense of ownership affirmed. This is why the apparent humility of the perform-ers at *X Factor* Tour concerts, when they acknowledge that they owe their success to the fans, has in the past gone down so well with the tribe. How-ever, the marketer's unwillingness or inability to implement a more authentic tribal approach may now be contributing to the tribe's demise. Tribes will flourish as long as you support the linking value rather than try to retain complete control over the brand, as may have been the case here. The only way to arrest the declining audience figures might be to hand more control over to the audience, via identifying and moving to support tribal linking values.

Cheffactor

For our final case in the chapter, we will now turn back to look at what can happen when a tribe are supported and have their creativity facilitated rather than restricted. Cheffactor was the brainchild of Cully and Sully, two entrepreneurs who initially launched the brand of the same name in 2004. The idea was very simple. The Cully and Sully brand was meant to symbolize wholesome, completely natural food, albeit in a very convenient easy-to-prepare form. The range included fresh soups, hot pots, and pies. In order to deepen the brand's association with the ethos and philosophy of preparing good food in a natural way, they decided to hold a competition to encourage consumers to prepare their own favourite dishes. The prize for the overall winner of Cheffactor was an opportunity to train as a chef at the renowned Ballymaloe Cookery School under the tutelage of celebrity chefs Darina and Rachel Allen. It was felt that this would help to maintain the brand's relevance to its target market at a time of changing marketplace conditions. As Campaign Director, a.k.a. Captain Cheffactor, Elaine Doyle explained, '*The plan was to stress that the competition was open to everyone, whether they were a whizz in the kitchen or not! So the call to action was a radio ad that literally started with the words "Hi! I'm Sully from Cully and Sully. We want to give you a once in a lifetime opportunity..." and went on to stress that all you needed to enter the competition was "a passion for good food".'*

In keeping with this theme of lucidity, in order to encourage entries, the design of the competition was kept very simple. Contestants just had to prepare their favourite meal and take a photograph of themselves with the resulting dish, with the words 'Cully and Sully' clearly displayed alongside them in the photograph.

The radio ad directed consumers to the Cheffactor.ie microsite, which was an offshoot of the main Cully and Sully website. Again while the microsite layout was kept uncomplicated and clear, it was also designed to draw visitors into the Cully and Sully online brandscape, so visually it was consistent with the features of the main site. The microsite was also designed to allow would-be entrants to upload their photographs with ease and enter short accompanying narratives to explain the details of their dish and why they deserved to win the competition.

A space was provided under each entry to vote and to allow other visitors and friends to comment on the recipes and wish the contestants luck. Cully and Sully – and Captain Cheffactor herself! – used this interactive space to encourage everyone and comment favourably on the entries – and the photographs.

So far, so good. What made things more interesting was the voting mechanism provided. Voting for entries on Cheffactor.ie was linked to Facebook so that votes on the microsite appeared as a 'like' on each voter's Facebook page, along with a photo of that entry. As Elaine noted afterwards, '*the exciting thing about this was that it was one of the first instances where Facebook liking as a voting mechanism was used on such a scale, and it allowed the competition to penetrate people's wider social networks. The design of the website also allowed every entrant to post the direct link to their own entry anywhere on the web.*' This was something of a contrast to the practice prevalent elsewhere whereby entrants appealing for support in web-based competitions could only post links to the overall website, rather than directly to their own personal entry. The initial competition design allowed for two finalists to be chosen via popular vote and one 'wild card' entry to be selected from those on the microsite by Cully and Sully.

The competition thus represented an opportunity for people to publicly express themselves via the idea of a shared passion for food. This arguably also tapped into the spirit of reciprocity that so often characterizes brand tribes. I will place myself on show in return for affirmation from you. Of course it also retained an element of individual narcissism in that it was a chance to show how creative you could be, while also literally putting yourself on show in your online photos. The other element in this process was the opportunity to receive immediate feedback and have this aspect of self affirmed.

What happened next was something completely unanticipated. Cully and Sully had no idea that people would take entering the competition so seriously. It was hoped that the competition would help drive traffic to the main webpage and that people would ask their family and friends to vote for them – which they did. But the tribe had ideas of their own as to how to canvas for votes!

From the early stages of the competition, entrants began to do anything they could think of in order to gain more votes. Some set up stalls outside supermarkets, handing out flyers and free samples of food in order to gain votes. Others handed out cupcakes or cooked dinners in exchange for votes. One person dressed up as a Jim Henson character and walked around a city centre handing out free lollipops in return for votes. Every single item of food had its own Cully and Sully label attached – it is worth noting that this was the initiative of the contestants; Cully and Sully had no idea people would start handing out treats, much less expect them to attach a Cully and Sully logo to each one.

One person even took out a series of radio ads, although this seems a little bit tame compared to the contestants who produced their own videos and ran them as online advertisements as part of their campaigns. The tribe had appropriated the Cully and Sully brand for themselves and had begun to spread the brand's message in ways that not so much exceeded the company's hopes but were absolutely outside the original frame of reference when deciding on the objectives for the competition.

The final numbers were impressive. In return for a modest outlay on web design and a short radio campaign, the competition attracted over 70,000 votes in its first year which of course meant that over 70,000 people had visited the microsite at least once in its first six months of existence. In addition the competition had also driven a significant level of traffic to the main Cully and Sully website. The response to the competition was also such that Cully and Sully decided to increase the number of finalists to five; three finalists to be chosen via popular vote and two 'wild card' entries to be selected as planned directly from the microsite.

The final of the competition, hosted at Ballymaloe, turned into something of a tribal celebration. It was used by Cully and Sully as a way to thank everyone who had entered the competition and of course it gave the entrants the chance to meet in person for the first time. The following year's approach involved refining the web page, giving each contestant their own blog wall, and generally expanding the ways in which the brand facilitated the tribe's creativity and proclivity for group narcissism. The numbers were even better, as word spread and the tribe spurred each other on.

What I like about this case (besides the heart-warming life stories the contestants have openly shared with one another, further enhancing the consciousness of kind that has come out of Cully and Sully Cheffactor.ie) is that it illustrates the potential of tribes and tribal marketing, even in those situations where the marketer has not necessarily followed the sort of approach that I would normally recommend. Cully and Sully Cheffactor didn't begin with a prolonged period of ethno-marketing – albeit that you could argue a strong case for the proponents already being members of the wider 'foodie' tribe, who may have already had an instinctive feeling for the linking value that could reside in the idea of 'a passion for food'. No, what happened here was that a few simple principles, such as facilitating and interacting with the tribe, were integrated with a flair for creative design, and then the tribe simply took over. In making use of the 'ghost script' the marketers had provided, they created the rest themselves. What I would say in conclusion, though, is this. If this is what can be achieved with a little facilitation, good design, and a determination to support the tribe, then what is the potential for tribal marketing on a larger scale when additional, albeit still modest, resources are available to implement a more comprehensive approach?

Concluding thoughts

Overall we have learned quite a lot from looking at these cases. The marketer can pursue a tribal agenda either deliberately, by initiating an ethno-marketing approach and altering their brand development strategy accordingly, or accidentally, whereby a tribe emerges in response to some

Table 7.1 Moving from data interpretation to brand implementation

Be humble – what does this mean?

Why is tribal marketing described as a 'humble' approach by Cova and Cova? Because it involves a willingness to accept that it is the *tribe* that are right about things. It is the *tribe's* perspective on the brand that matters. This is not the same thing as allowing the tribe to dictate all brand decisions, not in the least. But the marketer must infuse the brand with tribal values – and these values can only be understood if the marketer approaches the tribe in a humble way in order to learn to see the brand through their eyes.

Consider taking a low-key approach to brand communications

In tribal branding, it is very often the case that the best way to get across a message of brand authenticity is to stop trying to get your message across. Again, what does this mean? In practice it means – if you'll pardon the ancient chestnut – actions speak far louder than words. How did Salomon convince a younger generation of winter sports enthusiasts to adopt their brand? Not through a high powered media campaign, but by hitting the slopes alongside the tribe. How have Harley Davidson successfully conveyed the message of their iconic motor bikes as the very embodiment of the American Dream of freedom and the open road? Not just by setting up the Harley Owner Group but by immersing themselves in HOG events alongside their customers. This is not to say that brands should no longer be advertised but it is to argue that advertising needs to be infused with tribal values and accompanied by tribal immersion – otherwise what's the difference between your brand and the next?

Provide 'ghost' scripts (Kornberger 2010), not the whole script

Tribes need to feel that they are involved in the creation of their own experiences. Ordinary marketers try to provide the entire message, tribal marketers understand the need to propose possibilities and allow the tribe to decide what to do with them. However, instead of just asking in microsoftesque fashion 'where do you want to go today', tribal marketers – once they are familiar with tribal linking values – offer *experiential* propositions that resonate with the tribe's perceptions of the brand. Hence brandfest events such as the Posse Ride that provide a basic framework but allow the tribe to expand on it, or the Red Bull *Flugtag* – design your own wings! If you try to impose the entire script, without allowing the tribe enough latitude for creative play, you will end up with a scenario like the *X Factor* where a tribe starts to simply melt away.

Keep supporting tribal linking value in an authentic way

How do you hold on to your tribe, once one has emerged around your brand? This scenario can be a little more complex in situations where the marketer did not plan for or intend to bring about the emergence of a tribe. Sometimes – in fact probably most of the time! – marketers completely overlook the possible presence of a tribe and instead assume that they are dealing with a traditional audience, so instead of trying to support the tribe's linking value they instead engage in ever more frantic and artificial attempts to hold onto their audience's attention. Find out what your tribe's linking value is and support that, instead of resorting to tired old PR clichés and showbiz tricks in an effort to hold onto an audience who have begun to see through you and your lack of real interest in the things they care about.

Keep facilitating the tribe and supporting linking value offline and online

Members of tribes need the freedom to playfully interact with one another both online and offline. Take an integrated approach like Cully and Sully's – provide propositions and ghost scripts that can be expanded on in the offline world as well as virtually. Allow members of the tribe to share their stories with one another – this is how consciousness of kind becomes a self-perpetuating exercise and how the brand remains embedded in the network of social relationships. Similarly, if you look at 'Hog Tales' online, you'll see how the sharing of narratives is facilitated across a variety of tribal activities. Let the tribe build the brand for one another while you quietly continue to support them in this.

marketing initiative that lends itself to the establishment of shared linking value. In the latter case the example of the *X Factor* in particular suggests that where a tribe does emerge that the marketer needs to amend their approach to suit, or the tribe may begin to dissipate. However, in all cases the primary message here is that it is the tribe that decide what to gather around and for how long. As summarized in Table 7.1, tribal branding is implemented by gaining an understanding of the tribe's view of the world and then moving to support and uphold that. If the marketer wants to benefit from the existence of the tribe and goes about facilitating the tribe in the appropriate way, then the chances of the tribe continuing to thrive are greatly improved. In the concluding chapter of the book attention will focus on additional specific ways in which the marketer can implement support for tribal linking value. Prior to this we will take an in-depth look at the ethics of tribal marketing.

8 Towards an Ethics of Tribal Marketing

Introduction

In thinking about how to develop an ethical standard for tribal marketing, it seems sensible to begin by looking at some of the principles that inform any basic approach to business ethics. Commentators on business ethics usually begin by pointing to the main distinctions between the different types of ethical theory – absolutist, or traditional, ethical theory and relativist ethical theory. Most contemporary ethical theories are relativist and recognize the benefits to be derived from a non-absolutist approach. The non-absolutist nature of contemporary theory might in some ways make it a more appropriate starting point for the development of an ethical approach to tribal marketing – but this would mean overlooking the contribution of some key aspects of traditionalist theory to the development of an ethical approach to tribal marketing, so we will take a brief look at both perspectives before beginning to draw inferences for the approach recommended in this book.

Having looked at things from this wider perspective the chapter will then examine some additional principles that govern the manner in which tribal research should be conducted in order to comply with good ethical research practice.

Traditional and contemporary theories of business ethics

Crane and Matten (2010)[1] define ethical theories as 'the rules and principles that determine right and wrong for a given situation'. In practice, most business scholars and commentators on issues of business ethics would agree that it is difficult and perhaps even impossible to apply the same absolute rules in exactly the same way in all situations. *Ethical absolutism* is therein defined as adoption of a position whereby it is claimed that 'there are eternal, universally applicable moral principles (and that)...right and wrong are *objective* qualities that can be rationally determined'.

The difficulty with this position is that it doesn't offer a basis for compromise and doesn't seem to facilitate the reconciling of differing views so that decisions can be taken that all parties can at least feel some-what satisfied with. Furthermore – and perhaps most obviously – how can you possibly achieve a satisfactory compromise between differing parties when both insist on imposing their views and their morality in a particular context? Historically this has frequently resulted in the 'resolution' of dis-putes through conflict rather than consultation (the Crusades are just one example!).

Commentators in the contemporary, or relativist, tradition therefore argue that some form of ethical framework is required that recognizes the complexity of situations, and that also recognizes that when different stake-holders have differing ideas of what is right and wrong, some form of compromise is needed.

Ethical relativism is defined by Crane and Matten as the claim that 'morality is context-dependent and *subjective*. Relativists tend to believe that there are no rights and wrongs that can be rationally determined – it sim-ply depends on the person making the decision and the culture in which they are located'. Hence the notion that '...a moral judgement about behaviour in another culture cannot be made from outside, because moral-ity is culturally determined'. Ethical relativism places conflicting beliefs on an equal footing, that is it proposes that 'both sets of beliefs can be equally right'.

In keeping with this school of thought, Lisa Peñaloza (2012)[2] states that '(t)he cultural approach views ethics as emergent and negotiated within mar-ket systems, as members specify, evaluate, and enforce ethics using particular codes, symbol systems, and practices.... Members determine what is ethical as they define and regulate unethical practices (Peñaloza 2012:505)'.

Peñaloza also argues that 'it is imperative that marketing managers gain knowledge and understanding of the market system(s) in which they operate to do their job effectively and ethically' (Peñaloza 2012:506).

While this statement is made with a view to the development of a cul-turally informed approach to ethical marketing management in general, it can be argued that it is definitely applicable to tribal marketing in particu-lar. Marketing managers are far more likely to take better-informed ethical decisions when they possess an understanding of the values of the tribe. This should also be conducive to more effectively managing the relation-ship between the organization and members of a consumer tribe. Under this perspective, then, managers should recognize that the values and norms that prevail within a tribe are to be recognized and respected. How-ever, the fact that such 'locally' (i.e. tribally) produced norms may differ from the norms that prevail within the company or within other tribal clusters that relate to the brand and/or activity in a different way means that some sort of process is needed to not only identify differences but also to reconcile them in a way that promotes good decision-making. One way to do this is to recognize different tribes as potential forms of organizational stakeholder and to develop processes to relate to them accordingly.

From traditional theory to stakeholder theory

One of the most influential of the traditionalist thinkers was Immanuel Kant, who developed the theory of ethics of duties. As Crane and Matten explain, the imperatives outlined therein include the moral imperative to ensure that you treat every human being as an autonomous actor in their own right, that you respect their human dignity and autonomy, and that you do not use them as mere ends to achieve your own means. This does not imply that we never use each other as means, but rather that in using each other as means to achieve our own ends, we do not lose sight of the need to respect the other.

Hence the need to respect the freedom of others to make their own choices and develop their own expectations, for instance. This also implies that not only should the consent of the other actor be sought before expecting them to do something that benefits us, we need to ensure that they actually understand the implications of giving their consent.

In terms of applying this to an emergent code of ethics for tribal marketing, it would suggest that in researching and identifying the tribe's values, you then have a basis for treating/recognizing the members as ends in themselves and not just as the means to achieve your commercial objectives. If you remember to respect tribal autonomy and remember that their objectives may differ from yours, then you have a basis for implementing this particular theory.

Thus in seeking to implement this, you will effectively be tuning into the tribe's perspective and realizing that there is more at stake than your objectives or your view of the world. Other parties have something at stake too and may see things a little differently to you. Crane and Matten go on from their discussion of Kant to cite Evan and Freeman's (1993)[3] argument that the ethical basis of the stakeholder concept

> has been substantially derived from Kantian thinking... in order to treat employees, local communities, or suppliers not only as means, but also as constituencies with goals and priorities of their own, Evan and Freeman suggest that firms have a fundamental duty to allow these stakeholders some degree of influence on the corporation. By this, they would be enabled to act as free and autonomous human beings, rather than being merely factors of production (employees) or sources of income (consumers), etc. (this resonates with key aspects of SD Logic – see 'Discussion: Similarities and Differences between the Ethics of Tribal Branding and Service-Dominant Logic')

Discussion: Similarities and differences between the ethics of tribal branding and service-dominant logic

By now, in reading this, you may have noticed an overlap between the idea of tribes as brand stakeholders and some of the ideas proposed by Vargo and Lusch in their alternative marketing paradigm of service dominant logic, or as it has become more commonly referred to, SD Logic (2004).[4] It is certainly true that the need to recognize customers as ends in themselves is a fundamental part of the thinking behind SD Logic. Vargo and Lusch draw a useful and appropriate distinction between treating customers as operands (objects that can be operated on in order to achieve organizational objectives) and operants who are capable of acting autonomously and whose autonomy should be recognized by the organization in order to harness the potential of customers for co-creating value and achieving marketing objectives.

While I agree with the appropriateness of this philosophy, I would have a slight reservation about the way in which the SD Logic literature sometimes fails to clarify that marketers should not presume that customers want to lend themselves or their actions to the achievement of corporate objectives.

There may be times when the interests and objectives of a consumer tribe coincide with those of the company, but then again, there may be times when they do not. At such times, instead of making somewhat oversimplistic assumptions about consumer desires for collaboration, corporations might be better advised to retain a greater degree of cultural sensitivity towards consumer collectives and plan for the probability that corporate objectives may more often than not diverge from rather than converge with tribal objectives and goals.

It might even be the case that some tribes want to refrain completely from any form of relationship with the company and again this is something the company might just have to respect. Hence the slight lack of an overlap between some of the assumptions of SD Logic on the one hand and the ethics of tribal marketing on the other. Although both are inspired by the recognition of tribes as ends and not just means, an ethically informed approach to tribes recognizes that there may be times when tribal autonomy means just that. If consumers prefer to interact with one another without overt company involvement then the marketer's job may be to simply facilitate and not intrude (see Patterson and O'Malley (2006)[5] for a further discussion) – although if the marketer manages to restrict herself or himself to humble participation rather than attempting to dictate the agenda, they might be made to feel very welcome – and in the process come to learn a great deal about brand meaning co-creation!

The tribe as stakeholders?

Crane and Matten suggest that an effective solution to the problem of identifying stakeholders with a legitimate interest in the activities of any corporation is to adopt Evan and Freeman's (1993)[6] principles; the principle of corporate rights, meaning that the corporation is obliged not to violate the rights of others, and the principle of corporate effect, which views corporations as 'responsible for the effects of their actions on others'. Based on these principles Crane and Matten conclude that 'a stakeholder of a corporation is an individual or a group which either: is harmed by, or benefits from, the corporation; or whose rights can be violated, or have to be respected by the corporation'.

Under such a definition, consumer tribes can easily be regarded as a form of stakeholder – further, their identity as such potentially differs from the way in which customers have previously been related to as stakeholders. Crane and Matten also observe that inasmuch as stakeholders are seen as having a legitimate interest in any decision or action that affects them, that there should be a consultation process involved in the build up to any decision that substantially affects those stakeholders.

In developing an appropriate approach for the treatment of tribes as stakeholders we have to recognize that it may be impractical to try to consult with the tribe every time a decision needs to be taken that might have implications for them.

In practice, it might not always be feasible to 'consult' with the tribe in a formal sense. Some tribes might only exist in almost an implicit sense, whereby people feel themselves to be part of a community of some sort even if it has no formal structures whatsoever. In such cases it might be very difficult to ascertain the tribe's views. Approaches like Internet polling or surveys of tribal opinion are not the best way to go about it. It might be difficult to identify an exact population to target for random sampling, for instance.

This raises the question of how you might go about drawing up formal procedures for consulting with such a loosely defined tribe. It might be necessary to carry out a number of qualitative interviews with consumers who seem to be representative of the tribe and compare the findings from those to prior knowledge of tribal values. This of course assumes that the tribe are accessible and sufficiently stable in social structure to make this a meaningful exercise, which sometimes may not be the case.

In cases where tribal identity and/or location is unclear, the marketer should at the very least be sensitive to the possibility that a set of tribal values might exist, however tacit or implicit these values might be. A minority grouping on an official Facebook page who occasionally seem to dissent from the official view of things might constitute one example of this. Cultivating a sensitivity to minority or dissenting opinions might be one way to pick up on traces of tribal activity and then these sensibilities can at least be considered in decision-making.

Crane and Matten also recommend communicating with stakeholders via blogs. This makes perfect sense – this would be one way of consulting members of a tribe/brand community about decisions that could affect them. Blogs or even unofficial forums with high levels of interactivity – in short, those sites that meet some or all of Kozinets' criteria for netnography – might prove fertile territory for locating members of the tribe who can be invited to participate not only in consultation processes but also in the design of same.

Another way in which the marketer can reach out to different groups is to extend an invitation to interested parties to apply to become members of an official forum of some kind, where issues and decisions affecting customers can be discussed.

The approach taken by the new owners of Liverpool Football Club in the English Premier League in their establishment of a relationship with their fan base is particularly interesting in this regard. Given the backdrop of fan protests and an absolute breakdown in the relationship between the fan base and the club's previous owners, it made sense for Fenway Sports Group as the incoming owners to set up a forum to facilitate communication and consultation between the fan community and the club. The aspiration here was to cultivate a sense of transparency, to build a healthy relationship between the fans and the club's owners, and to facilitate strategic dialogue between fans and club, the better, presumably, to help realize the aims and objectives that all concerned shared – the future success of Liverpool FC both on and off the field of play.

The club decided that this new forum should be made up of representation from all valid categories of fan, as they saw it. This was to include representation from fans within the local geographical area of Anfield, fans from the greater Merseyside area, non-Merseyside UK fans, several categories of international fan, season ticket holders as a category, disabled supporters, women fans, fans who travel regularly to away games (travel costs and relationships with police forces in other parts of the UK and in other European countries being applicable as particular concerns here), LGBT fans, fans from ethnic minorities, and so on. This was thus a well-thought out initiative to construct a truly representative forum that could bring the concerns of a wide range of constituencies to the attention of the board of the club.

When initially establishing the forum the club engaged in a well-publicized drive to elicit applications. Fans were invited to apply online to represent a maximum of one particular fan category as listed. All applications were then considered by a selection committee made up of a small number of people including former player Ian Callaghan, Karen Gill (granddaughter of legendary former club coach Bill Shankly), several 'celebrity' fans whose credentials as lifelong supporters were nonetheless impeccable, and the (then) club Commercial Director Ian Ayre as club representative.

The forum meets frequently and has regular consultations with senior management whereby the concerns and issues considered by the forum can be discussed, decisions taken, and information fed back to fans who submitted queries or complaints or whom otherwise raised issues. Any fan can contact forum members, all of whom are volunteers, incidentally, via their email addresses as provided on the club website. Minutes from all forum meetings are posted on the club's official website, as is a full FAQ that delivers a further record of points raised and answers received. In all, this is a comprehensive effort at relationship-building and transparency to which the club seem genuinely committed.

If I was invited to make suggestions to improve this approach from a 'tribe as stakeholder' perspective, I would make a number of points. I would suggest that instead of just extending an invitation like this to all fans via the club website and then carefully 'vetting' the applicants, it would be more meaningful to approach not only the official Supporters' Club but also unofficial groups such as the Liverpool supporters' union 'Spirit of Shankly', and other groups, and seek their involvement in designing the entire process *before beginning the publicity campaign*. This would help to ensure that the fan

categories identified for inclusion in the forum included not only the relevant categories as determined or identified by the club but also as perceived
by the tribe.

I would also suggest that possible differences across different fan categories should be clarified via not only survey data but ethnographic research
that is better equipped to pick up on cultural nuances and differences across
tribal clusters. I would also advise that the position of those fans who have
done most over the years to contribute to the legendary atmosphere at the
club's stadium should not be marginalized by reduction of their representation to what is perhaps a disproportionately small number of positions
on the forum. It might be better to grant permanent representation to a
small number of unofficial groups that nonetheless speak for thousands of
match-going fans, *alongside* the existing categories in an *expanded* forum,
than to expect these groups to compete for representation on the forum
in categories where only one vacancy can be filled. As things stand, there
remains a certain level of scepticism among some members of unofficial fan
communities towards the official forum, along with some feelings of dis-
enfranchisement as a result of the process followed in designating categories
and selecting applicants. While to some extent such scepticism is an inevitable
part of a wider tendency to question anything 'official', it is possible that
more could be done to build up relationships across the entire fan community by efforts to include greater representation of these unofficial groups in
the official forum. Nonetheless the initiative does represent a step towards
more meaningful consultation with at least some clusters within the overall
fan tribe.

This also serves to reinforce the point about how necessary it is to implement the approaches mentioned earlier in the book with regard to picking
up on traces of tribal activity and identifying clusters of consumers who are
engaged in co-creation of meaning, particularly where the resulting meanings
may differ from the official party – or corporate – line. Once these clusters
are identified and approached, it becomes more feasible to consult with them
or at least retain an awareness that some tribal clusters may dissent from the
views expressed by those involved in the 'official' consultation process. It is
always better to be informed as to the existence of these groups and it may
even be possible to have some kind of informal dialogue with them, with a
view to hopefully developing the relationship further over time.

Types of stakeholder relationship?

Crane and Matten observe that relationships with stakeholders can take a
variety of forms, including challenge, where the relationship is characterized
by mutual opposition, sparring partners, whereby there is so-called 'healthy'
conflict, one-way support, whereby there is a one-way flow of supportive
resources, mutual support, project dialogue, strategy dialogue, or even joint
ventures.

While again none of these seem to provide a perfect or absolute 'fit' for the relationship between a corporation and a tribe, some of these descriptors do provide a *partial* fit.

The one-way support relationship category, for instance, provides a partial fit because it provides something of a match with the notion of company support for tribal linking values through the provision of sponsorship, for example. However, to regard the company/tribe relationship as solely grounded in one-way support overlooks the potential benefit to be derived from the effects of tribal support for and championing of company products, or tribal contributions to product innovation. Hence while much of the relationship may be characterized by one-way support, there will also be occasions and instances of benefits flowing back to the corporation, albeit that this will not always occur in a systematic or linear way.

In short, the tribe's legitimacy as stakeholders needs to be recognized, the independence of their views needs to be respected, and the decision as to the degree of formal contact and official relationship between them and the corporation is primarily theirs – and not the corporation's – to make. They are a different form of stakeholder – but they are a stakeholder nonetheless and it is far more appropriate to recognize this than to overlook them or trivialize their needs and priorities. Also, by recognizing the tribe and respecting their autonomy, some of the problems that can affect company/stakeholder relationships, such as culture clashes or lack of controllability, can be avoided or minimized.

Overall the advice to 'Be mindful and respectful of tribal autonomy' seems to be a good way of summing up what we've discussed so far. An additional argument in favour of implementing this philosophy is that it has other positive implications besides the maintenance of good ethical standards. Viewing the tribe as a *form* of legitimate stakeholder is useful because it recognizes the principle that brand meaning and brand value can be created and altered outside the boundaries of the organization, by other interested parties.

This has the additional implication that the appropriate methods for gaining an understanding of tribal values and aspirations are not an optional extra. In order to implement an ethical approach to tribal marketing, the marketer *has to* ensure that they are properly informed and aware of the tribe's perspective – and the only way to become fully informed is to use the methods and research tactics of ethno-marketing.

At the same time, it is a truism in the wider literature that the desires of one set of stakeholders should not necessarily be accommodated at the expense of other stakeholder categories. Hence decisions that are taken that are in contradistinction to the values and desired outcomes of the tribe are not necessarily unethical decisions.

(It also follows from this that marketers need to bear in mind that it is erroneous to assume that the tribe as brand stakeholder can be viewed as similar to the traditional, sometimes relatively limited way in which customers are defined as stakeholders. See Discussion Box on Treatment of Tribe as Stakeholder for some further thoughts on this.)

Discussion: Why the treatment of tribe as stakeholder needs to vary from the traditional treatment of customer as stakeholder – and how this also differs from the 'charismatic leadership' approach to tribalism

The stereotypical mindset of 'we don't need to worry about them not liking what we are going to do, they'll come round, customers always do' is not an appropriate approach here.

Tribal sensibilities need to be respected. It follows that rather than taking arbitrary decisions and expecting the tribe to follow you (and then being disappointed or worse, adopting a pompous stance of self-justification) you should find some way of at least assessing whether a decision you're about to take might clash in some way with the tribe's understanding of how things are meant to work or what the brand is meant to represent. Then you might at least have some insight into why people are upset and why some of them disengage from your brand.

It follows that the more you cultivate an understanding of tribal values, the more you might be able to come up with some way of reassuring the tribe, either during or after a decision has been taken that doesn't sit well with them. In short, some form of consultation with the tribe, whereby members of the tribe are respected as legitimate stakeholders, is a good idea if you want to avoid the risk of people becoming disillusioned or disengaging from the tribe.

Hence in those situations where a decision may need to be taken that is potentially at odds with tribal sensitivities, it is imperative to at least have some sense of how the tribe might react, and what measures might be needed to subsequently reassure them of their status as joint custodians of the brand. This is why the way in which Saab re-engaged with the Saab brand community post the community's hostile reaction to the launch of the Saab 9000 is interesting. While the community felt that this new model was fundamentally all wrong for the brand, and hence reacted against it rather than becoming early adopters and spreading the word about it, the company ultimately succeeded in bringing the community back on-side by seeking to involve them more deeply in future brand developments. This restored the relationship because it affirmed the tribe in their sense of joint ownership of the brand – without compromising or undermining the company's capacity to take decisions.

I also want to acknowledge that the idea of consultation as outlined in this chapter differs fundamentally from other approaches sometimes used to describe tribalism.

Where people see tribes as communities of consumers devoted to charismatic leaders, this idea of trying to consult with the tribe might seem questionable. Charismatic leaders are supposed to inspire devotion and are followed unquestioningly – allegedly. Hence one approach to charismatic leadership is to remain aloof and not to explain oneself. The tribe will follow you because of the strength of your personality and because everything you touch turns to gold, in their eyes at least. There is obviously some degree of truth in this. However, where this approach breaks down is in its inability to recognize that members of a tribe will actively re-negotiate and re-work the tribal narrative such a charismatic leader tries to present. Their reasons for following the leader might thus not be exactly the same as the reasons that leader imagines. When members of a tribe interact with one another, they may well be engaged in a collective re-working of their version of the narrative, their version of brand meaning, not the meaning presented to them with a flourish by the charismatic guru on stage.

It is thus worth noting that the innovations presented to the tribe by such a leader might be more important as a stream of novel resources from which the tribe will generate freshly re-worked narratives of their own than as a set of meanings that are received in 'cast in stone' mode and blindly adhered to as such. Tribes constantly re-write. It's what they do. Hence charismatic leaders can innovate but they should keep a close eye on the extent to which their innovations fit in with the tribe's pro-clivities and idiosyncrasies. By all means do things from time to time that surprise or maybe even challenge the tribe, but do not indulge in this kind of approach without continuing to maintain a sense of tribal feelings and values so that you can plan for a possible need to reassure the tribe if necessary. What this means in practical terms is that tribal consultation as described here should always be ongoing.

(For a more detailed discussion of tribal re-working of brand narratives in the case of one such 'charismatic leader' scenario, see Richardson (2013).[7])

Deciding against the tribe?

What should companies do if tribal behavioural norms seem to cause offence or clash with the values and norms of other customer categories?

In such instances, companies on the one hand should not make the mistake of automatically distancing themselves completely from the tribe in question but on the other hand should seek to avoid the alternative error of assuming that they must be deferred to, ahead of the interests or values of other types of customer. The marketer needs to ensure that the brand remains accessible to all potential customers and that wider ethical standards in relation to gender, homophobia, racism or similar must not be rendered subservient to the values of any tribal group, where those values are at odds with wider societal ethical norms, purely to cater to the whims of the group.

We know that tribes have their own value systems, their own systems of cultural, or what this book calls tribal capital. This implies that a tribal set of ethics (although tacit in nature) will be dictated and determined by such systems. In some cases these value systems can generate unacceptable outcomes. Hence the idea that practices like 'flaming', while distasteful in the normal run of things, may be deemed acceptable and appropriate in the context of tribal use of social media. Tribes will have their own ethical standards and norms and sometimes seek to enforce them in ways that individual customers may find offensive. Members of tribes and brand communities can sometimes engage in imposition of strong social pressures, even potential bullying, to ensure that members conform to group norms.

As Algesheimer, Dholakia, and Hermann (2005)[8] explain, consumers can often feel under pressure to adhere to the norms that prevail within a group and to participate appropriately in group rituals and so on. For the most part members of a tribe or brand community continue to adhere to such norms and practices for positive reasons such as enjoyment. However, sometimes members go along with practices they might feel very uncomfortable with, due either to overt or imagined pressure to comply with the expectations of the group.

Algesheimer et al. suggest that this can extend for example to members feeling under pressure to participate in derogatory discourse about outsiders. They cite the example of members of the Harley Owner Group making offensive remarks about 'rice rockets' (a derogatory nickname for Japanese motorcycles) for instance – this sort of remark, happily, does not seem to be characteristic of how the Harley Owner Group ethos has evolved into a more inclusive community. However, this example does serve to indicate how members of a consumer community cannot be guaranteed to behave in a way that complies neatly with corporate requirements for good public relations, an issue also raised by Gil McWilliam's commentary on developing brands via online communities (see McWilliam 2000).[9]

Another often referenced example of social pressure within a community is the case of the Straight Edge movement, as documented by Ross Haenfler (2004).[10] This group adopted a style of all or nothing commitment to their value system and infringements of the shared code of abstention from harmful substances were regarded as a complete betrayal of shared identity. Again this sort of extreme approach, the view that one violation of the rules justifies expulsion from the community, is not necessarily compatible with the more tolerant and relaxed approach that a corporation might feel they would prefer to be associated with!

This is clearly one of the issues that may cause potential discomfort for companies when it comes to the whole idea of tribes and tribal autonomy in the first place. Tribes can be portrayed as overzealous in their enforcement of group norms and this is due in part to the fact that from time to time some consumers have been subject to imposition of group norms that they found upsetting. While it is reassuring to bear in mind that social norms within consumer tribes are usually 'enforced' playfully rather than coercively (as per O'Sullivan et al.'s documentation of some of the more whimsical practices of the Beamish brand tribe as discussed in Chapter 3), it also follows that companies may need to dissociate themselves from actions that are offensive, and if necessary intervene directly to keep official company media and events free from offensive behaviours and to protect customers from bullying.

There is thus an onus on organizations to put their own systems in place to address this issue. Lisa Peñaloza (2012) mentions Facebook's deployment of a 'Hate and Harassment' team that actively intervenes in cases of cyber-bullying. The setting up of such teams is something that any company attempting to host tribal discussion forums on their own website needs to consider.

Also, if intervention is to be effective in cases of cyber-bullying, then some level of understanding of the values and norms that apply in that context is a prerequisite. In order for such interventions to be most effective, I would suggest that they need to be both culturally and sub-culturally informed.

In saying this, I am not advocating tolerance of inappropriate values and behaviour. Possible instances of cyber-bullying should not be over-reacted to by immediately assuming that the behaviour of one Internet troll is somehow representative of an entire tribal value system and that the company should immediately seek to disengage from its relationship with an entire tribe. It may be the case that just one, or a small number, of individuals are engaging in unacceptable behaviour. Hence the need to evaluate whether such behaviour is reflective of the values that prevail across the wider group. If this is the case, then a decision may need to be taken to disengage completely from the group in question.

In other cases, it might be possible to take a different approach to situations where group norms might not include unacceptable practices like cyber-bullying, but still include other behaviours that make it difficult to expand the appeal of the tribe to other customers. In the case of Harley Davidson it would have been commercially damaging for the company to simply seek to suppress the inappropriate, slightly offensive behaviour of the wilder elements of the Harley Davidson subculture – they'd have missed out on the opportunity to develop a wider market for the brand. As we know, they facilitated a relatively less brash version of brand identity performance instead, setting up the Harley Owner Group to allow members of a wider 'tribe' to enjoy consuming and performing the brand in something of a more family-friendly way, minus behaviours such as public nudity and so on. Harley Davidson now successfully supports biker groups of all orientations, so that women bikers for instance do not feel alienated by a brand culture that as originally practised by hard-core members of the Harley Davidson subculture was capable of being particularly sexist in orientation (cf. John Schouten, Diane Martin, and James McAlexander's (2007a)[11] research on the evolution of the Harley Davidson subculture). However, it's questionable whether this initiative would have succeeded had it not been informed by the ethnographic research carried out into the unofficial biker groups whose behaviour was of a slightly wilder nature than the family groups! This research helped to identify how the behaviour of the members of the unofficial tribe had given the brand an aura of rebelliousness which helped to render it irresistible to the members of the new 'official' tribe. The incorporation of brand meaning created outside the formal boundaries of the organization into formally developed marketing tactics is what good tribal marketing is all about.

In sum, tribal marketing entails taking a non-traditionalist, non-absolutist approach to ethics. Marketers should treat each tribal group as potential stakeholders, recognizing that not only do they engage in co-creation of their own values but that such values should be considered in a non-absolutist way. Rather than indulge in kneejerk reactions to apparently outlandish behaviours, use the methods and tactics of ethno-marketing to study the group before deciding on whether or not to disengage. Finally, it is worth reiterating that the vast majority of unofficial groups can readily be regarded as legitimate stakeholders and engaged with accordingly, provided they are happy to engage with the company.

Continued engagement with tribes in turn allows the marketer to derive other benefits from practices such as crowdsourcing. Hence some thoughts with regard to the ethical issues arising from tribal crowdsourcing are now considered.

Some thoughts on an ethical approach to tribal 'crowdsourcing'

How can a tribal marketer ensure that members of a tribe receive fair remuneration for original ideas and creative work that subsequently proves to yield commercial dividends for the company?

This is a complex issue. Members of tribes and brand communities can certainly create commercial value for organizations and, possibly because their own community or tribal objectives are being fulfilled, pay little or no heed to any thought of financial remuneration for their activities even where those activities result in commercial gain for the organization. Thriving brand-related Facebook pages that directly impact on brand loyalty are often run gratis by brand enthusiasts who derive huge intrinsic satisfaction from simply being active members of consumer communities. In some cases they have been known to turn down offers of financial remuneration!

I would suggest that a useful distinction can be drawn between such cases and cases where companies directly seek to obtain ideas for new products and services from members of tribes or brand communities. Referring again to Peñaloza's thoughts on the subject, she references a number of examples whereby competition winners are paid nominal sums for their ideas for new product designs while in return 'the companies get a free, perpetual, non-exclusive licence to practice every idea submitted' (Peñaloza 2012:507). In any case where the terms and conditions of competition entry stipulate that rights to new product ideas are signed over to the competition organizers this means that even non-winners might have their ideas used and receive no compensation whatsoever.

Apple's remuneration model for iPhone app development seems more ethical. Any app adopted for commercial distribution is the subject of a proper commercial agreement between Apple and the developer. The scale of this as a form of crowdsourcing suggests that the approach could be adapted to suit other contexts where the ideas of large numbers of people were all of potential commercial benefit.

One question that may well be posed here is why any company would go to such lengths to conduct the search for new product ideas in such an ethical way. Why come to formal commercial agreement with people when as things stand companies can just take ideas for free, provided rights to those ideas have been signed away? Why not just seek to benefit without cost from the sort of crowdsourcing outputs that tribes and brand communities so often spontaneously generate themselves, unprompted by any incentive on the part of any commercial organization? While certainly companies could try to do that, it does not seem to be compatible with what I would see as a symbiotic approach to the cultivation of good long-term relations with the tribe or brand community. I would suggest that more can be achieved in the longer term by a fully transparent approach to crowdsourcing, whereby at the very least companies clearly communicate to members the possibility of commercial benefits arising from community innovations and product ideas, so that members can make an informed decision as to whether or not to accept offers of remuneration before deciding on whether to relinquish rights or agree terms for royalty payments for instance.

Hence some sort of code of practice does seem desirable in relation to this particular aspect of corporate/tribal community relations, and Apple's approach seems to work.

The final point for discussion with regard to an ethics of tribal marketing is a consideration of the ethical issues that arise from the implementation of tribal research.

Towards an ethics of tribal research tactics

We have seen that there is much potential benefit to derive from ongoing engagement with the tribe via the methods and tactics of ethno-marketing. This in turn implies that a consideration of some basic principles of research ethics is necessary if we want to develop a more comprehensive overall view of the ethics of tribal marketing.

In trying to develop a simple set of guidelines for ethical conduct of tribal research it is easier in some ways to take a sort of common denominator approach rather than try to address all the nuances of research ethics, particularly those aspects over which there is disagreement. Hence my focus is on applying those principles over which there is agreement. Even if this is something of a basic approach, it has the advantage that it is clear.

The most basic principle is that research activity must not cause harm. According to Bryman and Bell (2003),[12] forms of harm include physical harm, harm to participants' development or self-esteem, harm to career prospects, or inducement to perform reprehensible acts. Researchers should assess whether the research has the potential to cause harm and minimize the possibility of harm occurring. One implication of this is that any issues relating to confidentiality should be negotiated and honoured.

The question of informed consent also arises. While covert observation completely transgresses this principle, the principle of not causing harm to those under observation is in practice regarded by some as a means of redressing concerns related to this. In practice a useful rule of thumb is also the principle that covert observation should only be applicable in contexts where those being observed are in a public space, are arguably aware that others can freely observe them, and are thus choosing to engage in observable behaviour. In any case it may be impossible to obtain consent from all parties in ethnographic research that involves observation of crowd behaviours, for example. It could similarly be argued that participants in public online forums are aware that whatever they post is essentially being posted in a public space – although if the content of a post is to be reproduced for any reason then consent should be obtained. Similarly if someone is identifiable in a photograph taken in a public space, their consent should be obtained before any such image is reproduced in a report.

The right to privacy applies with regard to non-public space and also applies in relation to the conduct of interviews. Participants should have the right to refuse to answer questions that they feel would breach their privacy or even to terminate an interview. Personal information of a sensitive nature should be kept confidential and some information should arguably not be recorded at all.

In terms of having some kind of checklist, a simple checklist might include the following points as outlined in Table 8.1:

Table 8.1   Checklist of ethics for tribal research practices

---

- Have you studied at least one set of professional research ethics guidelines and tried to incorporate them into your research design where appropriate? (Useful to study professional ethics codes, e.g. www.mrs.org.uk/standards/guidelines, www.britsoc.org.uk/about/ethic.htm)
- Have you familiarized yourself with your own institution's requirements?
- Have you ensured that there is no prospect of harm to any of your participants?
- Have you complied with the principle of informed consent, so that participants know, for example, what the research is about, how long their participation will take, and that they can withdraw at any time?
- Has someone else reviewed your proposed research activities to assess whether all ethical implications have been taken into account?
- Have you ensured that your participants will not be deceived about the research and its purposes?
- Are you confident that participants' privacy will not be violated in any way?
- Have you taken steps to preserve the anonymity of your participants (think of the consequences of someone being fired because of something they said on Facebook!!)

Concluding thoughts

Generally speaking, ethical theory is divided into two main approaches, the traditional absolutist approach on the one hand and the contemporary or relativist approach on the other. The traditionalist approach is not particularly applicable by itself in the current context, as its absolutist orientation fails to take into account differences in perspective from one group or culture to the next. Looked at from the outside, many consumer tribes might come across as having strange values, priorities, or norms that might seem contrary to prevailing norms within an organization. Hence the first reaction of organizations towards tribes might be one of keeping them at a distance or deciding that there was no scope to develop a relationship with groups whose values and norms seemed to diverge from those of the company's.

However, contemporary (relativist) ethical theory recognizes that values are culturally produced and thus the values of one culture may differ from others. The useful thing about this perspective is that it encourages us to be respectful of difference and it also reminds us not only that meaning can be created outside the formal boundaries of the organization, but that such meaning should be respected. Hence the suggestion that because tribes can create their own meanings around activities and brands, we should not insist on imposing our meanings but instead should respect theirs and endeavour to facilitate and support both these meanings and the processes that led to their creation.

When we combine this with a contemporary understanding of stakeholder theory (itself originally derived from traditionalist approaches) the argument for regarding tribes as legitimate stakeholders who should be consulted with on matters of mutual interest that affect all concerned is strengthened. Hence the argument in favour of a stakeholder approach and ongoing consultation as the appropriate ethical solution for tribal branding.

The adoption of a stakeholder approach should help to ensure that the tribe's values are taken into consideration whenever a decision is being taken that could affect the tribe, although of course it does raise the issue of how one might go about trying to ascertain what the tribe's values are, or what the tribe's stance on particular issues actually is. We've already seen that it is not simply a question of carrying out a survey in order to ascertain how members of a tribe might feel about an issue. It could equally be the case that there are differing factions, or clusters, in a tribe, whose views differ. Hence not only is some mechanism needed for identifying values, but also why the values and perspectives of different factions might differ, before taking a final decision that also takes into account the needs and perspectives of all stakeholders and audiences, not just the tribe's!

Fortunately if an ethno-marketing approach is ongoing, then not only should an adequate understanding of linking value be accessible, but any subtle differences in perspective across different factions *within* the overall tribe should be easier to identify. Ongoing dialogue, ethnographic interviews, ongoing analysis and interpretation of the data from participant and non-participant observation, and of course direct participant feedback, can and should be used as a means to gain insight into the views and values of this particular form of stakeholder. Dialogue with the tribe in relation to specific issues can also be reviewed in light of the ongoing insights derived from these methods.

Also, if as may well happen from time to time, the organization feels that it is necessary to take a decision or decisions that seem to conflict with tribal values, it should hopefully be easier to maintain an ongoing dialogue with the tribe, explain the reasons to them for particular decisions, and even find some alternative means to affirm the tribe and reassure them that their views matter. In the long run this should make it more likely that organization and tribe continue to enjoy the benefits of a symbiotic relationship, rather than either side missing out.

Furthermore, marketers should not assume that they only need to consult with official 'fan' clubs, or members of official organizations like the Harley Owner Group, to be sure that they have taken the tribe's views and values into account. There may be huge insight to be derived from trying to maintain some form of dialogue with other unofficial groups whose perspectives and practices might differ considerably from those of members of official fan clubs or owner groups. Certainly if we think back to the origins of the Harley Owner Group, we can recall that the brand's iconic status owes much to the legacy conferred on it by the actions of brand users whose values might differ considerably from the formal family-friendly values an organization might feel comfortable with.

Also, tolerance of and some form of support for those customers who prefer to remain outside the boundaries of official customer organizations is also highly advisable for the simple reason that tribal creativity and passion might be even more likely to flourish in such an informal environment. Given that this can help to (re)infuse the brand with a sense of originality and authenticity, this is not something that any tribal marketer should seek to discourage – even if at times both parties might prefer to keep some degree of distance from each other. It is a common characteristic of many brand communities that members feel that they are the true custodians of the brand and they are the ones who in the end are responsible for maintaining what is sometimes referred to as the 'spirit' of the brand. Muniz and O'Guinn documented this in relation to the Saab brand community, for instance, but it is a feature that has shown up again and again across all manner of consumer communities – members can treasure and even cultivate a shared feeling that they 'get' it but that the 'suits' do not.

As this may be part of what keeps renewing the cycle of special or even sacred feelings about the brand and the tribe, leading to renewed bursts of brand-related creativity, leading in turn to the renewal of these sacred feelings about who 'gets' it and who doesn't, it behoves the marketer to respect the desire on the part of some tribal members and factions to keep their distance from official customer groups. Not only is it more ethical, in a sense, to respect the desires of these tribal members to keep their distance, rather than try to impose membership of 'official' fan clubs or customer groups on them, ultimately it might also be in the best long-term interests of the brand, as it contributes to the regeneration of brand authenticity from outside the formal boundaries of the organization.

Another benefit to be derived from a benevolent approach towards any consumer tribe is that it can help with the avoidance of negative publicity. Instead of risking being seen as a corporate bully, by automatically acting in a heavy-handed way towards the tribe's use of company trademarks, companies should consider sympathetically investigating such usage of logos and so on.

If the tribe seem to be genuinely positively predisposed towards one or more of the company's products, and do not seem to be engaged in any antisocial behaviour, then there is a strong argument for the granting of permissions rather than the issuing of legal proceedings. Then, as in cases such as the relationship between Lego and the Lego brand community, the company is seen as accommodating its customers, and might be in a position to not only derive positive publicity from this but also be able to begin developing a relationship with the tribe – on the basis of recognizing them as legitimate brand stakeholders.

Finally, each tribal branding decision will potentially require some form of compromise between an absolutist outside view of what is morally and ethically correct, and a relativist view that places tribal ethics on an equal footing with the wider ethics prevalent in society as a whole – or at least recognizes that tribal ethics may differ from those in wider society. Companies need to find a balance between aligning their actions with all the normal expectations of society and respecting the idiosyncratic expectations of the tribe. For the most part this should be relatively unproblematic, but in any

Table 8.2 Elements of good ethical practice on the part of the tribal marketer

- Use of all appropriate research ethics principles when using ethno-marketing research techniques to identify tribal values and norms
- Respect for the tribe as legitimate stakeholders in the brand
- Respect for tribal values and norms – at a minimum, recognition of the principle that the tribe are free to create their own meanings, while simultaneously retaining the right on the part of the company to disengage from unacceptable meanings and practices
- This can extend into the practical detail of granting tribes permission for at least some use of copyright materials rather than taking legal action against them for breach of copyright (as in the case of Lego reaching agreement with the Lego brand community over the right to use images and other material online)
- Consultation with the tribe where possible and appropriate over corporate decisions that may impact on issues of concern to the tribe – in practice this consultation may resemble the sort of consultation exercise that many companies undertake in relation to other forms of legitimate stakeholder, but may have to be adapted depending on the composition of the tribe
- In keeping with this recognition of the tribe as stakeholders, fair procedures must be developed and implemented to ensure appropriate remuneration for innovations resulting from any form of 'crowdsourcing' activity, whether formal or informal.
- It should be made clear to all parties that the company are not obliged to defer to tribal preferences, or make the requirements or preferences of other stakeholders subservient to the demands or preferences of the tribe – nonetheless, if decisions are taken that seem contrary to the interests of the tribe, but those decisions are communicated in the context of a relationship characterized by consultation and transparency, then it should be possible to implement them without fundamentally undermining the relationship between marketer and tribe.
- Finally, where tribal behavioural norms are – even in light of contemporary or relativist ethical considerations – deemed to breach even pluralist standards of behaviour, then the company may be best advised to break off relations with the tribe and withdraw any legal permission granted.

cases where tribal value systems endorse forms of antisocial behaviour the company may need to have some form of distancing mechanism in place to disassociate themselves from these behaviours, while if possible not absolutely undermining the relationship with the tribe.

Ultimately this means that good ethical practice on the part of the tribal marketer will include all the following elements as outlined in Table 8.2.

9   Tribes and Tribal Branding – Where Do We Go from Here?

Introduction

By now we have covered a range of different aspects of the tribal approach to branding. As just reiterated in Chapter 8, two of the most crucial elements in this as a philosophy are respect for the principle that brand meaning can be created outside the formal boundaries of the organization and respect for the tribe's freedom to engage in this meaning creation process on their own terms. Everything else, including all the potential benefits to the company, really does stem from respect for these two principles. This implies, as we've seen, that companies who wish to engage with tribes need to do so patiently and humbly. There is a need to approach tribes in a respectful rather than arrogant way, using the principles for cultural entrée as defined by Robert Kozinets[1] and as explained in Chapter 3. There is a need to use the methods of ethno-marketing as outlined by Cova and Cova[2] to firstly identify traces of tribal activity (which clearly are sometimes very obvious but sometimes less so) and then identify tribal linking value. There may be a need to participate and not just observe, in order to be accepted as a presence in the community and in order to more fully understand the basis for the tribe's sense of social connection. This is important if the marketer is to succeed in developing communications and designing products, events, Facebook pages and even Twitter feeds that are perceived as supportive of tribal linking value. And while we have looked at refreshing examples of cases where vibrant and passionate tribes have emerged and endured with little or no input or support from a tribal marketer, we've seen that it is more advisable to fulfil an ethno-marketing approach, so as to at the very least understand the tribe's passions on their own merits. This is absolutely preferable to the possibility of undermining tribal linking value through trying to enforce an overly defined brand narrative that doesn't facilitate the tribe's desire to do their own thing, to re-work brand narratives as they see fit. When there is at least some freedom to re-work brand narratives, the results can be spectacular.

If you facilitate diversity of meaning – as with Red Bull, for example, where initially there *wasn't* a high-powered advertising campaign, this means that people can come up with their own imagined meanings. In the case of Red Bull, this brought about a situation where brand meaning was co-created and – as is so often the case – a tribe emerged around the brand without any prior intent on the part of the marketer to bring a tribe into being. Just getting the product out there and letting people come up with their own meanings really facilitated this entire process. To extrapolate from this example, as co-created meanings begin to emerge, the tribal marketer who is alert to the possibility of tribal activity can begin to support these meanings as created or re-worked by smaller clusters within an overall brand tribe.

We now think of the Red Bull tribe, even though the reality is that there are different social domains (or clusters) staked out, so to speak, underneath the wider Red Bull tribal umbrella. As we'll discuss later, Schau, Muñiz, and Arnould (2009)[3] identify *staking* as an important value creation practice in brand communities. In relation to Red Bull, different social domains that 'stake out' their own social space include the Red Bull Flugtag enthusiasts, the ravers/clubbers, the winter sports enthusiasts, and so on. In relation to each of these distinct social domains, Red Bull didn't impose a brand meaning, but instead gently suggested meanings. This allowed the members of each domain to appropriate those meanings as they saw fit, and as a result allowed them to assume that the brand was associated with their subculture. Once this association was established, Red Bull was seen as a legitimate presence and a legitimate sponsor of events that resonated with meaning for each cluster of the tribe. For example, the setting up and sponsoring of the Red Bull Music Academy was a typically clever move that was accepted as authentic rather than intrusive by the clubbing/DJ tribe. As the sponsoring brand already had a clear significance for tribal activity, which in this case was derived from Red Bull giving people the energy to keep dancing at all-night raves and parties, it is worth briefly speculating on how tribal sponsorship might be implemented in cases where the relationship between tribe and aspirational sponsor brand is not necessarily as obvious. Having discussed that, we can then revert to a review of some useful ideas on ongoing co-creation of brand value with tribes, before finishing up with some thoughts on what to do next.

Tribal sponsorship

How might tribal sponsorship work for a bank interested in benefitting from the opportunity to sponsor a successful rugby team like Munster, for instance? Clearly sponsorship arrangements between banks and sports teams already exist, but they are usually not implemented in a way that delivers the same depth of impact as tribal sponsorship.

There isn't really much in terms of an obvious, at-first-glance, authentic link between the bank's brand and the activity in question, certainly none that would be taken seriously by the tribe. Instead of focusing on low-impact goals such as increased awareness, the bank would have to take a long-term partnership approach, whereby branches of the bank formed closer ties to their local rugby clubs, and bank staff sports and social club members became more involved in not just supporting their local teams but also playing tag rugby and so on. It's worth stressing this as a suggestion because while the obvious answer is to encourage more staff to actually take up rugby, in practice this is probably not realistic for everyone. Tag rugby is more accessible and can thus give more people more of a sense that they are taking part in something. It would also help a little with important processes like empathizing and acquiring some of the tribal jargon.

The bank would also need to take on an altruistic role in terms of helping branches of the Munster supporters' clubs with things like getting to away games. Bank staff should have a visible presence in terms of travelling to away games – not just in the comfort and plushness of the corporate boxes and the VIP section but among the real fans travelling by plane, train, ferry, and automobile to get to matches the hard way, in order to support their team.

Bank loan products specifically geared towards the needs of fans, such as small loans to cover the cost of a season ticket, perhaps bundled in with the potential cost of attending the Heineken Cup Semi-Final or even the Final would then be perceived in a different light. The bank would have a little more credibility with the tribe if their staff were seen to be immersed in the same experiences as ordinary fans.

I hasten to add that this example is for illustrative purposes only! I've just chosen Munster rugby as an example because of the huge growth in their tribal 'Red Army' of loyal and colourful fans in recent years. Hence it's interesting to speculate on how a sponsor might try to support the linking value of such a tribe, rather than go for the conventional and relatively superficial option of sponsorship as an awareness – raising exercise. Because tribes usually place a premium on participation and commitment, I've suggested the above options as ways of giving sponsorship some much-needed credibility and added impact. However, it also follows that tribal marketing really involves far more than sponsorship or making guesses about linking value. In such a case, the sponsor would really need to engage in more of a commitment to all the phases outlined in the earlier chapters of this book. On this last point, as already suggested in Chapter 6, there is no need to wait till the conclusion of a full-blown two-year ethnographic study before beginning to implement changes to brand communications! Small changes or innovations can be implemented as soon as confirmed findings begin to emerge from the ethno-marketing process. What also matters is that changes are implemented in an integrated way, with more and more aspects of brand communication adapted to supporting tribal linking value as more of an understanding of tribal linking value is acquired. It follows that the same approach should be rolled out across the full range of tribal social domains that are relevant for the brand.

Correct use of social media

While it is imperative to get the basics right, in terms of offline support for the tribe, this needs to be done in conjunction with online support via social

media. There are plenty of examples of brands that already take a supportive and interactive role vis-à-vis the tribe with regard to offline activity. For
instance, the Football Association of Ireland's main sponsor, Three, take a
very supportive approach towards the needs of those Republic of Ireland
fans who travel to away matches. This in itself is a good example of a sponsor
actually supporting the tribe rather than just trying to raise brand awareness.
The FAI's close relationship with the 'You Boys in Green' fan community,
originally an entirely independent, fan-led unofficial supporters' organization, is a further indicator of good practice. In a different consumer activity
category, garage and auto parts retailer Full Stop Auto Centre also take a
proactive approach to sponsorship. Not only do they sponsor one of their
mechanics, who is a leading driver on the national car drifting scene, but
Full Stop proprietor Finghin O'Driscoll has actually been out around some
of the circuits himself, albeit as a passenger if not a regular competitor! The
point here is that he understands and can relate to the tribal 'buzz' from personal first-hand experience. Similarly, sports retailer John Buckley Sports has
a long-standing relationship with the wider athletics and triathlon communities in southern Ireland, not only because of the staff's expert knowledge and
ability to provide advice that specifically meets the needs of their customers,
but also because a number of the staff are active participants in triathlons
and similar events themselves, hence yet again the principles of empathy and
affinity between marketer and community.

What really enhances the effectiveness of the above approaches is appropriate use of social media to complement them. Hence social media content
needs to be grounded in a strongly developed sense of tribal linking value.
Using tribal linking value as your guide will lead to better informed decisions vis-à-vis things like Facebook page content, website content, the right
approach to take to Twitter, and so on, so that consumers will both engage
with the content and engage in conversation with one another regarding
the content. As Cathal Deavy, Global Brand Director with Unilever for
Cornetto Ice Cream, says, 'it's not just about the number of "likes" your
brand Facebook page gets, it's the number of people that you engage in conversation that *really* matters'. When people engage in online conversation
with each other on your brand's Facebook page, *then* you're implementing
tribal branding.

Hence from a tribal marketing perspective, social media need to be used
not to primarily promote product as such, but to serve as a *community hub*
whereby both aspiring and experienced members of the tribe are encouraged to linger, to contribute, and to interact. Blogs and news stories from
company staff and customers alike need to take their place alongside, and
to some extent in preference to the catalogue-type content that dominates
some retailers' approach to social media. (Two further points are worth making or reiterating at this stage – first, in using the term 'hub' here, I don't
mean it to refer to Fournier and Lee's definition of the term as discussed in
Chapter 1 but rather in the alternative sense that people are connected and
interact through it. Second – social media use should *not* be initiated without

a preceding and ongoing commitment to ethno-marketing to first identify and then begin to support tribal linking value. Social media content has to be reflective of tribal linking value and should be heavily contributed to by the tribe.)

It's also worth noting that when I refer to the need for an integrated approach, I'm clearly not talking about what is conventionally termed Integrated Marketing Communications (IMC). The conventional definition of IMC amounts to planning all marketing communications in a way that is intended to secure delivery of a consistent message across all media, including conventional broadcast media, Internet, P.R. activity, and so on. There is a compelling logic behind this, in that it makes sense to maximize the synergies to be derived from consistently conveying the same brand message via all media formats, rather than taking a fragmented approach. However, the inherent risk in attempting such a strategy without reference to any form of ethno-marketing lies in potentially succumbing to the fallacy that marketing communications should universally be characterized by a one-to-many broadcast-style approach, whereby the marketer retains absolute responsibility for brand meaning creation and message delivery. Similarly, an adherence to the sort of one-to-one 'personalised' messaging that digital media now offers the capacity to deliver should not be regarded as appropriate or optimal. It still smacks of a top-down approach to brand meaning development, rather than an authentic approach to supporting tribal linking value and tribal re-working of brand meaning.

The above might sound strange or even a bit controversial, so let me qualify what I mean by saying it. Brand image needs to be conveyed in a way that reflects and facilitates the *co*-construction of brand meaning. So when you are developing an integrated approach to social media, the tribal branding approach, where co-creation of brand meaning is facilitated via the brand communications strategy, is far more appropriate than the pushing – and pushy – approach to communications that characterizes the behaviour of so many organizations when it comes to media such as Facebook and Twitter. If a brand concept has been developed – via focus group research for instance – and social media are then used to 'push' this brand concept at a target market (even via software profiling of individual online behaviours), then a lot of potential for brand development has been lost. It is certainly true to say that an imaginative approach to Twitter and Facebook can generate very positive effects on electronic word of mouth (or word of mouse, as some commentators have called it) but this approach is not an optimal one for brand-building with and within a tribe, because it fails to acknowledge the co-creative abilities of consumers. Hence tribal marketing – including use of social media – is *not* the same as what we used to call word of mouth. In fact it couldn't be more different.

Tribal branding is not about pushing messages in the hope that these messages and positive sentiments will get relayed, it's about encouraging and supporting the process whereby the tribe compose, relay, and re-negotiate *their own* messages and practices. Channels must be created to facilitate genuine interactivity not just between consumer and marketer but *between consumers*. Marketers thus need to acquire and maintain an understanding of how consumers co-create brand-related meaning for each other. The only way to acquire and maintain this level of understanding is via ongoing use of ethno-marketing and integration of the resulting set of understandings back into the brand. If this is being done, then we can begin to speak of a holistic, properly integrated approach to brand development. Finally, this is not to say that all forms of online selling are to be excluded! Absolutely not. It's just that it's a question of proportion. You *should* have an online store on your website, to make it as convenient as possible for the tribe to acquire tribal-related items. You *should* use your Facebook page to keep the tribe informed of new products, special offers, and so on. You just need to keep this activity in proportion so that it *complements*, rather than crowds out, the other content forms that the tribe enjoy engaging with, such as videos, photos, blogs, and online conversations! So while it is perfectly appropriate to use social media to get your message out, you need to ensure that you do this in parallel with a properly integrated approach to social media vis-à-vis your tribe. If you confine your use of social media to the broadcasting approach – even on a one-to-one basis via the use of software algorithms to profile the interests of individual consumers and target them accordingly – you are selling yourself, your brand, and the potential of social media for brand development – incredibly short.

Ongoing co-creation of value

So far, we have looked at the processes involved in identifying and beginning to support tribal linking value. I now want to take a look at some more specific ideas on how to implement an ongoing joint approach to brand development. What else can a marketer do in order to encourage the processes of 'ghost script' appropriation, communal development of brand meaning, and communal provision of brand experience?

Schau et al. identify a number of ways in which companies can continue to co-create value with consumer tribes and brand communities on an ongoing basis. As their work builds in some respects on the work of Hagel and Armstrong (1997)[4] in respect of virtual communities, I'll begin by briefly reiterating some key aspects of Hagel and Armstrong's approach. For Hagel and Armstrong, one of the key principles in the development of virtual communities is facilitating the movement of community members along a sort of community career path so they move from being *browsers* (those who only occasionally visit your site) to *users/lurkers* (who visit more frequently and regularly pay sustained attention to site content) to *builders* (who comment on other peoples contributions and make contributions of their own that others may find interesting) and *buyers*, who may be either lurkers or builders but who also use the site to complete transactions. Builders are key to the whole enterprise because in contributing original material they help to ensure a stream of novel content that will help to draw in more browsers, hold the attention of lurkers, and encourage more people in turn to contribute themselves, thus becoming builders in their turn. A vibrant community thus emerges and also inclines towards using the site as an online retail outlet for buying, selling and exchanging community-related goods and services.

In order to encourage movement towards the point where people become builders, you need to facilitate this progression in an authentic and natural way. You need to facilitate conversation, you need to be culturally informed and culturally sensitized, and so on. In other words, you need to support the tribe and allow them to interact with one another. Participation by members of company staff is advisable as long as it is carried out in a transparent and authentic way – yet again, the clear implication is that staff should ideally be participants in the activities in question.

(At the risk of repeating myself, this also implies that it should be very easy to find and use the online store section of any brand's website, but there should not be an overemphasis on it. I would even go so far as to suggest that the proportion of website space devoted to the online shop should be in keeping with the proportionate amount of community time devoted to shopping for tribal goods and artefacts – that is, so that the rest of the website is taken up by things of interest to the community, including opportunities to contribute content and interact with one another. The tendency to over-crowd company websites and Facebook pages with catalogue-type content is one of the reasons why the potential of these media is unfulfilled. This is yet another case where less is more.)

The Ducati case as mentioned earlier is a perfect illustration of how to approach things. Ideally your brand's website and/or Facebook page should be a sort of virtual version of the kind of motorbike garage where people could hang out and talk about motorbikes, motorbike racing, their preferred brands, their experiences, and so on, without anyone trying to coerce them into buying things. However, the environment should be highly conducive to making purchases in that it should be attractive and easy to do so. Also, the tribal members 'hanging out' should not be allowed to create an excessively cliquish atmosphere that might discourage newbies – though in practice some 'official' websites tend to cater more for the 'newbies', letting the real hard core do their own thing elsewhere.

Furthermore, even official forums should attract people from all parts of the tribe, as this makes for a more authentic experience for everyone. One solution is to organize different online forums on the same website for each of the distinct social domains within the tribe, so that members can browse across all the forums before settling on the one that they feel most at home in. As Schau et al. note[5], a version of this approach has been used to great effect by the company behind the 'Twilight' saga ('Twilight' of course originally referring to the series of books by that name but now of course also referring to the monster hit TV and movie series). Among the practices that have been facilitated via the range of discussion forums on the official Twilight website are *staking* (facilitation of the Twilight Mothers subcommunity, for example, as a social domain in their own right within the wider fan community), *empathizing* (far from being confined to conversations that only consider the range of characters and events featured in the 'Twilight' stories, the official forum actively encourages members to engage in discussion on an eclectic mix of conversation topics), *customizing* (via active encouragement of fan efforts at writing their own short stories that feature the Twilight characters), and product *grooming* (in this case providing tips on how to care for first editions of the books). Schau et al. identify four overall sets of value creation practices in brand communities, into which the above practices fit (Figure 9.1).

The four sets of practices thus include *social networking, impression management, community engagement,* and *brand use. Social networking practices* include those practices that help to create, enhance, and sustain social ties among members of the community. As such, they include welcoming, empathizing, and governing. From a tribal marketer's perspective, it is important to support these practices while at the same time allowing the tribe the latitude to engage in these practices in a natural way. The bonds and ties that are formed via these practices tend to transcend temporal boundaries – community members who may over time have to disengage from tribal activities or move on from ownership of the community brand often tend to remain part of the social circle – and this sense of social connection can extend to marketing staff, itself a sign that the marketer has done something right in facilitating authentic participation.

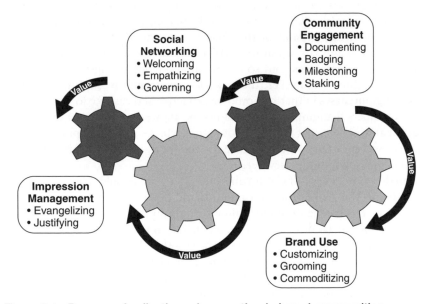

Figure 9.1 **Process of collective value creation in brand communities**

Source: Reproduced from Schau et al. (2009), by kind permission of American Marketing Association.

Impression management practices are defined as those practices 'that have an external, outward focus on creating favorable impressions of the brand, brand enthusiasts, and brand community in the social universe beyond the brand community'.[6] They include *evangelizing*, whereby 'members act as altruistic emissaries and ambassadors of good will', and *justifying*, which relates to the normalization of group identity and affirmation of its acceptability.[7]

The word 'altruistic' is key to the practice of evangelizing. How can a tribal marketer be perceived as altruistic? Douglas Holt (2002)[8] suggested that companies who feign altruism will have such pretence detected and deconstructed by consumers who have become cynical and jaded in relation to the various communications ploys of marketers. Two thoughts therefore come to mind. The first is that the marketer has to have a genuine interest in, or better still, a real passion for the product and/or activity.

For example, niche products that are seen as representative of authentic meanings and narratives, such as artisan food products, are among those that can lend themselves quite naturally to the sharing of passion for food. Sharing the passion means that the marketer can successfully be perceived as altruistic. One restaurant, La Cucina, in Limerick, Ireland, has already achieved semi-cult status through a blog published by the restaurant co-owner where she engages passionately with her blog followers about food. She doesn't use the blog to promote the restaurant, but the restaurant is perceived as a source of authentic, high-quality food because her followers can see the passion and care that she brings to both the online conversation around her blog and the food she prepares in her restaurant. So here, a sense of altruism refers to the authentic sense of care involved in preparing good food in a way that is really good for the restaurant's customers. There is a sense when you read the blog and customers' online responses to it that what matters is mutual enjoyment of food and taking care of customers as if they were family. When marketer and community have bonded via their mutual passion for good food – this is tribal branding.

What also comes to mind is that while at one level it is hard to envisage how a level of altruism can be achieved in a consistent way across the entire brand portfolio of a multinational corporation, the answer arguably lies in re-imagining each of the company's brands and finding new ways to engage with the users of that brand. Brands like Ben & Jerry's and Innocent drinks began with a sense of care and goodwill at the heart of their brands, and it certainly seems to have brought them a long way, so it isn't impossible. However, the strategy is dependent upon staying true to the core values of authenticity, passion, and showing that you care about the customer's lived experience because you are living the same experience yourself. Hence the second thought or principle is that the tribal marketer can only succeed in being perceived as altruistic when the marketer is seen to share the customer's experience and sharing their passion for the brand or activity at hand through taking part in usage activities.

Justifying is slightly different in that it is more concerned with the need to justify one's devotion to a brand[9]. For example, Apple Newton community members and Star Trek fans have a variety of practices that they draw from to justify their ongoing devotion. Members of the Apple Newton community continue to testify to the brand's incredible performance capacity, durability, and so on, while collectively managing to overlook potential problems (see Muñiz and Schau 2005[10] for a more detailed discussion of this case).

Brand communities need to be able to retain the belief that their faith is justified. As the example of the Apple Newton community shows, brand communities are capable of doing this by themselves, but tribal marketers may be well advised to pay close attention to such practices nonetheless – at the very least they may serve as particularly strong indicators of linking value and sources of singularity and distinction for the entire community.

Community engagement practices include *staking, milestoning, badging,* and *documenting*. They serve to 'emphasize . . . and safeguard . . . brand community heterogeneity or the distinctions among brand community members and subsets of members'.[11] These practices are thus an important source of cultural capital or if you prefer, tribal capital for members of the tribe or brand community.

Staking literally refers to staking out your domain and marking it as different to the other subgroups. It thus has to do with the social domain the community member sees themselves occupying within the wider domain, for example the lomography enthusiast who participates with a particular subgroup of fellow-lomographers, or the female Harley Davidson bikers who collectively see themselves as differentiated from the wider community of (male) Harley bikers.

One of the ways in which this is so useful for the tribal marketer is that strong, well-defined tribal clusters of this sort can help to maintain one another's collective devotion to a brand and/or activity even if the marketer needs to pursue alternative agendas to make the brand accessible to other sub-tribes. As long as a particular subgroup can maintain their own sense of territory, this could be enough to perpetuate their collective devotion to the brand, even if the marketer needs to engage differently with other groups in slightly alternate social spaces. However, the tribal marketer should still strive to facilitate the staking practices of all sub-tribes, rather than leaving it to individual clusters to act in an unsupported or unfacilitated way. The marketer still needs to affirm and acknowledge the specific linking values within each social domain, hence the need to be aware of the nature of each of these social domains and how they construct themselves as different from the others.

Milestones are the standout experiences related to the activity and/or brand, such as the time you bought your first motorbike or went to your first match or concert. In a consumer product context, upgrading to the latest version of a product, or realizing that this is the tenth time you have bought a Ford car, could also be a milestone.

It is really important to note that milestones need not be of a commercial nature at all and, to borrow an old phrase, 'no purchase is necessary'. Posting your 1000th post on an Internet forum is a milestone that can be celebrated, for instance. On many forums such milestones can trigger a status upgrade to a higher level of forum membership which of course may serve as an indicator of higher levels of cultural/tribal capital.

The key for the tribal marketer is recognizing milestones for what they are. It might cost little or nothing to recognize a milestone but leaving one unrecognized means that an opportunity to affirm the customer has been spurned. If you really cared about the stage someone has reached vis-à-vis an activity, you would recognize a milestone, wouldn't you? But there is also the question of recognizing it in an authentic way rather than attempting to do so in an overtly commercial way, for reasons that might be perceived as spurious. If I got a letter or text from my mobile phone network provider wishing me a happy birthday, for instance, I'd possibly feel a bit cynical about their motives. Why? The answer to this question lies in the de-contextualized nature of the greeting. I welcome birthday greetings from family, colleagues, and friends because these greetings and the recognition of these milestones (which can clearly come in different forms besides birthdays) comes in the context of an ongoing relationship where the people involved have proved themselves as friends over an extended period of time. Hence if companies want to benefit from the affirmative effects of milestone recognition they need to re-contextualize this recognition in some way.

One way of doing this might be to step back completely from direct provision of recognition, but to facilitate brand community recognition of milestones. If the company have trustworthy contacts within the tribe or brand community who can be relied on to submit authentic requests for resources when a milestone recognition social event of some sort is being planned, then the subsequent social occasion and process of milestone recognition takes place in the context of an ongoing, genuinely altruistic relationship and is thus perceived as an authentic gesture. So ensuring that the community doesn't lack for resources to celebrate these milestones, and of course an understanding of what the milestones are and why they are important, is a very useful thing. (It also follows that if I'd met a company employee at some kind of 'brandfest' event and we'd become friends then of course if I received a birthday greeting from them I'd receive it in a much more natural way, and their identity as a representative of the brand would have a more legitimate and welcome presence. Clearly, though, it isn't possible for company employees to meet and befriend every single customer – but in a tribe, they don't have to. Members of the tribe affirm the legitimacy of the brand for one another through every social contact they have.)

Badging is defined by Schau et al. as the practice of constructing 'semiotic signifier(s)'[12] of particular milestones. The changing of an avatar on an Internet forum, when it denotes a status upgrade, is an example of badging. Football fans buying club merchandise when they visit the club shop on a trip to Anfield or Old Trafford are also engaging in badging practices. The principle involved is the same – some way of being able to record that a particular milestone event has taken place. The question of how marketers ought to participate or facilitate this is therefore not dissimilar.

It's also quite probable that some way of bestowing recognition on the achievement of tribal milestones will have much more impact on the customer's relationship with a brand than any automatic triggering of a reward by means of a database-driven loyalty scheme. The key to this is recognizing that it will only be more effective to reward tribal milestones if the marketer has a culturally sensitized awareness of the milestones that have significance for the tribe. Better still, company staff who participate in tribal activities should demonstrate an enthusiasm for badging practices themselves and some proportion of staff should always be able to demonstrate a certain level of milestone achievement. Without wanting to overdo the number of times I refer to Harley Davidson, you can see the argument in favour of giving staff as well as customers some token of recognition to mark the achievement of a particular milestone – their fifth Posse Ride, for instance. This will have the requisite levels of credibility if it recognizes events that the staff member has actually participated in, so it is not something artificial that has been de-coupled from a real relationship. It also follows that it will be more meaningful for a customer to receive their symbol of milestone achievement from a staff member who has earned their respect through achievement of similar milestones themselves. The important element here is sharing the passion in an authentic way over a sustained period of time, so that when you do something it is seen as something done in the context of a relationship and not something done for contrived reasons and alterior commercial motives. The fourth community engagement practice is *documenting*.

> *Documenting occurs when brand community members construct a narrative of their brand experience, staking their social space, participating in milestones, badging the milestones for posterity, and finally evolving a cohesive personal brand narrative.*[13]

Documenting effectively means the sharing of brand stories and narratives. These include such stories and anecdotes as someone talking about how they customized their Mini and why. (This is the kind of contribution, incidentally, that Hagel and Armstrong would identify as typically coming from 'builders' in the context of a virtual community. The more you can encourage people to share these stories, the more that documenting is practised, the stronger your tribe will become.) Narratives are typically 'peppered', according to Schau et al., with references to milestones and examples of badging. Again a clear implication for the tribal marketer is to be able to interpret these narratives and perhaps even be able to relate some of their own (again it's important to note that the number of staff who might be able to do this might in practice be quite low, but it is important that someone at some level of the organization at least has the capacity to understand and empathize with these narratives. Also when recorded on community forums they are a very useful data source for the identification of tribal rituals and so on.)

The final set of practices relate to *brand use*. These include *grooming, customizing*, and *commoditizing*.[14] Grooming refers to the sharing of product maintenance practices – anything from how to clean hard-to-access parts of your Mini, to how to care for home-made costumes that are worn during Civil War re-enactments. Customizing refers to such practices as Apple Newton users tweaking their Newtons to perform functions other than those originally anticipated by Apple, or members of the Beamish brand community customizing and singularizing their Beamish 'tours' by varying the routes and varying the products consumed in conjunction with Beamish. Commoditizing refers to the practice of not only selling or exchanging community-produced goods but the related practice of actively monitoring and even restricting the prices charged for commodities produced and sold within the community. Within these communities, according to Schau et al. (2009), the overall objective is not profit, but community-building. To this conclusion I would add the further suggestion that such by-passing of an overt profit motive is also potentially a form of de-commoditizing in that it may serve to separate the tribe's identity from the profane commodifying influence of the official market for goods. Thus while there is certainly an intent to produce commodities for exchange and mutual benefit, there may also be an intent to signal that these are not to be confused with the normal commodities of the profane, de-sacralized, non-community marketplace.

In some cases, it is also easier to derive a sense of singularization in relation to the object or activity of tribal passion by producing your own customized version of tribal artefacts. In the case of hard-core football fans this often manifests itself in the production of home-made banners, unofficial t-shirts and other 'unofficial' goods that also have the advantage that they are slightly different to the official variants available from the club catalogue and thus confer a sense of distinction on their owner, or even the entire tribe (some fans pride themselves on their collective emphasis on home-made banners over the commodified equivalent that prevails among other allegedly less authentic fan bases). Incidentally, even though in some cases tribal feelings towards official merchandise and other official initiatives can be very negative, this should not be seen as a form of disloyalty to the brand. Rather, it is an alternative form of loyalty that is, incidentally, often expressed in ways that make the official brand and by extension the official merchandise all the more attractive to members of the wider fan community who will see 'official' products as perfectly authentic and legitimate. A very simple example of this is the way in which the atmosphere generated by die-hard football fans inside famous stadia such as Anfield or Old Trafford can inspire feelings of passion in 'newbie' fans from other parts of the country or even other parts of the world. Needing an outlet to express this newly felt passion, these fans turn to the buying of official merchandise and membership of official fan clubs as a way of expressing it. So the commoditizing practices of one hard-core tribal cluster, even in cases where these practices are designed to create a perception of distance between themselves and 'official' commodities, can effectively serve to authenticize those official commodities for other members of the wider tribe. In the case of other consumer subcultures, it has long been realized that product customization is a ready source of new product ideas that can be successfully commercialized due to demand among the wider community for something 'authentic'. The successful commercialization of the Harley Davidson 'Chopper' is a case in point, of course. Overall, this form of tribal crowdsourcing is just yet another example of the potential value to be derived from reaching out to and where possible developing relationships with the unofficial elements of the tribe.

Reinforcement of value creation practices

So far we have seen a variety of ways in which the tribal value creation process differs from more orthodox attempts to create or develop brand value. Table 9.1 now summarizes these differences.

It is also vital to remember that the various tribal value creation processes also differ in an overall way from more orthodox approaches to brand

Table 9.1 Some key differences between tribal brand development/tribal value creation and orthodox branding

Conventional sponsorship	Tribal sponsorship
Sponsors teams or events that the brand either wants to be associated with, or gain access to a large audience through, or both	Will only be effective if there is an authentic engagement with the activity in question
Objective – usually awareness and/or relationship-building in a conventional sense	Objective – to support the tribe and facilitate further acquisition of credibility for the brand as a legitimate participant in tribal activity
Conventional orientation towards social media	**Tribal orientation towards social media**
Delivery of predetermined meaning; either the same meaning to many target customers or a slightly adapted version of predetermined meaning to individual target customers	Facilitation of co-creation of meaning. Emphasis on interesting, co-created content rather than 'catalogue' type approach to Facebook, Twitter etc.
Value creation seen as marketer's responsibility	**Value *co-created* via practices such as social networking, impression management, community engagement, and brand use**
Marketer takes sole responsibility for creation of brand meaning, design of usage practices, and all forms of innovation in brand practice	Marketer and tribe *share the passion* – for food/science fiction/motor-cycling . . . they share narratives, share milestones, share brand use ideas and so on
Marketer tries to reinforce loyalty via e.g. rewards from loyalty schemes	Customer 'loyalty' – or more correctly, customer/brand *relationship* is reinforced naturally through integration of brand into social relationships and shared experiences

development in that their impact is greatly enhanced by the way in which they interact with each other.

As Schau et al. assert, each set of value creation practices helps to *drive* the other sets (as illustrated earlier in Figure 9.1), hence mutually reinforcing the overall value creation process. For instance, via the practice of 'documenting' (i.e. narrative-sharing) what consumers are doing is providing a template, or if you prefer Schau et al.'s term, a 'scaffolding'[15] around which the brand can be consumed. They then either overtly or tacitly invite others to replicate their behaviour. In practice this of course generates further practice innovations and members can then share even more stories with one another, generating more scaffolding around which more consumption can be constructed and so on. A very good example of this in the sports fan context would be the frequent sharing of 'away game' narratives where fans relate the experiences (both good and bad) they have had while following their team on the road. Stories of bars visited, beers drunk, and ballads sung offer a ready consumption template, rich in cultural capital, that other fans will eagerly seek to replicate and modify. Of course this is but one example of how the members of a brand tribe appropriate the basic 'ghost script' proffered by the marketer and re-work it to create their own narratives that, when shared, offer themselves to further re-workings by other members of the tribe.

Careful scrutiny of brand narratives is also useful for deriving an understanding of the stages in the tribal identity trajectory. For instance, what Schau et al. call the 'apprenticeship' stage can be mapped out with a higher level of accuracy by studying the milestone discourses around a member's first-time experience or encounter with the brand. Sometimes first-time encounters with the brand are subsequently related so fervently that they imply a form of epiphany, such as the sort of once-off conversion experience we saw in the Beamish tribe. However, these narratives need to be carefully unpacked and understood for the rhetorical devices they undoubtedly are. They confirm authentic membership of the community and not necessarily a sudden, intense, and permanent metamorphosis. An understanding of all the things that contribute to these conversion narratives is clearly important, so that the marketer can better understand whether it is possible for them to play a role in the facilitation of community entry for new members.

Marketers also need to track the insider jargon used in these narratives and try to retain an understanding of it, partly in an effort to ensure that the community remains open and accessible to new members. One of the ways in which this level of understanding can be maintained, naturally, is again via ethno-marketing in the form of participation as well as observation, so that terms can be noted, their usage tracked, and their meaning clarified. In practice the ability to use insider jargon appropriately also has the potential to greatly facilitate marketer access to the inner circle of the tribe or brand community. Correct usage of insider jargon authenticates the user. Thus with it, you are 'in' and without it, you are 'out'! Without some kind of ongoing commitment to ethno-marketing activity it might be difficult for the tribal marketer to hold on to their status as members of the tribe – hence the notion of ethno-marketing as ongoing, iterative, and evolving process rather than chronological or sequential activity with a definitive end point.

Schau et al. also provide an example of a member of the BMW Mini community exhorting another member to track the progress of their new car as it is shipped to the United States from Latin America, and to record this progress in his new car's 'baby book'[16]. While this is very much an example of how an idiosyncratic practice can become normative within a community and create value for a company as well as members of a tribe, two points are important; first, it should not be assumed that every brand community will want or even have any interest in the level of engagement and interaction with the company that BMW mini owners demonstrate in this example, and second, that the wider applicatory value of this, across different types of brand community, is the way in which brand community members constantly provide one another with a stream of brand-related innovations. This means that there is an ongoing sense of novelty associated with the brand. This helps to create an ongoing perception of singularity around the brand and the community, which in turn effectively differentiates the brand from other brands, other products, and other experiences. Therefore while it may be reassuring from a corporate perspective to see how members of the BMW Mini community collectively enforce the norm of positive relationships with the corporation, it should not be assumed that this practice will automatically prove replicable in the case of other brand communities. Members of tribes and brand communities may prefer to create value for one another independently of any relationship with the company. In such cases the role of the tribal marketer is obviously somewhat different, although there are clear benefits to be gained from identifying tribal linking value and occasionally proffering products and services to support it, albeit indirectly. Overall, then, the tribal marketer needs to remain sensitized to tribal values. By continuing to commit to at least some level of ethno-marketing activity, the tribal marketer can continue to make informed decisions as to appropriate levels and forms of support for tribal linking value.

Seeding practices

The approach to tribal branding is now – I hope – a lot clearer. Tribal branding means that the marketer seeks to contribute to the tribe's agenda – not take over responsibility for it. It is about allowing people to post about your product or service on Facebook themselves, because they feel like it – it follows that it is usually not about obtaining their permission for the brand to post as them! Nor does it mean that you try to assume responsibility for introducing individual consumers to one another – they make social connections with one another – you don't have to do this for them, you just facilitate it, via brandfest events, online media, and so on. It is essential to allow consumers to develop their own sense of what is different, unique, special, and important about the tribe and/or the brand – you don't seek to impose your sense of these things on each member of the tribe. Instead you sit back a little and allow them to affirm each other – while supporting this affirmation process through organizing social events and brandfests, hosting the tribe on brand Facebook pages and so on. You just need to make certain that you pay ongoing attention to how they define these things so you can adapt and evolve your support over time.

Therefore (to refer back to some of the terms used earlier on in the book), you need to continue to facilitate 'brand hijack' whereby tribes appropriate brands and engage in collective re-working of meaning, out of passion for the brand. You do need to organize events yourself but you should also consider sponsoring or co-sponsoring some of the unofficial events the tribe organize. All events, official and unofficial, are a really important facilitator of group narcissism whereby the tribe can enjoy putting themselves on show, creating a spectacle and as a consequence having something to gaze at (*X Factor* auditions, Harley Davidson Posse Rides, Beamish Tours as enacted and reproduced online, Red Bull Flugtag... the list goes on!).

Do remember people are here because they need to feel a social connection, and that you don't have to introduce people to each other! They are perfectly capable of doing this for themselves. However, if you engage in activities that undermine or damage the shared understanding of linking value then the social connection may be lost and many members of the community may begin to abandon the brand. The fall-off in audiences for the *X Factor* may be a case in point, where the tribal brand narrative (authentic discovery of natural talent) is increasingly perceived as subject to manipulation by the show's producers. In saying this I hasten to add that this is a question of perception and not proven fact. The underlying principle is really important though – if it is perceived that you are tampering with or attempting to manipulate the tribe's understanding of the narrative, you are risking a backlash, bad publicity, or even the break-up of the tribe. By all means retain the freedom to take brand-related decisions that may be seen as inconsistent with tribal linking values, but try to make sure that you do this in a transparent way, and try to accompany it with some meaningful gesture to affirm and reassure the tribe.

Tribal branding involves planting ideas, or 'seeds', and then allowing the tribe to cultivate those seeds into idiosyncratic, value-creating practices that reinforce consumer-brand relationships, generate new product ideas and usage practices, differentiate and support the brand, and so on. Hence Schau et al.'s advocacy of what they term 'seeding practices' whereby customers are provide not just with opportunities to customize but also the materials to do so. As we've seen, this is analogous to what Kornberger terms the provision of 'ghost scripts'[17] that consumer tribes can appropriate and re-work as they see fit.

Further, 'seeding' doesn't just refer to the facilitation of customization but facilitation of all the value creation practices discussed above. Schau et al. suggest achieving this by either setting up official online forums or approaching unofficial brand-related forums and either initiating or supporting as many of the various social networking practices, impression management practices, community engagement practices, and brand usage practices as possible, so that value creation begins to increase and the brand community begins to grow. Hopefully, this growth is paralleled by the development of a benevolent relationship between the community and marketer. Without the right initial processes of cultural sensitization, though, these initiatives are much more likely to fail.

In practice, seeding initiatives really stand a much greater chance of success if the marketer adopts the proper cultural entrée approaches as already detailed in this book. *Nothing* should be done without first having engaged with the community via an enthusiastic, respectful, and humble approach as outlined originally by Cova and Cova and expanded on in the various examples we've discussed. Further, by not only acquiring an understanding of the community's system of cultural capital, but having begun to actually *acquire* some of this capital via an immersed, ethnographic approach on the part of an adequate number of company staff, subsequent actions can be subculturally informed rather than just based on well-intentioned guesswork, and hence in their turn are more likely to be successful. Hence by taking an authentic interest and contributing something of value to the community, access may be gained and maintained provided there is an ongoing effort to participate and continue to share the tribe's passion for the brand and/or related activities.

A concluding caveat here is that you do not let the tribal 'tail' wag the corporate brand 'dog'. Brand communities sometimes start to go their own way and their take on things may not be appropriate for other segments of the brand market. As discussed earlier, you may need to develop alternative ways to maintain some form of relationship with the tribe or brand community in the event of it ever being necessary to take decisions that may conflict with their values.

Hence while it may prove possible to maintain a warm relationship with some or even most of the clusters within the overall tribe, it might not be possible or even advisable to achieve or retain such a relationship with them all. However, the marketer should certainly avoid contributing to relationship breakdown by engaging in any form of inauthentic or spurious activity that could undermine the relationship. Instead the aspiring tribal marketer needs to adopt a commitment to the practices of authentic tribalism as discussed.

This leaves us not with a neat, linear process of tribal branding but more a philosophy for creating brands with tribes. This philosophy is implemented through gaining ongoing insight into tribes, their behaviours, their values, and how to support them – hopefully for the benefit of both the tribe and the tribal marketer.

However, even if the process is non-linear, there are still some distinct stages and elements that contribute to it, and we can certainly identify those as follows (Table 9.2).

Table 9.2 Elements in the tribal branding process

- Identify tribal group or groups. Note that some tribes may either be so loosely defined that they do not really come together in a collectively observable way or only fragments of an almost totally unaffiliated wider social trend exist. In a case like that, just begin to observe some consumers whom you feel are representative of interesting trends. If on the other hand it is easy to identify an emergent or established community, then begin to work on gaining cultural entrée[18]
- Acquire initial understanding via background research and begin cultural entrée attempt (as discussed in Chapter 4).
- Take part in tribal events and activities, both as part of developing your understanding of the tribe and your relationships with members of the tribe (see for example Salomon's approach to the snowboarding tribe as outlined in Chapter 4) – keep collecting and interpreting your data while continuing to build social relationships with members of the tribe.
- Once accepted as a legitimate presence by members of the tribe, start to sponsor some of the events organized by the tribe – once this sponsorship is accepted, start to run your own events and invite/incentivize key members of the tribe to participate.
- In parallel with this, begin to adapt appropriate social media tactics (once tribal linking values are understood, begin to redesign your website and Facebook page accordingly)
- Don't just *facilitate* the tribe – instead *incentivize* social media participation, again by targeting key members of the tribe. You have to get people talking to each other, or there won't be enough of a discourse to encourage the community to frequent your website and Facebook page. (Not that the number of Facebook 'likes' isn't important! But without healthy numbers of people 'talking about this' then the tribal dynamic won't evolve).
- Instead of trying to set up their own online community from scratch some marketers simply approach an existing virtual community and ask them to agree to become the official website and forum (see e.g. Ducati as discussed in Chapter 2, or the FAI as mentioned above) – this is a perfectly good strategy as long as you have researched them properly and you can refrain from undermining their linking value after the takeover!
- The other dynamics grow from this. Your *ongoing role* is to stay in the background, make sure that some staff participate in tribal events, continue to monitor tribal linking value and thus *stay culturally sensitized* so that your ongoing tribal *seeding practices* will be in tune with and supportive of tribal linking value. Be sensitive to the possibility that different clusters within the wider tribe might have strong variations in linking value, hence necessitating alternative forms of seeding practice
- You should also run regular events (such as repeating the Posse Ride) so that 'official' event experiences and meanings can be appropriated by the tribe in a way that will blend in with events the tribe organize themselves – so that both official and unofficial events are used as a source of content and brand stories that members of the tribe can upload to social media and contribute to newsletters etc.

Concluding thoughts

There are a few things left that you need to bear in mind, such as the need to cater for different social domains within the overall tribe. If some brand initiatives seem to have potential to cause friction with or between different social clusters within the overall tribe, some kind of reconciliation/mutual affirmation exercise may be helpful. At all times be mindful of the need to respect the tribe as stakeholders and remember that this isn't some kind of neat, tidy linear process whereby you go out into the urban or online jungle in search of rare and elusive tribes, learn their ways and start to encourage them to integrate your brand into their lives – well, it sometimes is! But you also need to remember that sometimes a tribe will spring up around something you are already doing, even if you had no intention of initiating the formation of a tribe. If you decide to launch a new reality TV show and something about it resonates with people, they will begin to gather around it (*X Factor*). If you have a brand with some sort of interesting history or that lends itself to some kind of shared experience people might spontaneously appropriate it as a resource for relating to one another (Beamish). If you feel passionately that the thing to do is organize a competition that asks people to do something interesting and share it via social media, you could find yourself with a very enthusiastic tribe on your hands, faster than you can say 'Captain Cheffactor'!

What you need to keep in mind when a tribe spontaneously emerges around your brand like this are the following points:

▷ DON'T assume that the tribe has gathered round your brand for the exact reasons you've envisaged.
▷ DO make sure to begin to explore their linking values, using the methods of ethno-marketing as discussed, so that you can gain an insight into how they are appropriating the brand and re-working the narrative.
▷ DO begin to adapt what you're doing to support their re-working.
▷ DON'T seek to unilaterally impose your narrative at the expense of theirs – remember it's all about seeding, not coercing, and tribes deserve to be regarded as stakeholders in the brand.
▷ DO keep coming up with interesting and creative things yourself – novelty is healthy and tribes thrive on it.
▷ DO be aware that different specific forms of linking value may exist within individual social domains located within the overall tribe – and that you need to cater for diversity so that the brand doesn't become overly identified with one group – you don't want your brand ghettoised/perceived as tied to one demographic (the 'bikers are all fat old men' syndrome!) – you want a healthy diverse range of social domains (e.g. Red Bull!).

I'll conclude by acknowledging the possibility that in some respects the approach I've outlined herein might be regarded by some as more applicable to well-defined structures (official brand communities like the Harley Owner Group, official fan clubs like Lady Gaga's 'Little Monsters' or well-defined fan communities such as those associated with sports teams) than to the more elusive, ephemeral, and unstructured consumer tribes that continue to lurk in the tribal undergrowth. However, the approaches and practices we've just discussed really do apply to all tribes. Not all tribes dissipate as quickly as they emerge, for one thing. Not all consumer communities affiliate around only one brand, for another – some communities embrace a number of brands together for extended periods of time, making them neither pure ephemeral tribe nor absolutist, single-brand brand community. Huge numbers of consumer communities of all types continue to flourish, over timeframes that are definitively adequate for an application of the principles we've just discussed. Even for the most ephemeral and short-lived tribes, the approaches in this book sensitizes the marketer to the nature of tribal activity and the possibilities that exist therein. The application of this approach will help any marketer to comprehensively engage with the entire principle of brand meaning creation outside the formal boundaries of the organization. In short, if we are to fulfil the potential of brands as social creations, we really do need to engage with tribes. However, this book is ultimately just a set of thoughts and ideas about how to do that. The next step is up to you. Go and find a tribe and begin to engage with them yourself – and then let me know how you get on!

Notes

Chapter 1

1 Brown, S. 2007. Harry Potter and the fandom menace, in Cova, B., Kozinets, R. V. and Shankar, A. (Eds), *Consumer Tribes.* Burlington, MA: Elsevier/Butterworth-Heinemann (pp. 177–193).

2 Cova, B., and Pace, S. 2006. Brand community of convenience products: New forms of customer empowerment – The case 'My Nutella the community'. *European Journal of Marketing,* 40(9/10), 1087–1105.

3 Schau, H.J., Muñiz, A.M., and Arnould, E.J. 2009. How brand community practices create value. *Journal of Marketing,* 73(5), 30–51.

4 Muñiz, A.M., Jr., and O'Guinn, T. 2001. Brand community. *Journal of Consumer Research,* 27, 412–432.

5 Cova, B. 1997. Community and consumption. *European Journal of Marketing,* 31(3/4), 297–316.

6 Cova, B., and Pace, S. 2006. Brand community of convenience products: New forms of customer empowerment – The case 'My Nutella the community'. *European Journal of Marketing,* 40(9/10), 1087–1105.

7 Cova, B., and Cova, V. 2002. Tribal marketing. The tribalisation of society and its impact on the conduct of marketing. *European Journal of Marketing,* 36(5/6), 595–620.

8 O'Sullivan, S., Richardson, B., and Collins, A. 2011. How Brand Communities Emerge: The Beamish Conversion Experience. *Journal of Marketing Management,* 27 (9–10), 891–912.

9 Schouten, J.W., and McAlexander, J.H. 1995. Subcultures of consumption: An ethnography of the new bikers. *Journal of Consumer Research,* 22, 43–61.

10 Muñiz, A.M., Jr., and O'Guinn, T. 2001. *Brand Community* (ibid).

11 Kozinets, R. 2001. Utopian Enterprise: Articulating the Meanings of Star Trek's Culture of Consumption. *Journal of Consumer Research,* 28(1), 67–89.

12 O'Sullivan, S., Richardson, B., and Collins, A. 2011. *How Brand Communities Emerge: The Beamish Conversion Experience* (ibid).

13 Fournier, S. and Lee, L. 2009. Getting Brand Communities Right. *Harvard Business Review,* 87(4), 105–111.

14 Godin, S. 2008. *Tribes: We Need You To Lead Us.* New York: Portfolio, 2008.

15 Canniford, R. 2011. How To Manage Consumer Tribes. *Journal of Strategic Marketing,* Dec 2011, 19(7), 591–606.

16 Cova, B., and Cova, V. 2002. Tribal marketing (ibid).

17 Kozinets, R.V. 2002. The field behind the screen: Using netnography for marketing research in online communities. *Journal of Marketing Research,* 39(1), 61–72.

18 Schau, H.J., Muñiz, A.M., and Arnould, E.J. 2009. How brand community practices create value. *Journal of Marketing,* 73(5), 30–51.

Chapter 2

1 Muñiz, A.M., Jr. and O'Guinn, T. 2001. 'Brand community'. *Journal of Consumer Research*, 27, 412–432.
2 Fournier, S. and Lee, L. 2009. 'Getting brand communities right'. *Harvard Business Review*, 87(4), 105–111.
3 Schouten, J.W. and McAlexander, J.H. 1995. 'Subcultures of consumption: An ethnography of the new bikers.' *Journal of Consumer Research*, 22, 43–61.
4 Kornberger, M. 2010. *Brand Society. How Brands Transform Management and Lifestyle*. Cambridge: Cambridge University Press.
5 Cova, B. 1997. Community and Consumption. *European Journal of Marketing*, 31(3/4), 297–316.
6 Schau, H.J., Muñiz, A.M., and Arnould, E.J. 2009. 'How brand community practices create value'. *Journal of Marketing*, 73(5), 30–51.
7 von Hippel, E. 1986. 'Lead users: A source of novel product concepts'. *Management Science*, 791–805.
8 Mandelli, A. 2004, November. 'Ducati: Collaborative value and communities of consumers'. SDA Bocconi (Case No. 026/04).
9 Canniford, R. 2011. 'How to manage consumer tribes'. *Journal of Strategic Marketing*, 19(7), 591–606.
10 Mitchell, C. and Imrie, B. 2011. 'Consumer tribes: Membership, consumption, and building loyalty'. *Asia Pacific Journal of Marketing and Logistics*, 23(1), 39–56.
11 McWilliam, G. 2000. 'Building stronger brands through online communities'. *Sloan Management Review*, 41(3): 43–54.
12 Cova, B. and Pace, S. 2006. 'Brand community of convenience products: New forms of customer empowerment – The case "My Nutella the community"'. *European Journal of Marketing*, 40(9/10), 1087–1105.
13 Cova, B. and Shankar, A. 2012. 'Tribal marketing'. In Peñaloza, L., Toulouse, N. and Visconti, L. (Eds), *Marketing Management: A Cultural Perspective*. Oxford: Routledge (pp. 178–192).

Chapter 3

1 Cova, B. 1997. 'Community and consumption'. *European Journal of Marketing*, 31(3/4), 297–316.
2 Anderson, B. 1983 (1991). *Imagined Communities: Reflections on the Origins and Spread of Nationalism*. New York: Verso.
3 Kornberger, M. 2010. *Brand Society. How Brands Transform Management and Lifestyle*. Cambridge: Cambridge University Press.
4 Muniz, A.M., Jr. and O'Guinn, T. 2001. 'Brand community'. *Journal of Consumer Research*, 27, 412–432.
5 O'Sullivan, S., Richardson, B., and Collins, A. 2011. 'How brand communities emerge: The Beamish conversion experience'. *Journal of Marketing Management*, 27(9–10), 891–912.
6 Belk, R.W., Wallendorf, M., and Sherry, J.F., Jr. 1989. 'The sacred and the profane in consumer behavior: Theodicy on the Odyssey'. *Journal of Consumer Research*, 16(1), 1–39.
7 Schouten, J.W., McAlexander, J.H., and Koenig, H.F. 2007. 'Transcendent customer experience and brand community'. *Journal of the Academy of Marketing Science*, 35, 357–368.

8 Csikszentmihalyi, M. 1990. *Flow: The Psychology of Optimal Experience*. New York: Harper Collins.

9 Holt, D. 1995. 'How consumers consume: A typology of consumption practices'. *Journal of Consumer Research*, 22, 1–16.

10 Huizinga, J. 1955. *Homo Ludens: A Study of the Play Element of Culture*. Boston, MA: Beacon.

11 Algesheimer, R., Dholakia, U.M., and Herrmann, A. 2005. 'The social influences of brand community: Evidence from European car clubs'. *Journal of Marketing*, 69, 19–34.

12 Mitchell, C. and Imrie, B. 2011. 'Consumer tribes: Membership, consumption, and building loyalty'. *Asia Pacific Journal of Marketing and Logistics*, 23(1), 39–56.

13 Cova, B., and Cova, V. 2002. 'Tribal marketing. The tribalisation of society and its impact on the conduct of marketing'. *European Journal of Marketing*, 36(5/6), 595–620.

14 Cova, B. and Shankar, A. 2012. 'Tribal marketing'. In Peñaloza, L., Toulouse, N. and Visconti, L. (Eds), *Marketing Management: A Cultural Perspective*. Oxford: Routledge (pp. 178–192).

15 Canniford, R. 2011. 'How to manage consumer tribes'. *Journal of Strategic Marketing*, 19(7), 591–606.

16 Bourdieu, P. 1984. *Distinction: A Social Critique of the Judgement of Taste*. London: Routledge and Kegan Paul.

17 Holt, D. 1998. 'Does cultural capital structure American consumption'. *Journal of Consumer Research*, 25, (1), 1–25.

18 Thornton, S. 1997. 'The social logic of subcultural capital'. In Gelder, K. and Thornton, S. (Eds) *The Subcultures Reader*. London and New York: Routledge (pp. 200–209).

19 Mitchell and Imrie 2011. 'Consumer tribes': membership, consumption, and building loyalty. *Asia Pacific Journal of Marketing and Logistics*, 23 (1): 39–56.

20 O'Connor, S. and Richardson, B. 2006. *Stoked: An Ethnographic Study of Surfing*. Irish Academy of Management Annual Conference, 2006.

21 Holt. D. 2002. 'Why do brands cause trouble? A dialectical theory of consumer culture and branding'. *Journal of Consumer Research*, 29, 70–90.

Chapter 4

1 Cova, B. and Cova, V. 2002. 'Tribal marketing. The tribalisation of society and its impact on the conduct of marketing'. *European Journal of Marketing*, 36(5/6), 595–620.

2 Stewart, A. 1998. *The Ethnographer's Method*. Thousand Oaks, CA: Sage.

3 Kozinets, R.V. 2010. *Netnography: Doing Ethnographic Research Online*. Thousand Oaks, CA: Sage.

4 Schouten, J.W. and McAlexander, J.H. 1995. 'Subcultures of consumption: An ethnography of the new bikers'. *Journal of Consumer Research*, 22, 43–61.

5 Lofland, J. and Lofland, L. 1995. *Analysing Social Settings*, 3rd Edition. Belmont, CA: Wadsworth.

6 Fournier, S., Sensiper, S., McAlexander, J.H., and Schouten, J.W. 2001. *Building Brand Community on the Harley-Davidson Posse Ride*. Boston, MA: Harvard Business School Case, Reprint 501009.

Chapter 5

1 Belk, R.W. and Kozinets, R.V. 2005. 'Videography in marketing and consumer research'. *Qualitative Market Research: An International Journal*, 8(2), 128–141.

2 Sherry, J.F. 1995. 'Bottomless cup, plug-in drug: A telethnography of coffee'. *Visual Anthropology*, 7(4), 351–370.

3 Lofland, J. and Lofland, L. 1995. *Analysing Social Settings*, 3rd Edition. Belmont, CA: Wadsworth.

4 Stewart, A. 1998. *The Ethnographer's Method*. Thousand Oaks, CA: Sage.

5 Celsi, R., Rose, R., and Leigh, T. 1993. 'An exploration of high-risk leisure consumption through skydiving'. *Journal of Consumer Research*, 20(1), 1–23.

6 Arnould, E. and Price, L. 1993. 'River magic: Extraordinary experience and the extended service encounter'. *Journal of Consumer Research*, 20(1), 24–46.

7 Emerson, R., Fretz, R., and Shaw, L. 2001. 'Participant observation and fieldnotes'. In Atkinson, P., Coffey, A., Delamont, S., Lofland, J., and Lofland, L. (Eds) *Handbook of Ethnography*. London: Sage (pp. 352–368).

8 Arnould, E.J., and Wallendorf, M. 1994. 'Market-orientated ethnography: Interpretation building and marketing strategy formulation'. *Journal of Consumer Research*, 31(4), 484–504.

9 Kozinets, R.V. 2010. *Netnography: Doing Ethnographic Research Online*. Thousand Oaks, CA: Sage.

10 Muñiz, A.M., Jr., and Schau, H.J. 2005. 'Religiosity in the abandoned Apple Newton brand community'. *Journal of Consumer Research*, 31, 737–747.

11 McCracken, G. 1988. *The Long Interview*. Newbury Park, CA: Sage.

12 Wallendorf, M. and Arnould, E. 1991. 'We gather together: Consumption rituals of thanksgiving day'. *Journal of Consumer Research*, 18(1), 13–31.

13 Thompson, C., Locander, W., and Pollio, H. 1989. 'Putting consumer experience back into consumer research: The philosophy and method of existential-phenomenology'. *Journal of Consumer Research*, 16(2), 133–146.

Chapter 6

1 Glaser, B.G. and Strauss, A.L. 1967. *The Discovery of Grounded Theory*. Chicago, IL: Aldine.

2 Spiggle, S. 1994. 'Analysis and interpretation of qualitative data in consumer research'. *Journal of Consumer Research*, 21(3), 491–504.

3 de Chartonay, L., Drury, S., and Segal-Horn, S. 2005. 'Using triangulation to assess and identify successful services brands.' *The Service Industries Journal*, 25(1), 5–21.

4 Paul, J. 1996. 'Between-method triangulation in organizational diagnosis'. *The International Journal of Organizational Analysis*, 4(2), 135–153.

5 King, A. 1997. 'The lads: Masculinity and the new consumption of football'. *Sociology*, 31(2), 329–346.

6 King, A. 1998. *The End of the Terraces: The Transformation of English Football in the 1990's*. Leicester: Leicester University Press.

7 Belk, R.W., Wallendorf, M., and Sherry, J.F., Jr. 1989. 'The sacred and the profane in consumer behavior: Theodicy on the Odyssey'. *Journal of Consumer Research*, 16(1), 1–39.

Chapter 7

1 Cova, B. and Cova, V. 2002. 'Tribal marketing. The tribalisation of society and its impact on the conduct of marketing'. *European Journal of Marketing*, 36(5/6), 595–620.
2 Fournier, S., Sensiper, S., McAlexander, J.H., and Schouten, J.W. 2001. *Building Brand Community on the Harley-Davidson Posse Ride*. Boston, MA: Harvard Business School Case, Reprint 501009.
3 Kornberger, M. 2010. *Brand Society. How Brands Transform Management and Lifestyle*. Cambridge: Cambridge University Press.
4 Schau, H.J., Muñiz, A.M., and Arnould, E.J. 2009. 'How brand community practices create value'. *Journal of Marketing*, 73,(5), 30–51.
5 Godin, S. 2008. *Tribes: We Need You To Lead Us*. New York: Portfolio.
6 Holmes, S. 2010. 'Dreaming a dream: Susan boyle and celebrity culture'. *Velvet Light Trap*, 65, 74–76.
7 Papacharissi, Z. and Mendelson, A. L. 2007. 'An exploratory study of reality appeal: Uses and gratifications of reality shows'. *Journal of Broadcasting and Electronic Media*, 51(2), 355–370.
8 Kjus, Y. 2009. 'Idolizing and monetizing the public: The production of celebrities and fans, representatives and citizens in reality television'. *International Journal of Communication*, 3, 277–300.
9 Cortez, S. 2011. 'Cowell addresses "crazy" "X Factor" controversies'. Available at http://articles.nydailynews.com/2011-11-04/news/30361715_1_x-factor-nicole- scherzinger-producers (accessed on 9 January 2012).
10 Sweney, M. 2011. 'X Factor critics blame "finals fatigue" for ratings slump'. Available at http://www.guardian.co.uk/media/2011/dec/13/x-factor-ginals-fatigue-ratings-slump (accessed on 26 January 2012).

Chapter 8

1 Crane, A. and Matten, D. 2010. *Business Ethics*, 3rd Edition. Oxford: Oxford University Press.
2 Peñaloza, L. 2012. 'Ethics'. In Peñaloza, L., Toulouse, N. and Visconti, L. (Eds), *Marketing Management: A Cultural Perspective*. Oxford: Routledge (pp. 505–523).
3 Evan, W. and Freeman, R.E. 1993. 'A stakeholder theory of the modern corporation: Kantian capitalism'. In G. Chryssides and J. Kaler, *An Introduction to Business Ethics*. London: Chapman & Hall (pp. 254–266).
4 Vargo, S.L. and Lusch, R.F. 2004. 'Evolving toward a new dominant logic for marketing'. *Journal of Marketing*, 68, 1–17.
5 Patterson, M. and O'Malley, L. 2006. 'Brands, consumers and relationships: A review'. *Irish Marketing Review*, 18(1/2), 10–20.
6 Evanand Freeman. 1993. 'A stakeholder theory of the modern corporation'
7 Richardson, B. 2013. ' "It's a fix!": The mediative influence of the X Factor tribe on narrative transportation as persuasive process'. *Journal of Consumer Behaviour*, 12(2) 91–147.
8 Algesheimer, R., Dholakia, U.M. and Herrmann, A. 2005. 'The social influences of brand community: Evidence from European car clubs'. *Journal of Marketing*, 69, 19–34.

9 McWilliam, G. 2000. 'Building stronger brands through online communities'. *Sloan Management Review,* 41(3), 43–54.

10 Haenfler, R. 2004. 'Collective identity in the straight edge movement: How diffuse movements foster commitment, encourage individualized participation, and promote cultural change'. *The Sociological Quarterly,* 45(4), 785–805.

11 Schouten, J.W., Martin, D., and McAlexander, J.H. 2007. *The Evolution of a Subculture of Consumption,* in Cova, B., Kozinets, R. V. and Shankar, A. (Eds), *Consumer Tribes.* Burlington, MA: Elsevier/Butterworth-Heinemann (pp. 67–75).

12 Bryman, A. and Bell, E. 2003. *Business Research Methods,* Oxford: Oxford University Press.

Chapter 9

1 Kozinets, R. 2010. *Netnography: Doing Ethnographic Research Online.* Thousand Oaks, CA: Sage.

2 Cova, B., and Cova, V. 2002. 'Tribal marketing. The tribalisation of society and its impact on the conduct of marketing'. *European Journal of Marketing,* 36(5/6), 595–620.

3 Schau, H.J., Muñiz, A.M., and Arnould, E.J. 2009. 'How brand community practices create value'. *Journal of Marketing,* 73(5), 30–51.

4 Hagel, J. and Armstrong, A. 1997. *Net Gain.* Boston, MA: Harvard Business School Press.

5 Schau, Muñiz, and Arnould. 2009. 'How brand community practices create value'.

6 Ibid.

7 Ibid.

8 Holt. D. 2002. 'Why do brands cause trouble? A dialectical theory of consumer culture and branding'. *Journal of Consumer Research.* 29, 70–90.

9 Schau, Muñiz, and Arnould. 2009. 'How brand community practices create value'.

10 Muñiz, A.M., Jr. and Schau, H.J. 2005. 'Religiosity in the abandoned Apple Newton brand community'. *Journal of Consumer Research,* 31, 737–747.

11 Schau, Muñiz, and Arnould. 2009. 'How brand community practices create value'.

12 Ibid.

13 Ibid.

14 Ibid.

15 Ibid.

16 Ibid.

17 Kornberger, M. 2010. *Brand Society. How Brands Transform Management and Lifestyle.* Cambridge: Cambridge University Press.

18 Kozinets. 2010. *Netnography.*

Bibliography

Algesheimer, R., Dholakia, U.M., and Herrmann, A. 2005. 'The social influences of brand community: Evidence from European car clubs'. *Journal of Marketing*, 69, 19–34.

Anderson, B. 1983 (1991). *Imagined Communities: Reflections on the Origins and Spread of Nationalism*. New York: Verso.

Arnould, E. and Price, L. 1993. 'River magic: Extraordinary experience and the extended service encounter'. *Journal of Consumer Research*, 20(1), 24–46.

Arnould, E.J. and Wallendorf, M. 1994. 'Market-orientated ethnography: Interpretation building and marketing strategy formulation'. *Journal of Consumer Research*, 31(4), 484–504.

Belk, R.W. and Kozinets, R.V. 2005. 'Videography in marketing and consumer research'. *Qualitative Market Research: An International Journal*, 8(2), 128–141.

Belk, R.W., Wallendorf, M., and Sherry, J.F., Jr. 1989. 'The sacred and the profane in consumer behavior: Theodicy on the Odyssey'. *Journal of Consumer Research*, 16(1), 1–39.

Bourdieu, P. 1984. *Distinction: A Social Critique of the Judgement of Taste*. London: Routledge and Kegan Paul.

Bryman, A. and Bell, E. 2003. *Business Research Methods*. Oxford: Oxford University Press.

Canniford, R. 2011. 'How to manage consumer tribes'. *Journal of Strategic Marketing*, 19(7), 591–606.

Celsi, R., Rose, R., and Leigh, T. 1993. 'An exploration of high-risk leisure consumption through skydiving'. *Journal of Consumer Research*, 20(1), 1–23.

Cortez, S. 2011. 'Cowell addresses "crazy" "X Factor" controversies'. Available at http://articles.nydailynews.com/2011-11-04/news/30361715_1_x-factor-nicole-scherzinger-producers (accessed on 9 January 2012).

Cova, B. 1997. 'Community and consumption'. *European Journal of Marketing*, 31(3/4), 297–316.

Cova, B. and Cova, V. 2002. 'Tribal marketing. The tribalisation of society and its impact on the conduct of marketing'. *European Journal of Marketing*, 36(5/6), 595–620.

Cova, B. and Pace, S. 2006. 'Brand community of convenience products: New forms of customer empowerment – The case "My Nutella the community"'. *European Journal of Marketing*, 40(9/10), 1087–1105.

Cova, B. and Shankar, A. 2012. 'Tribal marketing'. In Peñaloza, L., Toulouse, N. and Visconti, L. (Eds), *Marketing Management: A Cultural Perspective*. Oxford: Routledge (pp. 178–192).

Crane, A. and Matten, D. 2010. *Business Ethics*, 3rd Edition. Oxford: Oxford University Press.

Csikszentmihalyi, M. 1990. *Flow: The Psychology of Optimal Experience*. New York: Harper Collins.

de Chartonay, L., Drury, S. and Segal-Horn, S. 2005. 'Using triangulation to assess and identify successful services brands'. *The Service Industries Journal*, 25(1), 5–21.

Emerson, R., Fretz, R. and Shaw, L. 2001. 'Participant observation and fieldnotes'. In Atkinson, P., Coffey, A., Delamont, S., Lofland, J., and Lofland, L. (Eds) *Handbook of Ethnography*. London: Sage (pp. 352–368).

Evan, W. and Freeman, R.E. 1993. 'A stakeholder theory of the modern corporation: Kantian capitalism'. In G. Chryssides and J. Kaler, *An Introduction to Business Ethics*. London: Chapman & Hall (pp. 254–266).

Fournier, S. and Lee, L. 2009. 'Getting brand communities right'. *Harvard Business Review*, 87(4), 105–111.

Fournier, S., Sensiper, S., McAlexander, J.H., and Schouten, J.W. 2001. *Building Brand Community on the Harley-Davidson Posse Ride*. Boston, MA: Harvard Business School Case, Reprint 501009.

Glaser, B.G. and Strauss, A.L. 1967. *The Discovery of Grounded Theory*. Chicago, IL: Aldine.

Godin, S. 2008. *Tribes: We Need You To Lead Us*. New York: Portfolio.

Haenfler, R. 2004. 'Collective identity in the straight edge movement: How diffuse movements foster commitment, encourage individualized participation, and promote cultural change'. *The Sociological Quarterly*, 45(4), 785–805.

Hagel, J. and Armstrong, A. 1997. *Net Gain*. Boston, MA: Harvard Business School Press.

Holt, D. 1995. 'How consumers consume: A typology of consumption practices'. *Journal of Consumer Research*, 22, 1–16.

Holt, D. 1998. 'Does cultural capital structure American consumption'. *Journal of Consumer Research*, 25(1), 1–25.

Holt. D. 2002. 'Why do brands cause trouble? A dialectical theory of consumer culture and branding'. *Journal of Consumer Research*, 29, 70–90.

Holt, D. (1995); "How Consumers Consume: A Typology of Consumption Practices", *Journal of Consumer Research*, Vol. 22, June 1995, p. 1–16.

Holmes, S. 2010. " 'Dreaming a Ddream: Susan Boyle and Ccelebrity Cculture'," *Velvet Light Trap*, 65 (Spring 2010):74–76.

Huizinga, J. 1955. *Homo Ludens: A Study of the Play Element of Culture*. Boston, MA: Beacon.

King, A. 1997. 'The lads: Masculinity and the new consumption of football'. *Sociology*, 31(2), 329–346.

King, A. 1998. *The End of the Terraces: The Transformation of English Football in the 1990's*. Leicester: Leicester University Press.

King, A. (1997); "The Lads: Masculinity and the New Consumption of Football", *Sociology*, Vol. 31 No. 2, 329–346.

Kjus, Y. 2009. 'Idolizing and monetizing the public: the production of celebrities and fans, representatives and citizens in reality television'. *International Journal of Communication*, 3, 277–300.

Kornberger, M. 2010. *Brand Society. How Brands Transform Management and Lifestyle*. Cambridge: Cambridge University Press.

Kozinets, R.V. 2002. 'The field behind the screen: Using netnography for marketing research in online communities'. *Journal of Marketing Research*, 39(1), 61–72.

Kozinets, R.V. 2010. *Netnography: Doing Ethnographic Research Online*. Thousand Oaks, CA: Sage.

Lofland, J. and Lofland, L. 1995. *Analysing Social Settings*, 3rd Edition. Belmont, CA: Wadsworth.

Mandelli, A. 2004, November. 'Ducati: Collaborative value and communities of consumers'. SDA Bocconi (Case No. 026/04).

McCracken, G. 1988. *The Long Interview*. Newbury Park, CA: Sage.

McWilliam, G. 2000. 'Building stronger brands through online communities'. *Sloan Management Review*, 41(3): 43–54.

Mitchell, C. and Imrie, B. 2011. 'Consumer tribes: Membership, consumption, and building loyalty'. *Asia Pacific Journal of Marketing and Logistics*, 23(1), 39–56.

Muñiz, A.M., Jr. and O'Guinn, T. 2001. 'Brand community'. *Journal of Consumer Research*, 27, 412–432.

Muñiz, A.M., Jr. and Schau, H.J. 2005. 'Religiosity in the abandoned Apple Newton brand community'. *Journal of Consumer Research*, 31, 737–747.

O'Connor, S. and Richardson, B. 2006. Stoked: An Ethnographic Study of Surfing. *2006 Proceedings of the Irish Academy of Management Annual Conference*, University College Cork, 2006.

O'Sullivan, S., Richardson, B., and Collins, A. 2011. 'How brand communities emerge: The Beamish conversion experience'. *Journal of Marketing Management*, 27(9–10), 891–912.

Papacharissi, Z. and Mendelson, A. L. 2007. 'An exploratory study of reality appeal: Uses and gratifications of reality shows'. *Journal of Broadcasting and Electronic Media*, 51(2), 355–370.

Patterson, M. and O'Malley, L. 2006. 'Brands, consumers and relationships: A review'. *Irish Marketing Review*, 18(1/2), 10–20.

Paul, J. 1996. 'Between-method triangulation in organizational diagnosis'. *The International Journal of Organizational Analysis*, 4(2), 135–153.

Peñaloza, L. 2012. 'Ethics'. In Peñaloza, L., Toulouse, N. and Visconti, L. (Eds), *Marketing Management: A Cultural Perspective*. Oxford: Routledge (pp. 505–523).

Richardson, B. 2013. '"It's a fix!": The mediative influence of the X Factor tribe on narrative transportation as persuasive process'. *Journal of Consumer Behaviour*, 12(2) 91–147.

Schau, H.J., Muñiz, A.M., and Arnould, E.J. 2009. 'How brand community practices create value'. *Journal of Marketing*, 73 (5), 30–51.

Schouten, J.W. and McAlexander, J.H. 1995. 'Subcultures of consumption: An ethnography of the new bikers'. *Journal of Consumer Research*, 22, 43–61.

Schouten, J.W., Martin, D., and McAlexander, J.H. 2007a. The Evolution of a Subculture of Consumption. In Cova, B., Kozinets, R. V. and Shankar, A. (Eds), *Consumer Tribes*. Burlington, MA: Elsevier/Butterworth-Heinemann (pp. 67–75).

Schouten, J.W., McAlexander, J.H., and Koenig, H.F. 2007b. 'Transcendent customer experience and brand community'. *Journal of the Academy of Marketing Science*, 35, 357–368.

Schouten, J.W., & McAlexander, J.H. (1995). Subcultures of consumption: An ethnography of the new bikers. *Journal of Consumer Research*, 22, 43–61.

Sherry, J.F. 1995. 'Bottomless cup, plug-in drug: A telethnography of coffee'. *Visual Anthropology*, Vol. 7, Issue (4), 351–370.

Spiggle, S. 1994. 'Analysis and interpretation of qualitative data in consumer research'. *Journal of Consumer Research*, 21(3), 491–504.

Stewart, A. 1998. *The Ethnographer's Method*. Thousand Oaks, CA: Sage.

Sweney, M. 2011. 'X Factor critics blame "finals fatigue" for ratings slump'. Available at http://www.guardian.co.uk/media/2011/dec/13/x-factor-ginals-fatigue-ratings-slump (accessed on 26 January 2012).

Thompson, C., Locander, W., and Pollio, H. 1989. 'Putting consumer experience back into consumer research: The philosophy and method of existential-phenomenology'. *Journal of Consumer Research*, 16(2), 133–146.

Thornton, S. 1997. 'The social logic of subcultural capital'. In Gelder, K. and Thornton, S. (Eds) *The Subcultures Reader*. London and New York: Routledge (pp. 200–209).

Vargo, S.L. and Lusch, R.F. 2004. 'Evolving toward a new dominant logic for marketing'. *Journal of Marketing*, 68, 1–17.

von Hippel, E. 1986. 'Lead users: A source of novel product concepts'. *Management Science*, 32, 791–805.

Wallendorf, M. and Arnould, E. 1991. 'We gather together: Consumption rituals of thanksgiving day'. *Journal of Consumer Research*, 18(1), 13–31.

Index of Tribes

Index of Topics

Note: Locators in **bold** indicate definitions or substantive treatment of a particular topic in the text.